edexcel
advancing learning, changing lives

BTEC National Travel and Tourism

Book 1

Core and specialist units

Andy Kerr

Victoria Lindsay

Diane Sutherland

Jon Sutherland

A PEARSON COMPANY

Contents

Why choose a career in travel and tourism?

One of the biggest industries in the UK

- There are an estimated **1.4 million jobs directly related to tourism activity,** some 5% of all people in employment in the UK (Visit Britain)

One of the fastest-growing industries in the UK

- **4% growth** a year

- Up to 1 in 5 new jobs in the UK are in Travel and Tourism sectors

Growing career opportunities

- Starting salaries of around £10,000 - £15,000

- Senior level salaries range from £20,000-£30,000, plus perks

- **66% of firms offer training**

- A new national skills strategy to improve skills and retention levels

A diverse industry

- Over **150,000 businesses**

- 80% of businesses are SMEs (small and medium sized enterprises) with an annual turnover of <£250,000

- A huge range of different sectors

Travel and tourism employment sectors:

Hotel management
Conference and event organisation
Customer services
Travel agencies
Tour management / operators
Holiday rep
Adventure tourism
Hospitality
Visitor attractions
Public sector
Heritage
Entertainment and leisure
Transport

Did you know...

Tourism worldwide

- There were over 800 million tourist arrivals worldwide in 2006

• The travel and tourism industry employs 200 million people worldwide

- Tourism generates over £500 billion worldwide every year

Tourism in the UK

- The UK is the world's fifth largest tourist economy

- Tourism generated £85 billion in 2005 and accounted for 3.5% of the UK's economy

• Over 32 million overseas visitors came to the UK in 2006

- UK residents took 59.3 million holidays

The world's top five tourism spenders

1. Germany $72.7 billion

2. USA $69.2 billion

3. UK $59.6 billion

4. Japan $37.5 billion

5. France $31.2 billion

Source: WTO, 2005 (International tourism expenditure (US$ billion))

World's top ten tourist destinations

1. France – 76 million	6. UK – 30 million
2. Spain – 55.6 million	7. Mexico – 21.9 million
3. USA – 49.4 million	8. Germany – 21.5 million
4. China – 46.8 million	9. Turkey – 20.3 million
5. Italy – 36.5 million	10. Austria – 20 million

Source: WTO, 2005 (World's top ten tourism destinations by International arrivals)

How to use this book

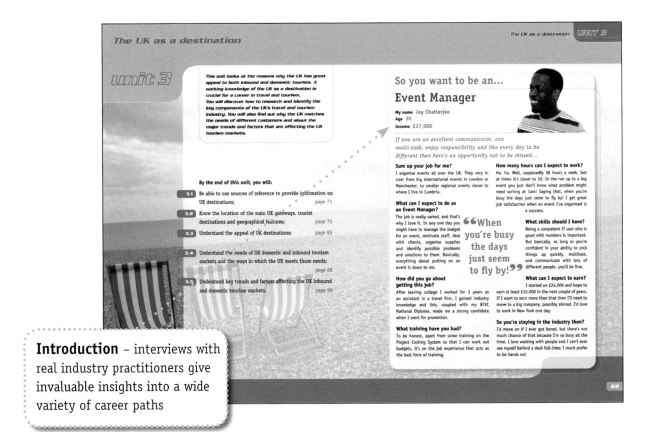

Introduction – interviews with real industry practitioners give invaluable insights into a wide variety of career paths

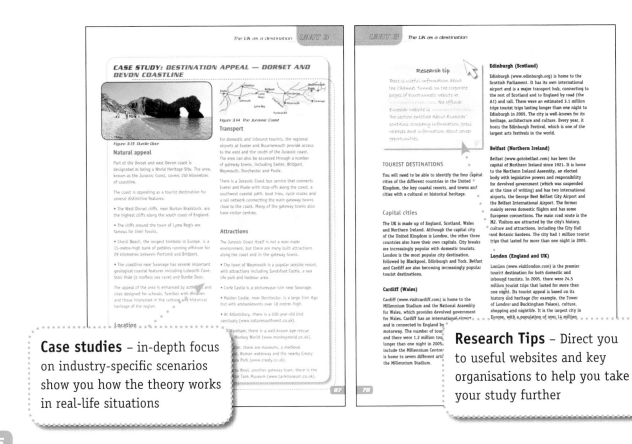

Case studies – in-depth focus on industry-specific scenarios show you how the theory works in real-life situations

Research Tips – Direct you to useful websites and key organisations to help you take your study further

Grading criteria – Learning outcomes and grading criteria at the beginning of every unit, so you know right from the start what you need to do to achieve a pass, merit or distinction

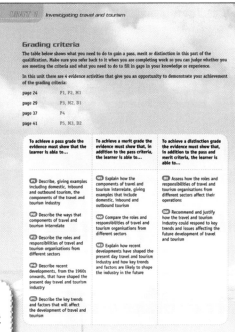

Evidence activities – short activities are spread throughout the unit giving you the opportunity to demonstrate your achievement of the grading criteria in small steps

Think – Questions help you reflect on your learning and to think about how it could be applied to real-life working practice

Key words – easy to understand definitions of key industry terms

Examples – industry-specific examples show you what the theory looks like in practice

Track your progress

This master grid can be used as a study aid. You can track your progress by ticking the level you achieve. The relevant grading criteria can also be found at the start of each unit.

To achieve a pass grade the evidence must show that the learner is able to...	To achieve a merit grade the evidence must show that, in addition to the pass criteria, the learner is able to...	To achieve a distinction grade the evidence must show that, in addition to the pass and merit criteria, the learner is able to...
Unit 1		
P1 Describe, giving examples including domestic, inbound and outbound tourism, the components of the travel and tourism industry	**M1** Explain how the components of travel and tourism interrelate, giving examples that include domestic, inbound and outbound tourism	**D1** Assess how the roles and responsibilities of travel and tourism organisations from different sectors affect their operations
P2 Describe the ways that the components of travel and tourism interrelate	**M2** Compare the roles and responsibilities of travel and tourism organisations from different sectors	**D2** Recommend and justify how the travel and tourism industry could respond to key trends and issues affecting the future development of travel and tourism
P3 Describe the roles and responsibilities of travel and tourism organisations from different sectors	**M3** Explain how recent developments have shaped the present day travel and tourism industry and how key trends and factors are likely to shape the industry in the future	
P4 Describe recent developments, from the 1960s onwards, that have shaped the present day travel and tourism industry		
P5 Describe the key trends and factors that will affect the development of travel and tourism		
Unit 2		
P1 Describe the features of a selected profit-making travel and tourism organisation	**M1** Compare the features of a profit-making and a non-profit-making travel and tourism organisation	**D1** Make realistic recommendations to resolve cash flow problems
P2 Describe the features of a selected non-profit-making travel and tourism organisation	**M2** Interpret the cash flow forecast, explaining how problems have occurred	**D2** Suggest and justify other ways either a profit-making or non-profit-making organisation could gain competitive advantage
P3 Complete a cash flow forecast for a travel and tourism organisation for a minimum six month period	**M3** Explain how a plan for a travel and tourism project enables the objectives to be met within the financial constraints	
P4 Plan a travel and tourism project within financial constraints	**M4** Compare how specified profit-making and non-profit-making organisations seek to gain competitive advantage	
P5 Explain how a chosen profit-making organisation seeks to gain competitive advantage to meet its aims		
P4 Explain how a chosen non-profit-making organisation seeks to gain competitive advantage to meet its aims		

To achieve a pass grade the evidence must show that the learner is able to...	To achieve a merit grade the evidence must show that, in addition to the pass criteria, the learner is able to...	To achieve a distinction grade the evidence must show that, in addition to the pass and merit criteria, the learner is able to...
Unit 3		
P1 Use appropriate reference materials to provide information on UK destinations	**M1** Analyse the appeal of destinations to domestic and inbound tourists	**D1** Evaluate the attraction of the UK for domestic and inbound visitors, making recommendations about how appeal to domestic and inbound tourism can be increased
P2 locate gateways, tourist destinations and geographical features of the UK	**M2** Explain how four specific UK destinations can meet the needs of domestic and inbound tourist markets	**D2** Evaluate the likely impacts of external and internal factors on the future of the UK inbound and domestic markets
P3 Describe the features that attract tourists to three UK destinations	**M3** Analyse external and internal factors influencing recent key trends in the UK inbound and domestic markets	
P4 Describe the needs of the UK domestic and inbound tourism markets		
P5 Describe external and internal factors influencing recent key trends in the UK inbound and domestic market		
Unit 4		
P1 Describe how the principles of customer service and methods used to evaluate it are applied in two different travel and tourism organisations	**M1** Compare the service provided by two travel and tourism organisations explaining how it meets the needs of different customer types	**D1** Evaluate the customer service provision in two organisations and make justified recommendations as to how improvements could be made to meet the needs of a wider range of customers
P2 Describe the benefits of good quality customer service and the consequences of poor service two different travel and tourism organisations	**M2** Independently demonstrate skills in handling customer service situations effectively and dealing with complaints to the satisfaction of both the customer and the company	**D2** Consistently and confidently handle customer service situations (including a complaint and a sale) showing a thorough understanding of customer types, needs and wants in different situations
P3 Describe how differing buyer behaviour and motivations can influence the service provided by two travel and tourism organisations	**M3** Demonstrate effective selling skills to meet differing customer needs in different situations	
P4 Use customer service skills to provide service to customers in two different travel and tourism situations		
P5 Deal with two complaints (one of which must be in writing)		
P6 Demonstrate selling skills in a travel and tourism situation		

To achieve a pass grade the evidence must show that the learner is able to...	To achieve a merit grade the evidence must show that, in addition to the pass criteria, the learner is able to...	To achieve a distinction grade the evidence must show that, in addition to the pass and merit criteria, the learner is able to...
Unit 7		
P1 Identify and locate countries, gateways and key leisure destinations within the European travel market	**M1** Explain how different factors influence the appeal of specific leisure destinations for different types of customer	**D1** Recommend how a European destination could increase its appeal for different types of customers
P2 Describe factors that contribute to the appeal of leisure destinations within the European travel market	**M2** Explain how specific European destinations meet the needs of different customer types	**D2** Evaluate the effects of current factors on the European travel market in the future
P3 Describe, with examples of destinations, European leisure experiences and their appeal to customer types	**M3** Analyse factors that shape development of the European travel market	
P4 Describe the development of the European travel market and its destinations and identify factors that have contributed to this		
Unit 8		
P1 Identify and locate continents, major long-haul tourist receiving areas, countries and destinations of the world using appropriate reference sources	**M1** Explain in detail why different long-haul destinations attract visitors with different motivations, and how travel factors can influence choice of destination	**D1** Assess the success of long-haul destinations in meeting the needs of different types of visitors, and make feasible recommendations as to how a destination could minimise the effects of the factors that negatively affect its popularity
P2 Select and describe different types of holidays offered by long-haul destinations for different types of customers identifying both travel and motivating factors	**M2** Assess the significance of the key features that influence the appeal of a selected long-haul destination	**D2** Evaluate how the selected destination could capitalise on its facilities in order to influence its future development
P3 Describe the features that contribute to the appeal of a selected long-haul destination	**M3** Independently plan a detailed multi-centre tour, clearly justifying selections for the chosen visitor profile	
P4 Plan a multi-centre long-haul tour to meet a given client brief, showing references used		

Research Skills

Before you start your research project you need to know where to find information and the guidelines you must follow.

Types of information

Primary Sources

Information you have gathered yourself, through surveys, interviews, photos or observation. This information is only as good as the questions and people you ask. You must get permission before you use someone's photo or include an interview in your work.

Secondary Sources

Information produced by somebody else, including information from the internet, books, magazines, databases and television. You need to be sure that your secondary source is reliable if you are going to use the information.

Information Sources

The Internet

The internet is a useful research tool, but, not all the information you find will be. When using the internet ask yourself if you can trust the information you find.

> Acknowledge your source! When quoting from the internet always include author name (if known)/ document title/URL web address/date site was accessed.

Books, Magazines and Newspapers

Information in newspapers and magazines is up to date and usually researched thoroughly. Books have a longer shelf life than newspapers so make sure you use the most recent edition.

> Acknowledge your source! When quoting from books, magazines, journal or papers, always include author name/ title of publication/publisher/year of publication.

Broadcast Media

Television and radio broadcast current news stories and the information should be accurate. Be aware that some programmes offer personal opinions as well as facts.

Plagiarism

Plagiarism is including in your own work extracts or ideas from another source without acknowledging its origins. If you use any material from other sources you must acknowledge it. This includes the work of fellow students.

Storing Information

Keep a record of all the information you gather. Record details of book titles, author names, page references, web addresses (URLs) and contact details of interviewees. Accurate, accessible records will help you acknowledge sources and find information quickly.

Internet Dos and Don'ts

Do ✓

- check information against other sources

- keep a record of where you found information and acknowledge the source

- be aware that not all sites are genuine or trustworthy

Don't ∅

- assume all the information on the internet is accurate and up to date

- copy material from websites without checking whether permission from the copyright holder is required

- give personal information to people you meet on the internet

Investigating travel and tourism

unit 1

The travel and tourism industry is made up of a vast range of different sectors. The industry is constantly developing and changing, with new factors and trends affecting the products and services it offers. This unit investigates the main features of the industry and how its different parts are related. You will also find out about different types of tourists and how the industry provides for them.

In this unit, you will learn about:

So you want to be a...

Travel Consultant

My name Jose O'Leary
Age 20
Income £11,000

*If you are organised, have a good telephone manner and
great people skills, this could be the job for you...*

So, what do you do?

I'm a Junior Leisure Travel Consultant. I book tailor-made packages for corporate clients; that's business travellers. They usually book short trips to European cities.

What does a typical day involve?

Customers tell me when, where and how they want to travel, then how long they want to stay and if they need a car. I usually get pretty clear requests from the customer. I'm responsible for booking everything, providing an itinerary, generating confirmations and so on.

How did you find your current job?

My job was advertised on the website Jobserve, they advertise hundreds of travel consultant vacancies. The job was also advertised in the local evening paper.

How did you get the job?

Seven people from my course applied for this job and we all had at least a pass on our BTEC National Diploma and a handful of GCSEs. I suppose I came across well at interview and I had a good reference from my tutor at college.

What training have you had?

I had three weeks induction training when I joined, which was a great help. I learnt about the computer systems and the booking software. I'm hoping to study for my Certificate in Travel (formerly known as ABTAC) soon.

What are the hours like?

I do a 35-hour week, that's five shifts of seven hours. On Tuesdays and Wednesdays I start at 12 and work through to 7. Sometimes I have to work Saturday morning, but I get a whole day off in the week in exchange.

> **❝I quite fancy staying in business travel; I like the buzz❞**

What skills do you need?

Patience! Customers are always changing their minds. We have major clients who spend a lot of money with us, so you have to remember that the customer is always right, even if they are totally wrong! You need to have a good telephone manner and excellent organisation skills. You also need to remain calm at all times.

How good is the pay?

It's not great, but it is my first year and my first ever job. I'll be looking for a promotion soon.

What's the likelihood of that happening?

There are plenty of opportunities. I would like to be a travel consultant in a couple of years. That would push my pay up to £16K plus commission; then after that a supervisor on £20K. I quite fancy staying in business travel though; I like the buzz.

Grading criteria

The table below shows what you need to do to gain a pass, merit or distinction in this part of the qualification. Make sure you refer back to it when you are completing work so you can judge whether you are meeting the criteria and what you need to do to fill in gaps in your knowledge or experience.

In this unit there are 4 evidence activities that give you an opportunity to demonstrate your achievement of the grading criteria:

page 24	**P1, P2, M1**
page 29	**P3, M2, D1**
page 37	**P4**
page 41	**P5, M3, D2**

To achieve a pass grade the evidence must show that the learner is able to...	To achieve a merit grade the evidence must show that, in addition to the pass criteria, the learner is able to...	To achieve a distinction grade the evidence must show that, in addition to the pass and merit criteria, the learner is able to...
P1 Describe, giving examples including domestic, inbound and outbound tourism, the components of the travel and tourism industry	**M1** Explain how the components of travel and tourism interrelate, giving examples that include domestic, inbound and outbound tourism	**D1** Assess how the roles and responsibilities of travel and tourism organisations from different sectors affect their operations
P2 Describe the ways that components of travel and tourism interrelate	**M2** Compare the roles and responsibilities of travel and tourism organisations from different sectors	**D2** Recommend and justify how the travel and tourism industry could respond to key trends and issues affecting the future development of travel and tourism
P3 Describe the roles and responsibilities of travel and tourism organisations from different sectors	**M3** Explain how recent developments have shaped the present day travel and tourism industry and how key trends and factors are likely to shape the industry in the future	
P4 Describe recent developments, from the 1960s onwards, that have shaped the present day travel and tourism industry		
P5 Describe the key trends and factors that will affect the development of travel and tourism		

1.1 *Travel and tourism components and their interrelationships*

TRAVEL AND TOURISM COMPONENTS

The travel and tourism industry provides the services, products and facilities to allow people to make full use of their leisure time or to facilitate business travel. The industry is made up of different components including:

- accommodation

- attractions and events

- tour operations and operators

- travel agents

- tourism development and promotion organisations

- ancillary or support services, such as insurance and car hire.

Between them, the components provide services for different kinds of tourist travel:

- holidays

- sightseeing trips

- visiting attractions

- visiting friends or relatives

- playing or watching sports events

- educational trips

- business trips and travel.

Accommodation

There are many different types of accommodation. The UK alone has around 50,000 hotels, guesthouses and bed and breakfast accommodation. Around 40,000 of these accommodation providers have less than 10 rooms each. There are two main categories of accommodation:

- serviced accommodation provides additional services, which usually means catering

for guests. Different levels of serviced accommodation are available. These include bed and breakfast, half board and fully inclusive.

- non-serviced accommodation provides room-only accommodation. If it is part of a holiday package, it is usually referred to as self-catering. Self-catering accommodation gives customers the means to cook their own meals in a basic, fitted kitchen. Non-serviced accommodation also includes motels (e.g. Travelodges). Most mass tourism resort accommodation overseas is non-serviced.

In the UK and most other economically-developed countries, there are a range of accommodation types.

Table 1.1 Accommodation types

Hotels	Fully furnished and serviced bedrooms.
Motels	Usually conveniently situated along major transport routes, offering basic facilities or those similar to hotels.
Guesthouses	Accommodation offered on a bed and breakfast or room-only basis.
Holiday homes	Houses, flats, villas or boats that can be rented and used on a self-catering basis.
Holiday villages	Chalets or caravans situated around facilities, such as swimming pools. They are usually provided on a self-catering basis.
Camping	Either brought by the customer or provided by the campsite and used on a self-catering basis.
Youth hostels	Basic accommodation, usually on a self-catering basis.

Key words

Half board – accommodation where only breakfast and an evening meal are usually provided
Fully inclusive – accommodation where all meals and most drinks are provided. Sometimes there are restrictions on drinks
Self-catering – accommodation provided on a room-only basis, with basic kitchen facilities available

Transport

Transportation is a key component of the travel and tourism industry. It is often referred to as the transport infrastructure, because it covers the road network, railways, sea transport and airports.

The choice of transport will very much depend on the type of travel and tourism being undertaken. The main ways to travel are by road, rail, sea and air.

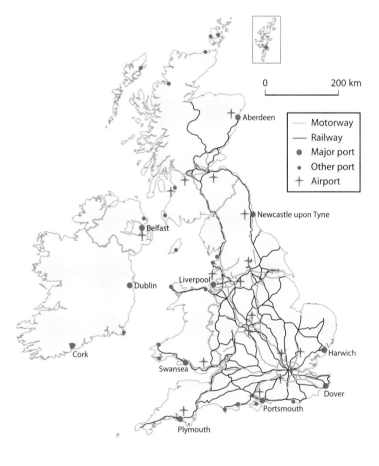

Figure 1.1 The transport infrastructure of the UK

Figure 1.2 Good road access is an important factor in the success of many tourist attractions

Road

Privately owned cars are the primary transport used by domestic tourists to make trips within the UK. Private cars can also be used in conjunction with sea travel to reach European destinations. For tourists abroad, car-hire is an increasingly popular means of travelling within a country. Fly-drive holidays, which include the flight to the country or region and car-hire for the duration of the holiday, are popular options, particularly for UK tourists travelling to America. Roads are also used by buses and coaches. This is a fairly small transport sector in the UK: coach travel within the UK accounts for only about 10% of tourist travel. Roads are important to the tourism industry because access to major tourist resorts and attractions frequently depends on the availability of a good road infrastructure, including motorways and adequate signage.

There are several advantages to road travel. It provides flexibility - for example, travel can be broken down over several days. Road travel is a relatively easy and safe way of travelling in the UK as the road network is maintained by the government and local councils. Road transport is very important in countries where rail and air transport is less developed. However, travelling by car is not always the most relaxing or reliable means of moving around a country. The existence of a safe and comprehensive road network is not guaranteed in all countries. This restricts the use of support services, such as car hire.

Rail

There is a comprehensive rail network in the UK. Most of the major routes pass through, begin or end at major cities. London, for example, can be reached from nearly every major city in the UK. Connections can be made in these major cities to other towns and cities on the rail network.

There are nearly 30 rail companies operating in the UK. Most of them are regional train companies, such as Merseyrail that serves the Northwest. Some, such as Virgin, provide national services, including connecting England and Scotland.

Most European countries have a comprehensive rail network, offering a fast and usually reliable service that allows customers to travel across Europe. Since 1994, UK tourists have been able to take the Eurostar train service through the Channel Tunnel to France and Belgium. Tourists can then connect with high-speed train services to reach other European destinations.

Sea

The UK is connected to the European mainland by numerous sea routes. The main routes are shown in Figure 1.3.

The most popular means of sea travel is by ferry. On some routes, passengers can either travel as foot passengers or they can take their vehicles on board.

A different form of sea transport is provided by cruises. These often involve two forms of transport as tourists usually have to fly to the starting point of the cruise. Popular cruises include the Mediterranean and Caribbean, where the ship docks at different places on the way. A popular non-stop cruise is the Atlantic crossing to North America.

River travel is available in some countries. In the UK, there are specific water transport-based holidays, such as canal boats and boats on the Norfolk Broads. Cruises operate on larger rivers overseas, for example, down the river Nile in Egypt.

Research tip

To find out more about the Channel Tunnel, visit Eurotunnel at www.eurotunnel.com.

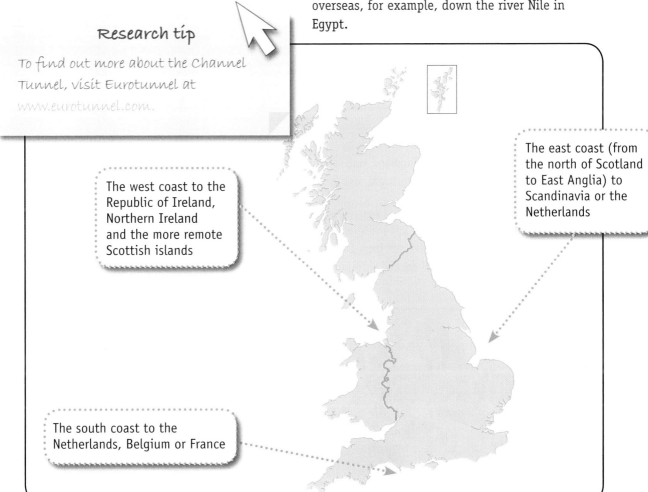

The west coast to the Republic of Ireland, Northern Ireland and the more remote Scottish islands

The east coast (from the north of Scotland to East Anglia) to Scandinavia or the Netherlands

The south coast to the Netherlands, Belgium or France

Figure 1.3 Main sea routes from the UK

Air

Airports act as hubs to bring tourists into a region or for residents of the area to leave it.

There are three different types of air transport.

- Charter flights are generally used by tour operators to fly package holiday customers. They usually operate on a seasonal basis to popular tourist destinations. Typical charter flights include those run by MyTravel and JMC.

- Scheduled flights are timetabled to run throughout the year and are used by independent travellers and business travellers. Typical scheduled airlines are British Airways, easyJet and Ryanair.

- Independent flights are largely used by business travellers and the aircraft are often relatively small. Typical independent operators include Centreline Air and Air Charter Service.

Air transport is limited by its capacity. Many existing airports are at bursting point in terms of flights and passengers. Regional airports offer a means of reducing the pressure on major airports and routes.

Key words

Hubs – transport centres, such as an airport, bus station or major railway station
Capacity – the maximum number of flights or passengers that the airport is able to deal with at any one time

Research tip

There are many regional airports. A comprehensive list can be found at www.azworldairports.com. Choose the country index and select 'United Kingdom'.

CASE STUDY: LEEDS BRADFORD AIRPORT

The airport first started scheduled services after the Second World War with flights offered to destinations including Belfast, Jersey and the Isle of Wight. The first daily service to London began in 1960 and the first package holiday flights started in 1976, when Thomson Holidays offered packages to Spain and Portugal, using Britannia Airways.

The extension of the runway in 1984 allowed the first transatlantic flights to take off from Leeds. Half a million passengers had passed through the airport by 1986.

In 1994, the airport was granted permission for flights to continue 24 hours a day, although there are restrictions on night-time flights.

Expansion of the terminal buildings, including the addition of a new check-in hall, improved customer facilities and better road access to the airport have facilitated its growth.

In 2006, the airport saw almost 2.8 million passengers flying out to over 65 scheduled and charter destinations. This was a 7% increase from 2005. In 2006, 18 new direct services began, including flights to Austria, Italy and Poland.

QUESTIONS

1. Look at a transport map of the UK. Where might the 2.8 million passengers using the airport have flown from before its development?

2. Visit the airport's web site and identify three other new direct services.

3. Suggest how the airport could attract and deal with more business passengers.

Figure 1.4 Leeds Bradford airport

Attractions

An attraction is a place or an event that attracts tourists to a particular destination. The appeal of attractions depends on other components of the travel and tourism industry, including:

- transport links

- convenient accommodation and catering facilities

- information services

- other local or regional attractions.

There are several different types of attractions.

Natural attractions

Natural attractions include mountains, forests, lakes and coastlines. Natural attractions draw tourists due to their beauty, landscape and natural and historical heritage. They require special management in order to maintain their beauty and identity.

There are 12 National Parks in England and Wales, and 2 in Scotland. There are also 40 places designated as Areas of Outstanding Natural Beauty (AONB) in England and Wales, and 9 in Northern Ireland.

Research tip

To find out more about the UK's National Parks, visit the website of the Association of National Parks Authorities at www.nationalparks.gov.uk.

Figure 1.5 Dartmoor National Park

Heritage attractions

Heritage sites are buildings and areas that are historically significant. (Confusingly, many of the undeveloped and unspoilt coastlines around England and Wales are called Heritage Coasts.) Heritage sites in the UK range from Stonehenge in Wiltshire to the Roman Baths in Bath, Holyrood Palace in Edinburgh and the many Shakespeare related sites in Stratford-upon-Avon. Some cities are famed for their heritage appeal, such as Oxford with its medieval colleges, world-class museums and botanical gardens.

Think What particular heritage is your local area associated with?

Research tip

To see the enormous variety of heritage sites in London, visit the website of the London Tourist Board at www.londontouristboard.com

Purpose-built attractions

Purpose-built attractions range from sporting venues to theme parks, zoos and museums. Most major towns and cities have important sporting venues and, from 2012, London will have Olympic venues and facilities that will remain major attractions for decades to come.

Popular theme parks include Alton Towers, Thorpe Park and Chessington World of Adventures. There are a number of zoos, including the famous London Zoo and the West Midland Safari Park.

Many museums are in major population centres, such as London or Oxford. Others can be found in more remote areas, reflecting the historical heritage of a particular area, such as the Ironbridge Museum near Telford.

Events

Events are an important component in the travel and tourism industry. There are many different types of events, including music concerts, theatre, comedy, heritage events, sports and specialist events, such as the Chelsea Flower Show.

The travel and tourism industry provides services for events including ticketing, event and accommodation packages, and transport services. In some cases, areas are geared up to regularly cope with an enormous number of visitors to popular events, such as Wimbledon.

> **Key words**
>
> Ticketing – the creation and distribution of entry tickets for major events

Tour operations

Tour operators are usually the main provider of travel and tourism packages. They bring together the various elements required in a holiday package, including:

- transport to and from the destination

- collection at the destination by the resort representative

- onward transport to the accommodation

- liaison with accommodation provider

- ongoing support, guidance and advice to the customer throughout the duration of the holiday

- excursions and additional services, such as car hire, while at the resort

- collection from accommodation and transport to the point of departure.

Many holiday packages involve a flight. Other tour operators may offer coach transport throughout the holiday.

Broadly speaking, tour operators fall into two different categories:

- mass market – those providing packages to domestic or overseas destinations, including transport, accommodation and, in some cases, meals

- specialist – those providing tailor-made holidays to match customers' specific requirements, or themed holidays, for example, diving, cookery or art-related holidays.

Travel agents

Travel agents act as intermediaries between tour operators, airlines and accommodation providers and their customers. They offer customers a wide range of choice by selling products from their preferred business partners.

> **Key words**
>
> Intermediaries – businesses or organisations that deal with products or services somewhere in the chain of distribution. They are sometimes called middlemen

There are a number of different types of travel agents.

Table 1.2 Types of travel agents

Retail	High street travel agencies offer a range of holidays from different tour operators. They can book all parts of a customer's holiday requirements.
Business	Agencies that cater for business travel, specifically targeting other businesses.
Call centres	Calls from customers are usually generated by advertising, for example, through newspapers or brochures. They can book all parts of a customer's holiday requirements.
Online	Agencies that provide services through a website rather than through high street presence or a call centre. Customers can select, book and pay for a wide variety of different travel and tourism services, including full package holidays through the company's website.

Tourism development and promotion

All countries that experience tourism have their own tourist boards that try to encourage tourists to visit through advertising, promotion or events. In the UK, there are national and regional tourist boards, which aim to develop and promote tourism to both domestic and overseas tourists. They market both the UK as a whole and specific regions or destinations.

Tourist Boards provide information on their websites. In popular tourist areas, there are often Tourist Information Centres (TIC), which act as information and advice points for visitors to the area.

Trade associations act as an information point for businesses in the industry and set out the minimum levels of service required by their members. In the UK, there are over 100 different trade associations that are directly related to the travel and tourism industry. These range from organisations concerned with conferences and events to the British Incoming Tour Operators Association.

Key words

Trade association – an organisation made up of member businesses that perform services on their behalf. They represent the industry as a whole

Research tip

The Association of British Travel Agents website is www.abta.co.uk. The website of the Association of Independent Tour Operators can be found at www.aito.co.uk.

ABTA

Some trade associations are also regulatory bodies. This means that checks have been made on their members to ensure they comply with UK and European regulations. Members of travel and tourism regulatory bodies are required to guarantee that they give accurate descriptions of their holidays and offer choice, quality and high levels of customer service. If members do not meet basic minimum standards, the trade association's approval can be removed.

There are also government regulatory bodies. The local Trading Standards Office can investigate customer complaints and government organisations, such as the Competition Commission, can investigate complaints of unfair business practices.

Key words

Regulatory bodies – independent or government organisations that seek to control the activities of a particular industry

Ancillary services

In addition to essential services such as accommodation, transport and attractions, other services and products are required by tourists. These are known as ancillary services. Insurance is the most important example. In many tour operators' packages, insurance can be purchased on a holiday-by-holiday basis, but other insurance companies offer year-round insurance to cover an unlimited number of trips. The type of insurance needed depends on the type of holiday and the risks involved. Insurance is more expensive for activity holidays, or for travel to areas where there is a significant risk from crime or to health.

The other two main ancillary services are:

- currency exchange – travel agents, banks, post offices and bureau de change at airports and resorts offer exchange services

- car hire – this can either be booked as part of the initial booking, through the tour operator representative at the destination or independently by the tourist at their destination.

INTERRELATIONSHIPS IN THE TRAVEL AND TOURISM INDUSTRY

No single component of the travel and tourism industry can operate alone without relying on other parts of the industry. A hotel, for example, relies on transportation links and the attractions in the local area to bring tourists to them. Some of these interrelationships have brought different components of the industry together.

Chains of distribution

A chain of distribution is the means of getting a product to a customer. A traditional chain of distribution in the travel and tourism industry might look like this:

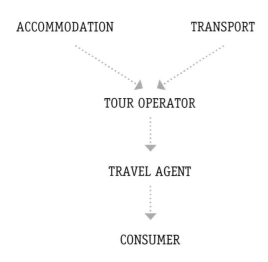

Figure 1.6 A traditional chain of distribution

However, developments in the industry mean that chains of distribution are now often far more complex.

Example

Many airlines, with the possible exception of British Airways, easyJet and Ryanair, rely on tour operators and travel agents to sell seats on their aircraft. The tour operator often owns the airline; Thomson and MyTravel have their own aircraft to fly their customers as part of their package holiday. Even if a tour operator does not own the airline, the airline may rely on a particular tour operator using their services in their packages. In turn, the tour operators' packages are sold through various travel agents. Where all the different components within a chain of distribution are owned by the same company, these are known as fully-integrated chains of distribution.

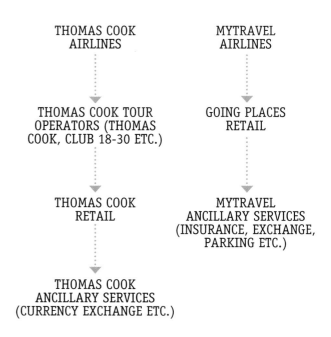

Figure 1.7 Two examples of fully-integrated chains of distribution

Of course, there are also much simpler chains. For example, accommodation-only holidays, such as villas in France, are sold through businesses that promote France as a destination for a holiday. The properties appear in the business's brochure and bookings are made via the business, which then handles the payment.

Integration

Until fairly recently, booking a holiday could mean having to deal with a number of businesses, which all provided different parts of the package. As we have seen, chains of distribution are changing as businesses increasingly expand their area of operations. This process is known as integration.

The advantage to businesses is that by offering all or most elements of a holiday the business is able to control its costs and ensure that their customers receive a guaranteed high standard of service. There are two main types of integration:

- horizontal integration – where businesses at the same level in the chain of distribution merge together or are purchased by another business

- vertical integration – where a business at one point on the chain of distribution purchases or acquires a business at a higher or lower level of the chain of distribution.

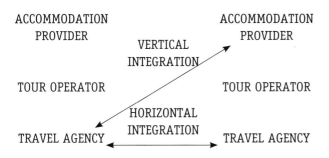

Figure 1.8 Types of integration

Example

The tour operator, Thomson, acquired Lunn Poly, a chain of travel agents, in 1972. The Lunn Poly brand name was kept until 1994, when the company was rebranded as Thomson Holidays.

Interdependencies

Several additional options are offered when you book a flight on easyJet, including accommodation and car hire, as well as ancillary services, such as insurance and airport car parking. These are all examples of interdependencies within the travel and tourism industry.

Businesses enter into arrangements like this with one another so that they can all benefit from a single booking. If a customer has purchased a flight, they may also need accommodation or a car. By providing booking services for these two components of the trip, easyJet can earn more from the initial booking of a flight. The customer benefits from these arrangements because they offer convenience.

Think When you went on your last holiday or school trip, how many different components of the travel and tourism industry were involved?

Figure 1.9 The easyJet homepage shows the different ancillary services offered

TYPES OF TOURISM

There are basically three different types of tourism. They are all significant within the travel and tourism industry, but each has their own unique features.

- Domestic tourism. People who are resident in a country travelling within it. For example, a person from London taking a holiday to the Yorkshire Dales.

- Inbound tourism. People entering a country to visit. For example, French residents visiting the UK.

- Outbound tourism. People leaving a country to visit a different country. For example, UK residents visiting France.

> ***Think*** Which type of tourism is most likely to bring money into the UK?

The different needs of domestic, inbound and outbound tourists determine the role played by the different components of the travel and tourism industry. For example, out of 151 million domestic tourist trips in the UK in 2003, 34 million were visits to friends and relatives. This means that components such as transport or attractions would be more important for these tourists than accommodation or tour operators.

For inbound or outbound tourism, components such as accommodation, tour operators and tourist boards would play a more important role.

EVIDENCE ACTIVITY

P1 – P2 – M1

Your employer has asked you to prepare a presentation that can be given to new employees, which will help explain the travel and tourism industry.

1. Describe all the components of travel and tourism. (P1)

2. Describe the nature of domestic, inbound and outbound tourism. (P1)

3. Give examples of each component, naming a particular business or organisation. (P1)

4. Link your description of them to one or more domestic, inbound or outbound tourism types. (P1)

You can use the following table to help you organise your presentation:

Component	Business or organisation example	Type of tourism
Accommodation		
Attraction		
Tour operator		
Travel agent		
Development and promotion		
Ancillary services		

5. Describe the way in which different parts of the travel and tourism industry interrelate, mentioning distribution, integration and interdependencies. (P2)

6. Explain rather than describe the components of the travel and tourism industry and the way in which those components interrelate. (This means that you need to give clear reasoning behind your examples. A good example would be the relationship between local accommodation providers and tourist boards, or the integration of airlines, resort transfer transport and accommodation brought together by tour operators as a complete package for customers). (M1)

1.2 The roles and responsibilities of travel and tourism organisations

ROLES AND RESPONSIBILITIES

Organisations in the travel and tourism industry fall into two different sectors: the profit sector, which is usually a private business that is involved in the industry to make money, and the not-for-profit sector, which does not need to make a profit or generate sales because the money to run it comes from elsewhere.

The vast majority of organisations in the travel and tourism industry are in the profit sector, but all of them have two key roles and responsibilities:

- meeting the organisation's aims and objectives

- providing services or products.

We will be looking primarily at businesses in the profit sector in the following sections.

Meeting the main organisational aims

Every organisation has a series of goals that are the organisation's objectives. They are designed to state what the organisation wants to do or achieve in the short, medium and long-term.

A short-term objective is usually one that can be achieved within a year or so. A medium-term objective could take two to five years, while a long-term objective may not be achieved for many years.

The objectives of the organisation will depend on the type of organisation it is, how old it is, how big it is and, of course, what the trends are in the market in which it operates.

Key words

Market – the total number of people who might want a particular product. In travel and tourism, a market might be people who go skiing, the total number of tourists booking holidays to Spain or the total number of visitors to a particular attraction

An organisation's aims may also be affected by factors beyond their control, such as high interest rates or unemployment. There are many different types of aims, but they really boil down to just two things:

- making enough money to cover costs

- making enough money to make a profit.

Making a profit

Making a profit means ensuring that the income of the organisation, or its revenue, is greater than the costs of the organisation, or its expenditure.

Key words

Interest rates – the cost of borrowing money, as set by the Bank of England on a monthly basis
Revenue – money coming into the business
Expenditure – money going out of the business

Profit can be measured in two different ways. The first is a simple calculation that involves subtracting the costs from the income of the organisation. The result is called the gross profit. However, businesses have to pay tax on their profits. The profit left after the tax has been taken off is called the net profit.

The owners of private businesses in the travel and tourism industry will want a return on their investment. Depending on what type of business is involved, these individuals will receive a share of the profit in proportion to the amount of money that they have invested in the business.

Key words

Return on their investment – this means that the investors want to make money from the investment they have made. This is usually a share of the profits

Maximising sales revenue

Maximising sales revenue means attracting as many customers as possible and encouraging them to spend money. This can be achieved by attracting new customers through advertising and special offers or by convincing existing customers to buy more products and services.

Businesses that show increases in sales tend to be more profitable, but this is not always the case in the travel and tourism industry. Take, for example, a tour operator that has already made a commitment to airlines and accommodation providers to sell a certain amount of seats or rooms over the summer period. It might find itself having to discount unsold holidays in order to fill the aircraft and the rooms. Although sales figures would look high, they would make less profit for every holiday that they have sold because the prices have been cut.

Key words

Discount – offering money off the price of a product or service in order to encourage customers to buy

Increasing market share

Market share is how much of a particular market is controlled by a business. Market share is calculated by comparing the sales of a particular business with the total sales in the market.

Example

If we wanted to know a particular tour operator's market share of the Spanish package holiday market, we would have to know how much the whole Spanish holiday market is worth to all tour operators. We can use the following formula:

Market share (%) = sales by the business/total sales in the market x 100

Let us suppose that the total holiday market is worth £800 million. If the business has total sales of £16 million, then we can calculate their market share in the following way:

£16m/£800m x 100 = 2%

By periodically checking the total amount of sales in the market compared to the current sales figures of the business, it is possible for the business to monitor their market share. If the total sales in the market increased, then the business would have to increase their sales in order to maintain their market share.

Ensuring compliance with regulations

Any business or organisation in the travel and tourism industry has to ensure that they comply with a wide range of different laws and regulations. Some are industry-specific, but many apply to all types of businesses. If the business is based in the UK, it will have to follow any laws or regulations set out by the UK government and, in many cases, also by the European Union. However, businesses operating abroad have to comply with local laws and regulations.

Example

Some of the major laws affecting the travel and tourism industry include:

* The Package Travel, Package Holidays and Package Tours Regulations 1992. These set out the responsibilities of travel and tourism businesses towards their customers and what rights their customers have.

* The Consumer Protection (Distance Selling) Regulations 2000. These cover any product or service sold over the Internet, digital television, mail order, catalogue, telephone or fax.

* The Enterprise Act 2000. This sets out consumer codes of practice and consumer law, and it aims to make all businesses trade in a fair way.

* The Data Protection Act 1998. This is the most recent version of a law that seeks to protect individuals from the misuse of their personal information by businesses.

Research tip

If you want to see any of the laws in detail, visit www.opsi.gov.uk. This is part of the Office of Public Sector Information and contains all laws relevant to the UK

In addition to these laws, the Association of British Travel Agents (ABTA) lays down the minimum standards required of its members. It represents 6,000 travel agencies and 850 tour operators in the UK.

The Association of Independent Tour Operators (AITO) represents many of the UK's specialist tour operators. They are all bound by AITO's code of business practice.

Providing services and products

Regardless of an organisation's particular involvement in the travel and tourism industry, they all provide either products or services to different customer groups. It is mainly a service-based industry. Services are things that customers purchase, such as an aircraft flight, insurance or an entrance fee to an attraction, but they are not physical products. Products do exist in the travel and tourism industry, but they are usually restricted to catering, souvenirs and other physical items.

Not all travel and tourism organisations deal directly with the public. Some deal with other organisations that are not related to the industry at all. Hotels, airlines and travel agents may deal with other organisations or businesses, providing services to them as customers.

> **Think** Businesses that operate between the provider and the consumer are called intermediaries. Why might it be in a hotel's interests to use an intermediary?

Other organisations in the industry deal solely with organisations within the travel and tourism sector. An airline may only deal with tour operators; a coach company may deal directly with travel agents or owners of attractions.

However, many parts of the industry deal with customers on a daily basis, for example, through retail travel agents, attractions, different types of transport and accommodation and through information services provided by tourist boards.

As we have seen, if an organisation does not deal directly with customers, it probably has representatives or business partners to sell its products or services. For example, an airline would use a tour operator and the tour operator would use a travel agent.

SECTORS OF THE TRAVEL AND TOURISM INDUSTRY

As far as the travel and tourism industry is concerned, we can identify two key sectors, these are:

- the profit sector – includes most accommodation, transport and attractions (unless entrance is free), and all tour operators, travel agents and ancillary services, such as insurance and car hire

- the not-for-profit sector – includes tourist boards, regulatory bodies, such as ABTA, conservation and heritage groups.

The important distinction between the two different sectors is the way in which the organisations are funded and their main roles and responsibilities.

Profit sector

In terms of sheer numbers, the profit sector dominates the industry. We should really use the word business rather than organisation to describe them as they are involved in the industry in order to make money. They provide products and services to other organisations inside or outside the industry or directly to customers.

Research tip

Thomas Cook is not just a travel agent, but also a tour operator. Their website is at www.thomascook.com

Profit sector businesses will seek to provide services and products at the cheapest cost to themselves and sell them at the highest price that customers are willing to pay. Once they have taken all other costs into consideration, the difference between a business's costs and its selling prices represents its profit.

These businesses play an important role in the economy. The UK's travel and tourism industry alone is worth over £70 billion. Worldwide, the industry employs 221 million people or 8.2% of total employment. A new job is created every 2.4 seconds.

Not-for-profit sector

Not all travel and tourism organisations are in the profit sector. Some do not need to make a profit. They simply need enough funds to carry out their work.

The regulatory bodies, such as ABTA and AITO, receive fees from members. Tourist boards receive money from local and central government to publicise the region for which they are responsible. Conservation groups receive money from donations and from their members.

CASE STUDY: RSPB

Figure 1.10 An RSPB reserve

The Royal Society for the Protection of Birds is a UK charity that works to secure a healthy environment for birds and other wildlife. Its total income in 2006 was £88.28 million with over £24 million coming from membership subscriptions and over £23 million from money left to them in people's wills. Over the same period, they spent over £82 million, mainly on species and habitat conservation, as well as on their nature reserves and education. They rely almost exclusively on support from the public and from their members in order to continue their work.

Adapted from www.rspb.org.uk

QUESTIONS

1. Visit the RSPB website and find out six other sources of income for the charity.

2. RSPB reports and accounts contain the phrase "costs of generating voluntary income". What do you think this term means?

3. Use the RSPB's website to find out how much it had in the bank at the end of 2006.

EVIDENCE ACTIVITY

P3 – M2 – D1

Your employer has asked you to select one organisation from the profit sector and one from the not-for-profit sector and prepare a follow-up presentation, looking at the various roles and responsibilities of at least one organisation from each sector. You need to choose organisations that give you the maximum opportunity to talk about a wide range of roles and responsibilities. Bear in mind that it is unlikely for an organisation to have just one major role or responsibility.

1. Describe the organisation's aims. (P3)

2. Describe the products and services it offers. (P3)

3. Describe the organisation's typical customers. (P3)

4. Identify which sector the organisation belongs to. (P3)

5. Compare your two organisations. You should look at the similarities that they have in their roles and responsibilities, as well as the key differences. Both will have organisational aims, but these may be different, as one organisation is in the profit sector and the other is in the not-for-profit sector. Both, however, will be concerned with providing products and services, either to organisations, the industry or customers. (M1)

6. Assess how the roles and responsibilities are affected by being in either the profit or not-for-profit sector. A tour operator would, for example, want to increase its sales revenue and profits by adopting a fairly aggressive sales strategy. This might also be true of a tourist board that has acquired a considerable marketing budget in order to promote their region or area of the country. However, it is the local travel and tourism industry that will benefit directly from their actions, rather than the tourist board itself. (D1)

1.3 How recent developments have shaped the present-day travel and tourism industry

RECENT DEVELOPMENTS

Changes in the travel and tourism industry are broadly driven by customer demand or by technological or product development. Significant developments since the 1960s include:

- the growth of package holidays and mass-market tourism

- the opening-up of long-haul destinations

- the establishment of high street travel agents

- improved aircraft technology

- the development of new transportation, including the Channel Tunnel, hovercraft, car ferries and high-speed ferries

- the post Second World War building of resorts like Butlin's and the decline of traditional seaside resorts.

Research tip

To find out more about Butlin's, visit their web site at www.butlinsonline.co.uk.

Legislation

We can trace the demand for travel and tourism services back to 1871, when the British government passed the Bank Holidays Act. This established the first real holidays and thousands of people flocked to British seaside towns. Later, in 1938, with the Holidays with Pay Act, British employees for the first time were guaranteed payment of their wages while on holiday.

British tourism itself really came into its own in 1969 when the Development of Tourism Act was passed. This established the tourist boards.

In terms of legislation, the following changes have been significant to the development of travel and tourism in the UK:

- employee entitlement to paid annual leave

- the opening-up of the countryside through Right to Roam legislation

- the facilitation of the development of tourism facilities and purpose-built areas through planning permission, often supported by government grants and assistance

- the Package Holidays and Package Tours Regulations that spell out the requirements of tour operators

- consumer protection legislation that protects customers in their dealings with businesses in the travel and tourism industry

- the free movement of people throughout Europe as a legal right and as a benefit of joining the European Union

- the availability of visas (a certificate in a passport giving permition to enter a country) to enter most countries in the world by the UK entering into agreements with those nations.

Research tip

To find out more about visas, visit www.ukvisas.gov.uk.

Example

Two more recent destinations in Europe are Krakow in Poland and Prague in the Czech Republic. Prague attracted 650,000 UK visitors in 2005, while Krakow attracted 60% more visitors in 2005 than in 2003, most of whom were on short city breaks.

Product development

A major product development in the industry is the increase in the different types of holidays offered. From the 1960s onwards, there was a huge growth in the package holiday business. All-inclusive package deals were offered to European destinations for the first time.

Things have gradually changed, although the mass-market package holiday is still very popular. Specialist holidays have developed with island cruises, short city breaks, and holidays to all-inclusive resorts and new destinations becoming increasingly popular. Many of these are long-haul destinations as the flight time from the UK is significantly more than the three or four hours to traditional Mediterranean resorts. The availability of long-haul flights has opened up tourism in countries as far away as Brazil, Thailand, Australia and New Zealand.

Figure 1.11 Krakow, in Poland, is a destination rapidly growing in popularity with UK tourists.

CASE STUDY: THOMAS COOK

The English publisher, Thomas Cook, is credited for having created the first travel package. He organised a journey by train for 500 people in July 1841. Over the next few years, the Cook family gradually developed their business, taking travellers to America and on steamboat cruises down the river Nile in Egypt. After Thomas Cook died in 1892, the business continued to grow and thrive. In 2005, the business celebrated its 150th anniversary of taking Britons abroad. From small beginnings, charging the equivalent of 5p for their first ever rail package, Thomas Cook now offers holidays to a thousand different locations. The company employs 11,000 people and there are nearly 600 high street shops, 7 travel warehouses, 3 call centres and over 120 bureau de change. The business is the third largest vertically-integrated travel group in the UK. It owns its own airline, tour operations and sales outlets.

Figure 1.12 In 2007 Thomas Cook ran 574 high street shops

QUESTIONS

1. What do you understand by the term 'vertically-integrated travel group'?

2. Thomas Cook is the third largest travel group in the UK. Find out which are the largest and second largest.

3. Visit Thomas Cook's web site at www.thomascook.com and visit the Corporate section to find out their mission statement.

Destination development

Barely a week goes by without tour operators or airlines announcing that new transport links will be established to new destinations around the world. Direct flights to major European cities provide new destinations with opportunities to attract tourists in large numbers for the first time.

Whenever a destination is opened up to direct flights and the possibility of package holidays or the arrival of independent travellers, a number of issues need to be addressed by the destination. Often the development will take place with the guidance of the tour operators who can advise on key facilities that will be demanded by their customers. The destination needs to ensure that its infrastructure is capable of dealing with the influx of tourists and that the resort facilities match the requirements of customers. In some cases, destinations have developed their tourism services in order to appeal to and become associated with particular types of holiday.

Key words

Independent traveller – an individual or a group of people who book their transport (e.g. airline flights) themselves and organise their transport and accommodation at their destination

Technological development

Technological developments have revolutionised the travel and tourism industry by enabling greater access to information and booking opportunities for customers. They have also facilitated the development of more streamlined systems in order to process bookings more efficiently. The four key technological developments are as follows.

- Computerised reservation systems – databases that can block in bookings by customers so that immediate availability, cost and other factors can be relayed back to the customer. The reservation system acts as a confirmation system for the tour operator, the airline and for the accommodation providers.

- Teletext – shows lists of up-to-date holiday information, providing the customers with the opportunity to browse available offers to find the right dates, destination and price for their trip. The travel and tourism industry, particularly tour operators and travel agents, often use this system as a means by which they can sell off any under-capacity at discounted prices.

- The Internet – many customer-facing tourism businesses have web sites where bookings can be made online, along with secure payment systems. Automated booking confirmations are sent to the customer. The tickets and holiday details can be posted to the customer shortly before the holiday using a computer reservation system. Tour operators' web sites only sell their own holidays, while other web sites, such as lastminute.com, offer holidays and packages from a variety of different providers. Some web sites focus primarily on selling flights from a variety of airlines, such as Flightline.

- Call centres – advertising and brochures produced by tour operators or travel agents prominently display call centre numbers. Customers can call to enquire about bookings. The call centre operator can confirm availability and make or change bookings by using a computer reservation system. Call centres are also proactive in the sense that they will call customers who have previously booked with them to offer discounts or special offers to encourage another booking.

Research tip

Lastminute.com's web site is www.lastminute.com. The website for Flightline is www.flightline.co.uk. Both websites offer the opportunity to book a flight only or to book flight and accommodation with ancillary services, such as car hire and insurance.

Transport development

Aircraft technology has improved substantially over the last two or three decades. Aircraft are now considerably larger and faster, and they are also capable of landing in much more restricted spaces.

Think What do you think the consequences of these changes would be?

There are also more flight options for passengers, allowing them to choose from first class, business class and economy class. For many long-haul flights, this has meant that the cost of seats caters for a much wider range of customers.

There has been a significant change in the number of airlines with the rapid growth of low-cost airlines, such as easyJet, Ryanair and Flybe. These no-frills airlines offer affordable transport to a wide variety of destinations in Europe and beyond. This has been accompanied by the development of new or improved airports. There are now many more regional airports operating in the UK and across Europe that fly to a greater number of destinations. These airports provide alternative transport routes and enable low-cost airlines in particular to operate into countries by flying to airports near major cities, even when the main airport serving that area is at full capacity.

Ryanair operates flights to Treviso airport in Venice, 30 kilometres from the city. Buses then transport visitors into Venice. By comparison, the main city airport is only 8 kilometres from the city.

Research tip

To find out more about low-cost airlines, visit these websites:

www.easyjet.com

www.ryanair.com

www.flybe.com

There have also been developments in other forms of transport. The railway system was privatised in the mid-1990s in the UK, bringing an increased investment in rolling stock. The Channel Tunnel was finally completed in 1994, allowing direct rail travel from London to northern Europe.

As an island, the UK traditionally depended on sea travel to reach other countries. The development of cheaper and faster alternatives, such as air travel and the Channel Tunnel, means that the once-popular sea travel has declined. Traditional ferry services have also faced increased competition from faster forms of transport, such as hovercraft and high-speed catamarans.

The other significant change in transport in the past 50 years has been the massive growth in private car ownership, which has increased year-on-year. Cars are now the most important means of transport for domestic tourism and they are used in outbound tourism using the Channel Tunnel, ferries or hovercraft.

Key words

Privatised – the sale of a publicly owned organisation to private individuals.

Lifestyle changes

The UK currently has a low rate of unemployment and levels of home ownership are at the highest point ever. These two trends mean that many people now enjoy high levels of disposable income. Many choose to spend money on travel and tourism. People are taking holidays more frequently, with the average duration of each holiday being ten days.

Between 1996 and 2005, the number of visits abroad each year by UK residents had increased from just over 42 million in 1996 to 66.4 million in 2005. Spending abroad had also doubled. In 1996, UK tourists spent £16.2 billion on their holidays. In 2005, they spent £32.1 billion. UK tourists spent nearly 450 million nights abroad in 1996; this had increased to nearly 669 million nights by 2005. It is estimated that 6 million Britons will be living abroad by 2020.

It is clear that major lifestyle changes are taking place. This has meant increased demand for the industry in the traditional package tourist market and alternative types of holiday, such as adventure travel and new destinations.

Research tip

For up-to-date statistics on the travel and tourism industry, go to www.statistics.gov.uk.

THE PRESENT-DAY TRAVEL AND TOURISM INDUSTRY

Today the travel and tourism industry continues to develop in terms of its structure (with vertical and horizontal mergers) and the products and services it offers.

Products and services

There has been a significant growth in mass tourism as well as the emergence of specialist travel services, particularly in the long-haul market. In the past, many people holidayed at British seaside resorts, but travel and tourism is now a global industry. Each year, new tourist destinations are being discovered. All governments now realise the significant impact that tourism can have on their country's income.

Business operations

Traditionally, businesses only operated in their particular part of the chain of distribution. Producers manufactured their products, which were then passed on to wholesalers that would then sell them to retailers. Consumers purchased finished goods from retailers. Chains of distribution in the travel and tourism industry are slightly different.

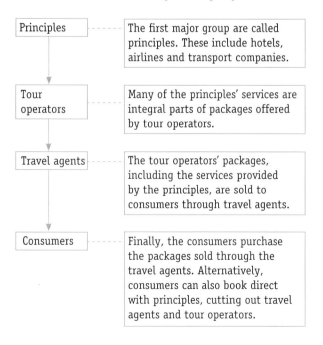

Principles	The first major group are called principles. These include hotels, airlines and transport companies.
Tour operators	Many of the principles' services are integral parts of packages offered by tour operators.
Travel agents	The tour operators' packages, including the services provided by the principles, are sold to consumers through travel agents.
Consumers	Finally, the consumers purchase the packages sold through the travel agents. Alternatively, consumers can also book direct with principles, cutting out travel agents and tour operators.

Figure 1.13 A chain of distribution

Today the travel and tourism industry has to operate in a very flexible way. Principles can sell their services directly to the consumer through advertising, the Internet and call centres. More commonly, principles still rely on tour operators to sell their products through their brochures or through Internet and television advertising.

Many businesses no longer operate solely in one part of the chain of distribution. They will buy or merge with other businesses.

Other companies will buy businesses in different parts of the chain of distribution or in different countries so that they can tap into new consumer markets.

Example

In 2006, First Choice, a tour operator, made 13 acquisitions, costing them over £145 million. They bought out other tour operators.

Key words

Acquisition – a business buying the assets, know-how and customer database of another business

Consumer demand

Consumer demand continues to increase year-on-year.

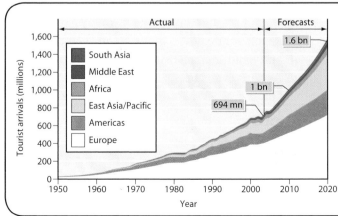

Figure 1.14 Projected international arrivals up to 2020

Source: World Tourism Organisation: Tourism 2020 Vision

Types of organisations

The industry in the UK is dominated by a handful
of businesses, including tour operators, such as
Thomson, First Choice and Thomas Cook, and

airlines, such as British Airways. The vast majority
of these businesses are privately owned. There is,
however, room in the industry for a large number of
small businesses. Of the 127,000 travel and tourism
businesses in the UK, 80% have a turnover of less
than £250,000. Many of these are in the specialist
holiday market or cater for independent travellers.

> **Key words**
> -------------
> Turnover – the amount of income a business makes in
> a financial year

Table 1.3 Types of organisations in the travel and tourism industry

Type of organisation or component of the travel and tourism industry	Description and current situation	Useful websites for further information
Airports	The major airports, including Heathrow, Gatwick and Stansted, are owned by the British Airports Authority.	www.baa.co.uk
Airlines	British Airways is the largest airline in the UK and the second largest international airline. Other major British airlines include British Midland, Virgin Atlantic, Monarch, and the Irish-based Ryanair and easyJet.	www.flybmi.com www.virgin-atlantic.com www.flymonarch.com
Ferry travel	Ferry travel operators include Norfolk Line and Trans Europa.	www.norfolkline-ferries.co.uk www.transeuropaferries.co.uk
Car hire	The major car hire businesses in the UK are Hertz, Avis and Europcar.	www.hertz.co.uk www.avis.co.uk www.europcar.co.uk
Railways	Network Rail owns the national rail network, although there are many different train operating companies, including Virgin, Central and One.	www.networkrail.co.uk www.virgintrains.co.uk www.centraltrains.co.uk www.onerailway.com
Other rail services	Other major rail systems include London Underground, the Docklands Light Railway in London and the Eurostar service that uses the Channel Tunnel.	www.tfl.gov.uk www.eurostar.com www.eurotunnel.com
Tour operators (the major ones)	Tour operators that have contracts with hotels, airlines and transport companies are dominated by four major businesses. These are Tui, MyTravel, First Choice and Thomas Cook.	www.tui.com www.mytravel.com www.firstchoice.co.uk www.thomascook.com
Tour operators (independent)	Cosmos is the UK's largest independent tour operator and owns Avro and Monarch Airlines.	www.cosmos.co.uk
Trade and regulatory bodies for tour operators	The support services for tour operators include the Association of Independent Tour Operators, the Association of British Travel Agents and the Federation of Tour Operators.	www.fto.co.uk
Travel agents	There are 6,500 travel agents' shops in the UK. The biggest chains are Thomas Cook, Thomson, Going Places and the Co-op's Travelcare.	www.goingplaces.co.uk www.travelcare.co.uk
Attractions (entrance fee payable)	The top three paid admission attractions in the UK are British Airways' London Eye, the Tower of London and the Eden Project in Cornwall.	www.londoneye.com www.hrp.org.uk www.edenproject.com
Attractions (free entrance)	The top three free admission attractions are Blackpool Pleasure Beach, the British Museum and National Gallery.	www.blackpoolpleasurebeach.com www.thebritishmuseum.ac.uk www.nationalgallery.org.uk
Hotels	Major hotel chains include The Hilton, Radisson and Holiday Inn. There are also motel chains, including Travelodge and Premier Travel Inn.	www.hilton.co.uk www.radisson.com www.holidayinn.co.uk www.travelodge.co.uk www.premiertravelinn.com

Competition

Competition is strong throughout the travel and tourism industry. Businesses must compete for customers.

> **Think** There is a term called 'the grey market'. They are the main customers of cruise liner companies. What do you think the grey market is? What other travel and tourism products might this group demand?

Employment

The major factors that have allowed the travel and tourism industry to grow are the development of new destinations and new customer markets around the world. China is the biggest market for new customers in the industry. The USA is beginning to become very important to the industry once again. Business travel continues to grow at a rate of around 5% a year.

The travel and tourism industry provides directly over 74 million jobs worldwide. However, when we include other industries that rely on travel and tourism in some way, such as construction (building hotels and infrastructure) and agriculture (producing food), the total indirect employment is around 221 million jobs.

Around 2.2 million people are employed by the travel and tourism sector in the UK alone. Just over 2 million of these are employees. The remaining 160,000 are self-employed or run their own businesses.

Contribution to Gross Domestic Product

The Gross Domestic Product (GDP) is a country's total earnings. GDP refers to all income generated within a country, whereas Gross National Product (GNP) is a country's total income, including money earned abroad. The travel and tourism industry accounts for about 4.5% of the UK's GDP. For many economically-developing countries, it represents a significant proportion of their earnings. Botswana's GDP has grown by nearly 500% over 10 years as a result of travel and tourism. Tourism is a principle earner for 83% of all economically-developing countries.

CASE STUDY: WHALES CONTRIBUTE, TOO

Figure 1.15 Dolphin watching in Scotland

Tourism brings £4.4 billion into Scotland every year and provides thousands of jobs. Each year 250,000 tourists are attracted to the west of Scotland to see the whales and dolphins. The region earned £1.7 million from direct whale-watching activities and £5.1 million from accommodation, food and travel.

Nearly 20% of the tourists stayed extra nights in the area after whale-watching, bringing in another £0.9 million.

In rural areas of Scotland, marine tourism can bring in up to 12% of the local income. Over 72% of the people employed are locals.

Tourism is the single most important employer on the island of Mull and whale-watching brings in £0.65 million every year.

Adapted from www.whaledolphintrust.co.uk

QUESTIONS

1. Why is whale-watching important to Scotland?

2. Why is it important for Scotland to make sure that tourism is sustainable?

3. Find out what other aspects of tourism occur on the island of Mull.

EVIDENCE ACTIVITY

P4

Your employer is holding a special meeting for shareholders. Some of the shareholders have owned shares in the company for twenty or more years. Your employer believes that some of them do not understand very much about recent developments in the travel and tourism industry. Your employer has therefore asked you to prepare a briefing on recent developments, many of which will be gradual developments.

1. Identify and describe the recent developments in the travel and tourism industry (perhaps product, destination, technological or transport). (P4)

2. Describe how the current travel and tourism provision has been affected by these developments over time. (P4)

1.4 *Trends and factors affecting the development of travel and tourism*

TRENDS

There are several key trends that can be identified as affecting the development of the industry.

- The increased frequency of holidays. This has been driven by cheaper flights and accommodation, higher competition driving prices down and people having higher levels of disposable income.

- Greater flexibility. Customers are able to state precisely what type of product they want and they can purchase it in different ways. This means that holidays can be tailored to the specific requirements of customers without having to buy a generic package that only partly meets their needs.

- Greater numbers of independent travellers. Customers book airline flights, accommodation and car hire directly rather than using package holiday tour operators. Initially, this was mainly to countries that were not served by tour operators, but it is now common practice, even for mass-market destinations, such as Spain and Greece.

- Growing popularity of adventure travel. Holidays include physical activities (e.g. mountaineering, trekking, backpacking or rafting) and cultural exchange. This growth has been made possible by the increased accessibility of remote areas.

- Growth of new destinations. These are often opened up by the availability of direct or near-direct flights. The destinations are appealing because they are viewed as exotic or unusual and they are often largely undeveloped without the trappings of mass tourism.

- The growth and expansion of regional airports both in the UK and across Europe. This has made air transport more accessible to more people. In the past, international flights were only available via a few airports in the UK. Now it is possible to fly from your local airport to mass tourism resorts as well as more unusual destinations.

Research tip

Your local regional airport is likely to have developed several internal domestic airline connections, as well as direct flights abroad. What is new this year? What are the new projected destinations during the next couple of years?

FACTORS AFFECTING THE DEVELOPMENT OF TRAVEL AND TOURISM

Some factors affecting the industry are events or circumstances that are beyond its control. (Many of the trends, on the other hand, are driven by developments in the industry or by the changing tastes and demands of customers.)

Natural disasters

Climatic disasters have had a drastic impact on the industry, as well as on the destinations and the residents living there. Two major recent disasters were Hurricane Ivan, which struck Grenada in 2003, and the tsunami that hit southeast Asia in 2004. The tsunami has had the longest-lasting effect on the industry. Many of the resorts in the Maldives, for example, were devastated as the infrastructure and accommodation were destroyed. The eastern coast of the popular destination of Thailand also suffered widespread destruction.

Health warnings and epidemics

The travel and tourism industry is affected by occasional health warnings and other scares, which can lead to the virtual closing-down of particular destinations, sometimes for a relatively long period of time. The most recent major incident was the outbreak of the SARS virus.

Research tip

The Tourism Emergency Response Network, or TERN's, website can be found at www.ternalert.org.

The Tourism Emergency Response Network monitors worldwide problems. For example, at the beginning of 2007, there were bird flu outbreaks in the Philippines, Indonesia, Egypt and Hungary.

Terrorism

Despite the fact that areas such as the Middle East have been dangerous for many years as far as tourists are concerned, the terrorism attack that has had most effect on the worldwide travel and tourism industry were the attacks on the World Trade Centre in 2001. The number of Americans travelling overseas declined and only began to recover after 2004.

Specific locations, such as Bali, have also suffered very badly from terrorist attacks. It took two years for Bali to recover from the terrorist attacks that killed 200 people in 2002. Recent attacks in Turkey, Kenya, Egypt, Madrid and London have all had a negative impact on domestic, inbound and outbound tourism.

Figure 1.16 Airport staff screen passengers arriving in Hong Kong for the SARS virus

Environmental issues

Many scientists believe that some natural disasters, such as the increased frequency of hurricanes in the southern United States, are partly caused by travel and tourism.

The industry has taken steps to promote responsible tourism, and specifically eco-tourism. Eco-tourism means visiting environmentally sensitive areas, but ensuring that the tourist trade does not adversely affect the area. This is also known as sustainable tourism, where the development of resorts or tourism infrastructure is built to a limited level in order to preserve natural habitats and ways of life.

> ### Research tip
>
> For further information on eco-tourism and useful links, visit www.peopleandplanet.net.

> ### Research tip
>
> To find out more about responsible tourism, visit the website of the International Centre for Responsible Tourism at www.icrtourism.org.

Cost of travel

The cost of travel has fallen over recent years. Once the domain of the wealthy, travel is now within the grasp of almost everyone, helped by the availability of cheap transport, such as low-cost flights.

DEVELOPMENT

During the 1990s, the top four British tour operators dominated mass-market travel, sharing 50% of the package holiday market. The growth of the independent travel sector means that it now accounts for 30% to 44% of the overall tourism market. This change seems to have been driven by low-cost airlines, use of the Internet and increased ownership of second homes abroad. As a result, the package holiday market is generally in decline, but the overall travel and tourism market is growing at a rate of around 6% per year.

New products and services

In terms of key developments in the industry, the following are growth areas:

- the general improvement of air and ground transport infrastructure

- improved environmental management

- community-based tourism development

- eco-tourism development

- heritage and cultural tourism development.

Retail and business travel operations

The number of travel agents has decreased by approximately 100 retail outlets every year since 1991. In 1991, there were 2,800 outlets in London alone, but this figure is now under 1,500. Many smaller chains were bought up by the big four operators. Nationwide, travel agents on the high street peaked at 7,000, but nearly 1,000 have closed since then.

Example

To read the press release from First Choice Holidays about the sale of their retail and business travel operations, visit www.firstchoiceholidaysplc.com. Click on the Media link and select Press releases and archive years. Click on 2003 and select the Disposal of Spanish Leisure Retail and International Business link.

The UK's business travel market is worth around £6.8 billion. Business travel incorporates the following:

- scheduled flight reservations

- executive aircraft and helicopter charter

- rail travel

- journey planning

- reservation services

- worldwide hotel reservation services

- self-drive and chauffeur-driven car rentals

- car ferry reservations.

In addition to this, business travel providers handle travel insurance, passport and visa services, parking services and leisure services, such as the booking of theatre and special event tickets. One of the largest business travel providers is Business Travel International (www.bti-worldwide.com).

Consumer demand

Strong consumer demand continues to transform the industry. In 2006, the online travel and entertainment retailer, www.lastminute.com, was sold for the second time in just over a year for £2.2 billion. The new owner, Sabre Holdings, also owns www.travelocity.co.uk, which is the second largest online travel booking business in the United States.

According to the World Travel and Tourism Council, total consumer demand grew by 4.6% in 2006. Between 2007 and 2016, the demand is expected to grow at a rate of 4.2% per year. On average, consumers spend 9.5% of their total personal income on travel and tourism-related products and services. This is expected to reach 9.8% by 2016. In terms of the world's total demand for travel and tourism, the European Union leads the way, followed by North America and northeastern Asia.

Research tip

Visit the World Travel and Tourism Council's website at www.wttc.org to find out more about future trends and consumer demand for travel and tourism.

Distribution methods

The greater frequency of travel has led to the creation of new businesses at different levels of the industry. Many of the large operators, including Thomson, have significantly restructured, so that they have several different brands with each one focused on a different market (e.g. higher value holidays and niche market holidays).

The development of the Internet has changed distribution methods by enabling the development of e-tourism. As a result, there is a transition underway from offline to online distribution. Internet sales are growing at a rate of 35% to 40% each year.

> ***Think*** What are the advantages of e-tourism to consumers? What are the disadvantages?

Another significant change in the distribution method has been the so-called low-cost frontier. This has been driven by the arrival of low-cost airlines, encouraging independent travel, improving access to more destinations, and increasing demand for low-cost travel in general.

This has caused some concern for traditional tour operators. With customers that are increasingly tending to opt either for low-cost travel or for luxury travel options, the market for the standard middle ground is shrinking.

> ***Think*** Do you think the middle ground of products will eventually disappear?

EVIDENCE ACTIVITY

P5 – M3 – D2

Your employer also feels that it would be useful to explain to the shareholders the key trends and factors that are currently affecting the travel and tourism industry. They must be relevant and relatively up-to-date.

1. Describe three key trends affecting the development of the travel and tourism industry. (P5)

2. Describe three key factors affecting the development of the travel and tourism industry. (P5)

Your employer feels that some of the shareholders already know about recent developments, but do not understand their relevance. For example, the end of hostilities in the Former Yugoslavia and the rebuilding of resorts and infrastructure in the area have opened up countries like Croatia and Montenegro as tourist destinations. Another example would be increased choice in the package holiday market, where customers can mix and match flights, accommodation and duration.

3. Explain how recent developments have shaped the present travel and tourism industry. (M3)

4. Explain how key trends and factors are likely to shape the industry in the future. (M3)

Your employer also realises that the shareholders will not be satisfied with a description and an explanation of the current trends and factors. They will want some recommendations and justifications regarding future strategies. For example, the increased concern of long haul travellers leaving a high carbon footprint. A part of this would be the increased environmental tax levied on travellers, the impact on the destination and on global warming.

5. Suggest how the industry could adapt to trends and factors affecting it. (D2)

6. Describe in detail how organisations or sectors could benefit if they are able to adapt to identified trends and factors. (D2)

The business of travel and tourism

unit 2

To be successful in any business you need to understand and develop the competitive advantage of your business over that of the competition. In this unit, you will be learning about how a business manages and develops a competitive advantage. You will also be looking at how an organisation can manage the cash flow of the business and how this cash flow management is vital to the organisation's success.

You will also be able to plan a project in the workplace and adapt it to fit within the financial constraints while meeting the project's objectives.

Lastly, you will be investigating how different organisations compete with each other within the marketplace.

By the end of this unit, you will:

2.1 Know the features of different types of travel and tourism organisations   page 45

2.2 Be able to complete a cash flow forecast   page 49

2.3 Be able to plan a travel and tourism project within financial constrains   page 54

2.4 Understand how a travel and tourism organisation gains competitive advantage to achieve its aims   page 62

So you want to be a...

Hotel Manager

My name Nathan May
Age 28
Income £26,000

Managing an organisation is hard work, but if you relish a challenge, hotel management could give you the responsibility and rewards you've always wanted.

What does a Hotel Manager do?

I manage the day to day running of all aspects of the hotel and ensure that the hotel's standards are maintained. I have overall responsibility for each department in the hotel: kitchen, restaurant, housekeeping, receptions, porters, conference and banqueting and the bars. Budget setting and high-level recruitment are also part of my job.

That sounds like a lot – what skills do I need?

People skills are vital in any management role. You also need a good understanding of finance, like cash flow and income statements. You need to be able to think on your feet, resolve conflicts and problems for both guests and staff and keep a level head.

How did you get into the job?

I went to College and studied a GNVQ Advance in Travel and Tourism, then started working in a local travel agency but soon realised it wasn't for me. I quit and went University, where I got a Degree in Hospitality Management.

I joined a two-year graduate training scheme with a large hotel group and started my role here; I've been here 4 years now.

If I want a career in hotel management, where should I look for jobs?

I saw an advertisement for it in the *Caterer and Hotelkeeper*, although it was also advertised on the company website and in a local newspaper. We advertise for staff at the local college.

How good is the training?

I had a two week training session at a sister hotel before I started here to learn the company's systems and procedures.

I've heard the hours are demanding – what's it really like?

It depends on the time of year – December is incredibly busy, what with all the Christmas parties. The rest of the year is less manic - I usually work 50-60 hours a week.

Are there any extra perks?

There are a number of benefits like free accommodation, profit share schemes and meals allowances.

What about career development?

Eventually I would like to open my own restaurant or a country pub, but for now I'm happy working here. The advantage of working for a big company is that there is the possibility of promotion to area manager or moving into a head office management role.

> **❝ You need to be able to think on your feet ❞**

Grading criteria

The table below shows what you need to do to gain a pass, merit or distinction in this part of the qualification. Make sure you refer back to it when you are completing work so you can judge whether you are meeting the criteria and what you need to do to fill in gaps in your knowledge or experience.

In this unit there are 3 evidence activities that give you an opportunity to demonstrate your achievement of the grading criteria:

page 48	P1, P2, M1
page 52	P3, M2, D1
page 61	P4, M3
page 67	P5, P6, M4, D2

To achieve a pass grade the evidence must show that the learner is able to...	To achieve a merit grade the evidence must show that, in addition to the pass criteria, the learner is able to...	To achieve a distinction grade the evidence must show that, in addition to the pass and merit criteria, the learner is able to...
P1 Describe the features of a selected profit-making travel and tourism organisation	**M1** Compare the features of a profit-making and a non-profit-making travel and tourism organisation	**D1** Make realistic recommendations to resolve cash flow problems
P2 Describe the features of a selected non-profit-making travel and tourism organisation	**M2** Interpret the cash flow forecast, explaining how problems have occurred	**D2** Suggest and justify other ways either a profit-making and non-profit-making organisation could gain competitive advantage
P3 Complete a cash flow forecast for a travel and tourism organisation for a minimum of a six-month period	**M3** Explain how a plan for a travel and tourism project enables the objectives to be met within financial constraints	
P4 Plan a travel and tourism project within financial constraints	**M4** Compare how specified profit-making and non-profit-making organisations seek to gain competitive advantage	
P5 Explain how a chosen profit-making organisation seeks to gain competitive advantage to meet its aims		
P6 Explain how a chosen non-profit-making organisation seeks to gain competitive advantage to meet its aims		

2.1 *Know the features of different types of travel and tourism organisations*

TYPES OF ORGANISATIONS

All organisations can be categorised as one of two types: profit-making or non-profit-making.

> **Think** Create a list of five organisations that you think are profit-making, and five that you think are non-profit making. Use the Internet to check your answers.

Profit making

These are organisations that are in business to make money for the owners. The owners could be an individual, partners or shareholders.

Key words

Partner – a member of a partnership, which is an organisation that can have from 2 to 20 owners who have equal liability

Shareholder – an owner of one or more shares, which are small parts of a company

Non-profit-making

These organisations are not in business to make a profit. The sector includes charities and government organisations.

Example

The National Trust is a charity and it is completely independent of the government. Its income depends on membership fees, donations and legacies, and revenue raised from its commercial operations. More than 72 million people visit a National Trust destination every year. The organisation also looks after forests, beaches, farmland, islands, archaeological remains, castles, nature reserves and much more.

> **Think** Why is the National Trust not interested in making a profit?

Research tip

Find out more about the National Trust and its business by looking at its website www.nationaltrust.org.uk.

CASE STUDY: VIRGIN

Virgin Atlantic sells the transportation of passengers from one destination to another while making a profit for its shareholders in the process.

Figure 2.1

Virgin, one of the leading brands in Britain, is also one of the major global brand names of the 21st century. We are involved in planes, trains, finance, soft drinks, music, mobile phones, holidays, wines, publishing, space tourism and cosmetics. These diverse businesses are tied together by the strong brand names.

Virgin have created over 200 companies worldwide, employing over 35,000 people. Their total revenues around the world in 2002 exceeded £4 billion.

Source: www.virgin.com

FEATURES

Every organisation will have a number of features as regards the way in which the company is managed. This section will be looking at ownership, liability, distribution of profits, control, sources of finance and the documentation that you need to set up the business.

Ownership

There are a number of different ways in which an organisation can be owned. Types of ownerships are:

- Sole traders: they own the business themselves in a similar way that you own a house or car.

- Partnership: each partner owns a specific amount of the organisation, which is set out in the partnership agreement.

- Limited companies: these are owned by shareholders who are individuals or organisations that have invested money in the company by buying a share(s).

- Members: these tend to be non-profit-making organisations that have membership. The members are the owners of the organisation. They may or may not take part in the day-to-day running of the organisation.

Liability

The level of liability that an owner of an organisation has depends on the type of organisation itself. A sole trader is liable for all debts that the organisation may have. This level of liability is the same for a partnership with the exception that all partners are liable for the debts of the organisation. For limited companies, as the name suggests, there is a limit to the level of liability. A shareholder is only liable for the amount that they have invested into the organisation.

Distribution of profits

For profit-making organisations, the profits have to be distributed between the owners of the organisation. For a sole trader, this is straightforward as the sole trader is the only owner. The profits, minus the taxation, belong to the sole trader. For a partnership, the distribution of profits will be set out in the partnership agreement before the company starts operating. For limited companies, the profit needs to be split between the owners and the shareholders. This is paid in the form of dividends to shareholders.

Not all the profits from a profit-making organisation will be given to the owners, some of the funds may be retained to reinvest in the organisation. If a non-profit-making organisation has a surplus of funds, this money will also be reinvested in the organisation or put into a contingency fund.

Key words

Debts – any payments owing from the company
Dividend – the amount that each owner will get for every share they own of the organisation

Control

As far as the law is concerned, a sole trader has total control over their business. This is reflected by the level of liability discussed above.

Boards of directors have strategic control of their organisation. However, they are answerable to the shareholders of the organisation and have to work within the guidelines set out in the Companies Act. This includes publishing of annual accounts and registration of company and directors at Companies House.

Key words

Board of directors – the collective term for all the directors in an organisation
Companies Act – refers to a number of pieces of legislation that are used to regulate trade. The most recent version is the Companies Act 2006

Research tip

Find out more about Companies House by visiting the website www.companieshouse.gov.uk. Use the WebCheck service to learn about any travel or tourism company that you've learned about so far.

Figure 2.2 Board directors are answerable to shareholders

Trustees are the people who act as the governing body of a charity.

The Charity Commission states the responsibility of a trustee as follows:

Trustees have and must accept ultimate responsibility for directing the affairs of a charity, and ensuring that it is solvent, well-run, and delivering the charitable outcomes for which it has been set up.

> **Think** What are the benefits and disadvantages of each type of ownership?

Sources of finance

Organisations require capital to set up or expand the organisation and sometimes even to help with everyday expenses. There are a number of places that this money can be sourced. Banks are organisations that make profit for shareholders through the lending of money to businesses and individuals. The two main types of loans that you are likely to receive from a bank are overdrafts or business loans. An overdraft is a facility that allows money to be taken out of your account if there is actually no money there. Limits are agreed before an overdraft is issued on an account. A business loan is the lending of a specific amount of money over a fixed period of time with an agreed repayment plan and timescale.

Friends and family can also be willing to help, but this can put pressure on your relationship if the business does not go well.

Another method of raising funds is to sell shares or part ownership of the company, either publicly or privately. This is a good way for a small company to generate a large amount of capital to expand, but it does lead to the ownership of the company being handed over to the shareholders.

Grants are amounts of money paid by the government to encourage organisations to behave in a particular way. There have been a number of grants available recently for small businesses to pay for staff training and development. Grants can also be used to encourage growth in particular areas of the economy or country to help increase employment.

> **Key words**
> Capital – money invested in the business rather than generated by trade. It is usually used for significant amounts of money

Documentation needed to set up a business

No specific documents are required to set up as a sole trader. You will, however, need to inform the tax office as you will have to self-declare income tax. For a partnership, a partnership agreement will need to be written. This should be done by a solicitor and state the relationship between partners and responsibilities. The following documents are required to set up a limited company: Certificate of Incorporation, Memorandum of Association, Articles of Association.

Key words

Incorporation – the process of setting up and registering a company

Certificate of Incorporation

This is obtained from Companies House by lodging a Memorandum of Association and Articles of Association with the Registrar of Companies. This can take some time and you may not trade under the company name as a limited company.

Memorandum of Association

This is the company's charter and will contain the following information:

- The name of the company and location of the registered offices.

- The objects of the business, which are the objectives why the company is being formed. It will also cover the area of business.

- The limits of liability of the shareholders.

- The share capital, a statement of the amount of share capital that is authorised and how this makes up the price of each share.

- The name of signatories. All companies must have two signatories at the time of incorporation with one signatory being a director.

Articles of Association

This document contains information about the management of the organisation. It includes the appointment of directors with their areas of responsibility and contains details of the procedure of company meetings. The Articles of Association is also concerned with relationships between the organisation and its shareholders.

Although these are the only documents required to set up a company, you will need to have sales and cash flow forecasts and budgets to approach a bank or an investor to acquire capital. You also need to keep financial records of the actions of the business.

Research tip

Most high street banks will give you information packs about the documentation that they require and standard forms to use for setting up a business bank account.

EVIDENCE ACTIVITY

This activity could be used as evidence for the following assessment criteria: P1, P2 and M1.

1. Describe the features of one profit-making and one non-profit-making travel and tourism organisation. (P1, P2) If you are planning to use this as evidence for your qualification, check with your tutor that the two organisations are suitable. You should include the following features: Ownership, Liability, Distribution of profits, Control, Sources of finance and Documentation needed to set up the business.

2. Compare the features of a profit-making and non-profit-making travel and tourism organisation that you describe in previous task. (M1) Your description could be in the form of a report or a presentation.

2.2 *Be able to complete a cash flow forecast*

CASH FLOW FORECAST

Every organisation will have money coming in and going out of the business. It is vital that the business manages the flow of cash into and out of the business. If you do not have the funds that are required to be able to pay for supplies or bills, then it possible that the organisation will cease trading and it may be declared bankrupt.

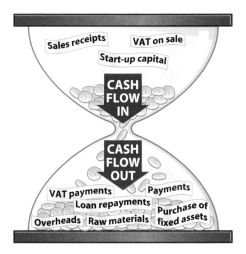

Figure 2.3 Examples of cash flow in and cash flow out

Cash inflows

An organisation requires cash to flow into the organisation to cover the expenses of everyday business. This inflow of cash comes from three main sources.
1) Receipts on sales.
2) VAT on sales.
3) Start-up capital.

Receipts on sales

Only a few travel and tourism organisations make all their sales in cash. Sales are increasingly done by credit cards or credit sales. Obviously, cash sales mean that the money earned can be used again immediately for the business. This is called liquidity. However, credit cards may take a little longer to receive payment, usually 3–5 working days. Credit sales take much longer to get the money into your bank and therefore the liquidity of credit sales could cause cash flow problems.

VAT on sales

Most products sold in the UK will have some element of Value Added Tax (VAT) added to them. Current rates run at 0%, 10% or 17.5%, depending on the items. As a business, you have an obligation to collect this VAT from your sales and then to pay this collected taxation to the Inland Revenue four times a year. The taxation that you collect never belongs to your organisation and you are only collecting it on behalf of the government. Depending on the size of turnover, an organisation can claim VAT back off the government for any VAT paid on purchases against the amount collected from sales.

Start-up capital

Start-up capital means the money that is invested in the organisation to set up the business. Businesses might also require capital to expand the business. This may come from additional investment from current owners or from share capital coming from incorporation.

> **Key words**
> ---
> Credit sale – a sale where the customer will pay the account at a later date. This is particularly common in business-to-business transactions. Typical credit terms could be 30 days
> Liquidity – the ability to use cash or debts within your organisation

TOTAL CASH INFLOWS

Total cash flow is the sum of the three inflows of cash that have been covered on this page. In a cash flow forecast this will be shown as a total of the cash inflow column.

Table 2.2 Cash flow forecast to show total income

Month	January	February	March	April	May	June
Receipts on sales	10,000	10,000	10,000	10,000	15,000	15,000
VAT on sales	1,750	1,750	1,750	1,750	2,625	2,625
Capital	20,000	0	0	0	0	0
Total income	31,750	11,750	11,750	11,750	17,625	17,625

CASH OUTFLOWS

Every business must have money flowing out of the company to pay for bills, supplies etc. This part of the cash flow forecast will look at the major types of outflows that a business can expect to have.

Payments

Payments are any outgoings that pay for a service that your organisation has received. This could be as simple as a payment to the window cleaner for cleaning the travel agency windows or fees for a management consultant that has been working for the organisation.

Raw materials

These are the materials that the product is made from. In most cases in travel and tourism, we do not generate products from raw materials. The only exception is food production in hotels. It is worthwhile considering that the components of the package holiday (accommodation, transportation and connections) could be viewed as the raw materials that a tour operator uses to make the package holiday.

Figure 2.4 Aviation fuel is considered to be a raw material

Loan repayments

Many organisations require financial support from banks or investors. This support is usually in the form of a loan. These loans will require repayment to be made in regular instalments. This is made clear in the loan contract and is part of the terms on which the money is loaned to the organisation.

Overheads

Overheads are the everyday costs of running a business. These include heat, light and power, rent and rates, water rates, staff wages, stationery costs, hiring of equipment and petty cash. Some organisations look at these together in a cash flow forecast and others will itemise them, depending on the size of the business and the level of the costs. Wages tend be the largest of all overheads in a hotel, for example, and they are often kept separate in a cash flow forecast as this is a key operating indicator of the control of overheads.

Overheads can be viewed as two different types: fixed and variable. Fixed overheads remain the same, regardless of the amount of trade your business does and includes costs such as water rates, rent and staff wages. Variable costs will change depending on the amount of trade in the business and could include material costs.

Purchase of fixed assets

A business will need to buy equipment, fixtures and fittings, vehicles and buildings. These assets are referred to as fixed because they will remain in the organisation for more than one year's accounting period. However, the purchasing of these assets may have a substantial effect on the organisation's cash flow. Some organisations in the travel and tourism industry have huge amounts of money invested in their fixed assets.

> **Think** How much do you think it would cost to buy a Boeing 747 or a hotel with 100 rooms?

> **Key words**
> Asset – property that has monetary value, which is owned or part-owned by the business

VAT payments

The VAT payments that you have collected on behalf of the government will need to be paid every three months. It is worth remembering that the money that is collected for VAT is never the property of the business. As you can see from the example below, this can have a significant effect on the cash flow of your business and needs to be considered in your cash flow forecasting.

Total cash outflows

Similar to total cash inflow, total cash outflow is the sum of the total of cash outflows.

Net cash flow

The net cash flow is the balance between cash flow in and cash flow out of the business in the time period. This is a useful figure to have as it does help you to understand the balance of the cash flow in the business. However, as the business operates continuously and not in isolation from one time period to another, the cash flow at a set point might not give the whole picture.

Balance brought forward

This is the opening balance for the month's cash flow. As the first of this month followed the last day of last month, the balance carried forward from last month is the balance brought forward for this month. Or in other words, it is the amount of money you have or do not have in the bank at the beginning of the month.

Balance carried forward

The balance carried forward is the closing balance of the cash flow for a particular period. This is made up of the balance carried forward, plus the net cash flow for the period. If the business purchases an expensive fixed asset, this might make the cash flow forecast look less attractive than having money in the bank. However, money in the bank is not actually working for the business, whereas money invested in an asset might be generating profit for the business. Therefore, we have to make a judgement on what level of cash reserves we need to keep in the bank and at what level the money should be reinvested into the organisation or paid out to owners and/or shareholders.

Table 2.3 Total cash outflow

Month	January	February	March	April	May	June
Payments	1,000	1,000	1,000	1,000	1,000	1,000
Raw material	500	750	750	750	1,000	1,000
Loan repayments	250	250	250	250	250	250
Overhead	2,000	2,000	2,000	2,000	2,000	2,000
Purchase fixed assets	0	0	10,000	0	0	0
VAT payments	0	0	5,250	0	0	7,000
Total cash flow out	3,750	4,000	19,250	4,000	4,250	11,250

Table 2.4 Cash flow forecast showing net and balance figures

Month	January	February	March	April	May	June
Receipts on sales	10,000	10,000	10,000	10,000	15,000	15,000
VAT on sales	1,750	1,750	1,750	1,750	2,625	2,625
Capital	20,000	0	0	0	0	0
Net cash flow in	31,750	11,750	11,750	11,750	17,625	17,625
Payments	1,000	1,000	1,000	1,000	1,000	1,000
Raw material	500	750	750	750	1,000	1,000
Loan repayments	250	250	250	250	250	250
Overhead	2,000	2,000	2,000	2,000	2,000	2,000
Purchase fixed assets	0	0	10,000	0	0	0
VAT payments	0	0	5,250	0	0	7,000
Total cash flow out	3,750	4,000	19,250	4,000	4,250	11,250
Net cash flow	28,000	7,750	(7,500)	7,750	13,375	6,275
Balance brought forward	0	28,000	35,750	28,250	36,000	39,375
Balance carried forward	28,000	35,750	28,250	36,000	39,375	45,650

Key words

Brackets ( ) – used in accounts to symbolise a negative amount. This makes it clearer to see which figures are negative as a minus sign could easily be missed in a table of figures

Research tip

Look at some different companies accounts online. (Try PLCs as they should be published.)

Example

Traditional National Carrier (TNC) is a European airline that was set up in the 1950s. It was formerly the national airline of a small central European country that was privatised in the 1980s. In recent years, the profit margins on flights have reduced due to competition from low-cost airlines and increased competition on the routes that TNC fly.

Due to the reduced profits and the need to pay dividends to shareholders, the amount of money that TNC has been able to invest in its fleet has reduced year on year. TNC's fleet is now ageing and it is not ready to compete with the new super-jumbos, such as the Airbus A380, that its competitors are investing in.

Think What could the management of TNC do to stop this decline?

EVIDENCE ACTIVITY

This activity could be used as evidence for the following grading criteria: P3, M2 and D1.

1. Complete the cash flow forecast for a travel and tourism organisation for a minimum of six months. (P3) (see blank cash flow chart on the next page)

Flyway Travel is a small independent travel agency based in your town, owned by Mr Cox. It has come up with the following information and Mr Cox has asked you to complete a cash flow forecast for the company as he knows that you have been studying cash flow at college.

Use the following information to complete the cash forecast for Flyway Travel:

a) The bank balance at the beginning of the year was £10,000.

b) The forecast for sales for the year is £240,000. This does not include VAT, which is charged at 17.5% on all the holidays sold.

c) They expect 25% of their sales in January and 25% of sales in February and the other 10 months to have equal sales.

d) Mr Cox plans to invest £50,000 capital in June. This money is to be used in August to buy a new computer system for the agency at a cost of £50,000.

e) Flyway Travel has no outstanding loans that need repayment.

f) Flyway Travel plans to have a computer consultant to help install the new computer system. His fee will be £5,000 a month for the three months of June, July and August.

g) Raw material costs and the cost of holidays from tour operators are 75% of the receipts.

h) VAT is payable in every third month: March, June, September, December.

i) Flyway Travel Overheads run at £6,000 a month and tend not to vary during the year.

2. Interpret the cash flow forecast, explaining how problems have occurred. (M2)
From the cash flow you have produced for Flyway Travel, can you explain any issues and problems that Flyway might have in 2008?

3. Make realistic recommendations to resolve cash flow problems. (D1)

4. Make a list of recommendations of how you would solve this cash flow issue.

Cash flow forecast for Flyway Travel												
Month	Jan	Feb	March	April	May	June	July	Aug	Sept	Oct	Nov	Dec
Receipts on sales												
VAT on sales												
Capital												
Net cash flow in												
Payments												
Raw material												
Loan repayments												
Overheads												
Purchase fixed assets												
VAT Payments												
Total cash flow out												
Net cash flow												
Balance brought forward												
Balance carried forward												

2.3 Be able to plan a travel and tourism project within financial constraints

Travel and tourism organisations tend to break their structure down into small teams. This could be a cabin crew on a flight working for a large international airline or a resort team looking after customers on holiday for a tour operator. These are the front line teams that the customers see delivering the services that they have paid for. There are also a large number of teams supporting the service delivery teams. These include marketing teams that promote the product and finance teams that control and keep financial records. This learning outcome aims to give you a better insight into the working of some of these teams when planning a project.

PROJECT PLAN

Earlier in this unit, we looked at organisations and the fact that they are made up by groups of individuals working together towards a specific goal. In order to achieve a goal, especially if the aim is complex, the goal needs to be broken down into specific projects that work towards achieving the overall goal of the organisation. For example, one of its many aims of a privately owned company is to make money for the owners or shareholders. There are many privately owned

organisations in the travel and tourism industry that all have the same fundamental aim, but they all work in different ways to achieve this.

A plan is a structured idea of how a team will achieve its aim. There are a number of issues that have to be set and agreed on before you draw up a project plan.

Objectives

A team requires well-defined objectives to be able to pull together in a united force to create a plan.

An objective is a specific target that can be worked towards. Modern business tend to use the anagram SMARTER as a structure to help to set these objectives.

SMARTER stands for:
Specific
Measurable
Achievable
Realistic/Relevant
Timeframe
Evaluated
Recorded

This structure helps teams to set objectives that are achievable, but challenging. The issue of being measurable helps the team by being able to measure success and its progress towards the objective.

CASE STUDY: HOTEL OCCUPANCY

It is common practice in hotels to have daily room occupancy targets. These targets are set so that all members of the hotel reception team know what the daily target is for the number of rooms that should be sold.

This might seem to be quite a strict way of working and it could be said that it is impossible to increase the number of people booking into a hotel because people will only want a room when they want it and advertising will not increase occupancy in the short term.

In the case of a small hotel in Oxfordshire where the owner offered the reception staff a £5 bonus for every room sold after 5pm for that evening's

occupancy, it was found that, through contacting other hotels in the area and the local tourist information centre to swap room occupancy figures, it was quite possible to find customers.

It might seem quite strange that you would want to swap such confidential information with your competition. As room occupancy is a key operating indicator of the success of failure of the business.

QUESTION

Why do you think this help all the hotels in the area?

Although a long-term target is needed when setting objectives, it is always better to break objectives down into smaller goals. This makes them seem more achievable and it also helps teams to remain focused on the target.

This is best demonstrated by the fact that a 400 metre race is easier for a 4 x 100-metre relay team member than a 400-metre runner.

Figure 2.5 Breaking tasks down into smaller sections helps to keep teams focused

---

Example

It becomes an easier target to increase sales by 1% per month for each month of the year. Whereas to increase sales by 15.9% in a year seems a harder target to achieve and the staff are more likely to lose interest, although the financial targets are the same.

Timescales

All projects need timescales. These timescales are usually dictated by the circumstances and outside pressures. For example, in a theme park and many other seasonal visitor attractions and resorts, the timescale may require that a new ride or attraction is completed before the reopening of the park or attraction in the closed session.

The timescale may also need to be short to minimise disruption or to fit into the needs of a business. The most important time to advertise summer holidays is after Christmas. Most of the large tour operators have promotional campaigns set to start on Boxing Day. This is because a large number of people, who work and only have four weeks holiday every year, start to think about their summer holiday after the Christmas holiday is over.

It is important to set a schedule that includes the timescales of key performance indicators.

> ### Key words
> --
> Key performance indicators – points that you can measure achievement by for the project's objectives. These inform whether you are on track to achieve the targets

Finances

Almost every project has financial constraints. As money is one of the key aims of a private business, the expenditure of finances has to be controlled and set for a project.

A budget will be set for the project and it should be broken down by expenditure within different areas of the project. Detailed quotes from suppliers should be used to help to set the budget. It is important not to estimate cost, but to find actual prices. It is also a good idea to have a contingency fund, which is an amount of your budget put aside in case of an unforeseen expense.

Finance control is also a huge issue in the non-profit-making sector as the monies have to be found either from organisations' savings or from raising more funds from members or cancelling other projects.

This is also an issue for the public sector where money is raised through taxation.

CASE STUDY: COST OF LONDON OLYMPICS SET TO RISE

Figure 2.6 Initial celebrations have turned to concern about the mounting cost of hosting the Games

There were great celebrations when London won its bid to host the 2012 Olympic Games; but it looks as though the organisers have under-estimated the cost of staging the games

The Games are now expected to cost an estimated £3.3 billion; up £900 million from the original estimate and representing a rise of 40% in just over a year.

Culture Secretary Tessa Jowell broke the news to MPs at the Commons' Culture, Media and Sport Committee, leading to opposition party members blaming the government for mis-management of the finances.

In defence, Ms Jowell protested that the rise was due to a revised figure for transport costs and a 100% increase in the price of steel, of which hundreds of tons will be needed to build the necessary arenas and stadiums.

This has not satisfied all MPs, however. Many believe these extra costs were predictable at the time of the bid and that the Government presented a purposefully low estimate so as to avoid public criticism.

Despite the government's reassurances, many critics believe that this increase in over-heads will be the first of many and that the final figure could be as much as £10 billion.

It is expected that extra funds will be achieved through a combination of increased London council tax, lottery funding and investment from private businesses.

QUESTION

What do you think the effects of this increased cost will have on the people of London and UK in general?

Actions required

Apart from identifying the cost involved and the overall aim and specific objectives, it is also important to identify the actions that are required to achieve the project. This could be looked at as a plan of what tasks are needed to achieve the objective of the project.

This will have an effect on the project, both in terms of timeframe and cost. Some actions cannot take place before others. This creates an order in which the tasks have to be completed and a timeframe can be added to this. It is also important to identify whom the action is to be taken by. This is a good point to delegate specific responsibilities to members of the team. It is usually done by assigning responsibilities to staff with a specific role, skill or expertise. For example, when a tour operator designs a new brochure, each member of the team will have a specific responsibility. This could be the photography or the page design, writing the information or editing the text.

PROJECT

All projects should go through a process that is called the planning and implementation loop. This process has a number of different steps and, although the amount of detail that you might gain at different stages will differ for different projects, you will find that you tend to use most of them.

Objective setting stage: the object or goal of the project is either agreed or set by a senior member of the team.

Research stage: research what options and solutions there are for the objective set in the previous stage. It could include research into provision and services of competitors.

Planning stage: an action plan is set in order to achieve the project's objective.

Resource stage: this is where you work out which resources you have and which are needed in order to complete the project. It is not unusual to reconsider the plans when the cost implications are taken into account.

Final planning stage: a final plan is considered at this point that takes the information into account from the research stage, as well as resources available to solve the problem.

Implementation stage: the stage of the process where you put into your final plans into action. This is run in parallel with the monitoring stage.

Monitoring stage: progress towards the objective is monitored, as is every detail of the project while it is being implemented. It is easier to solve problems at this stage than at the end of the project.

Evaluation stage: when the project has been completed, it is important to monitor its success and also to identify any issues that went well or poorly. This is so that these lessons can be taken into account for future projects and the same mistakes are not made again.

Recording stage: You have identified the strengths and weaknesses of the project that needed to be recorded throughout the evaluation stage. This record may be used at a later date when a similar project is being considered.

Up until now, we have been looking at the components of a project. We are now going to look at two different projects that you might work on in the travel and tourism industry.

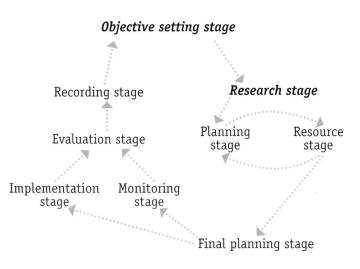

Figure 2.7 Planning and implementation loop

Promotional campaign

The selling of travel and tourism products has its own unique issues. The services that you are selling are intangible in most cases. Unlike selling a car that the customer can test drive before buying it, most travel and tourism products have to be purchased in advance of the experience.

Promotion is vital to the selling of holidays as you need to communicate a lot of information about the product or service to the consumer before the customer feels confident with the product or service.

Figure 2.8 Promotional material selling different types of holidays

We are going to look at an example of a promotional campaign for a small independent privately owned travel agency.

Objective setting stage

A travel agency may have a number of different objectives from a promotional campaign. These could include:

- increasing awareness of the agency or products
- introducing a new product or outlet
- explaining the unique selling point of services offered
- combating rumours
- increasing customer numbers
- increasing sales.

Research stage

The travel agency will both look internally and externally at the research stage. Internally, it will look at previous campaigns and use these to identify which marketing communication methods were the most effective.

Example

Some stables in Buckingham that specialise in pony trekking for beginners found the advertisement that generated the most bookings was not the expensive radio publicity in the local area, but magazine advertisements in *The Lady* and *Country Life*.

Think Why do you think the magazine advertisements generated the most sales?

The travel agency also needs to look at what its competitors are doing in the form of promotion. There seems little reason to offer the same as the competitors when it comes to discounts or special offers. It makes more sense to offer a differentiated range of offers.

Planning stage

All the promotional material needs to be planned. This includes identifying the types of advertisements and communication that they plan to use. It is very unlikely that the agency will be successful in its promotion if it only uses one method of communication. In Unit 5: Marketing Travel and Tourism Products and Services, you will learn that different types of marketing communications have a different purpose. The length of time that each method of communication will run for also needs to be considered.

Key words

Intangible – something that is impossible to touch

Differentiated – to develop a product or service that is specifically different from any of the competitors'

Resource stage

All resources need to be planned. This not only includes budgeting for the cost of the resources, but the development and production of the material required for the campaign. It could also include designing and printing flyers, posters and leaflets, recording radio advertisements, writing press releases and direct mail letters, preparation of any promotion displays and window displays.

Final planning stage

All the plans need to be confirmed at this stage. This involves having all the promotional material ready and any events organised, including the materials and any bookings etc. It is also the stage at which the material should be looked over thoroughly to ensure that the materials produced all have the right message and that there are no errors.

Example

Last September, while working in a restaurant, John was asked to organise the Christmas party promotional menus. He spent a long time planning the menus with the chef, spelling all the dishes correctly and making sure that the prices were accurate. John had 20,000 leaflets produced in the shape of Christmas trees with all the menu information and the extras that could be offered, such as discos and live bands. Imagine John's disappointment when he was told by the owner that the leaflets were wonderful, except he had forgotten to include the restaurant's name and address.

Think What could John have done to stop him making such a silly mistake?

Implementation stage

This is the stage where you run the campaign. This should run smoothly due to all the planning that you have done beforehand.

Monitoring stage

You need to monitor what is happening throughout the implementation stage. This includes checking that any paid-for advertisements that you have used are correct in terms of location and size. It is also important to start monitoring each promotional activity to help evaluate the success of the campaign.

Evaluation stage

It is important to monitor the success during and at the end of the campaign. Not everything you have done will have been successful. The agency needs to identify which communication methods worked well and which did not. In order to do this, the agency will build some way of monitoring how successful each promotional method was into its system. For example, giving a discount to customers that come in with a flyer will mean that you can record how many flyers were redeemed for discounts at the end of the campaign. This information can be used to work out if the flyers were a worthwhile promotional method.

Recording stage

All of the successes and failures need to be recorded during the campaign. In the future, this information will be used to consider which methods of promotion to use for the next campaign. This will lead to a concentration of resources into the success methods of market communication. Be careful not to disregard new methods. This will give your promotional campaigns more 'bangs for your bucks' in the future.

Arranging a visit

This is a common task for a tour operator, independent travel agencies and coach companies.

Objective setting stage

All visits must have an objective, whether it is to see a particular attraction or a particular type of attraction. The setting of the objective has a direct effect on the type of visit being planned.

Research stage

For a trip you need to identify which location or attraction you are going to and check that the attraction has the facilities to be able to cope with your party and their needs. You also have to think about the transport that is available and the accommodation needs of the group.

Example

Rusty runs a small tearoom in Guernsey near to a popular attraction. The tearoom sits approximately 50 people inside and 50 more outside in the gardens. Every few weeks, a large cruise ship pulls into the port with up to 3,000 customers disembarking for the day.

Think Rusty does not want to turn people away, but how can he and his two helpers cope with this huge number of customers?

Planning stage

When you are arranging a visit, the planning stage involves selecting the destination and the trip's itinerary. This must include an estimated timeframe for the trip. At this point, you should also consider what you are going to offer to make the experience unique. For example, a trip to the theatre could include a backstage tour.

Resource stage

This is the stage at which you organise the facilities that you need to be able to operate the visit. It could involve booking tickets on public transport or organising transportation to the attraction or destination. For tour operators, this may include the chartering of aircraft and coaches. Resources will also include communicating with the resort, destination or attraction that is being visited to book places. For example, if you are visiting a popular museum, you may need to reserve a number of tickets.

Key words

Itinerary – a list of steps and times involved in a project

Final planning stage

Plans from the initial planning stage may need to be altered to fit in with the requirements of the attraction, destination or resort. There is no point in arriving at an attraction if it is not open or ready to cope with your party. The cost implications of the visit will also become apparent at this stage as you have enquired into the cost of transportation and entry to the attraction at the resource stage. Risk assessment should also be carried out. More information on risk assessments can be found on the Health and Safety Executive website (www.hse.gov.uk).

Key words

Risk assessment – a process whereby health and safety risks are identified for each activity. Precautions can be added to reduce risk or if the risk deemed to be too high, the activity may not take place

Implementation stage

This is when the bookings for resources are made and tickets sold for the visit. It could include a promotional campaign, to help to sell the tickets. It also involves the running of the visit.

Monitoring stage

During the implementation stage, it is important to monitor the work and make any changes that are required. This could include implementing contingency plans if necessary.

Evaluation stage

The success or failure of the trip needs to be evaluated. Some visits are more successful than others. Like the promotional campaign, this information can be used by the team to help to reduce problems and build on strengths.

Recording stage

The evaluation needs to be recorded so that it is available to other members of the organisation to help them in the planning of any visits.

Example

Tour operators such as Thomas Cook have a team of people called a Disaster Management Team. They are responsible for any Thomas Cook customer that might find themselves in difficult circumstances in the case of a major incident while on holiday.

Think Can you list a few of major incidents that have happened recently?

Research tip

Some national newspapers, such as The Guardian and the Independent, have news archives that you can search to find out about major incidents:
www.guardian.co.uk,
www.independent.co.uk.

FINANCIAL CONSTRAINTS

Most projects will have some level of financial constraint. This is often referred to as the budget. In the example of a promotional campaign, the budget will vary massively from organisation to organisation. The promotional budget that First Choice has for a year will be very different from that of a local independent travel agency.

However, this is not the case with visit planning. Tour operators are in business to make profits, so the cost of planning the trip must be less than the income from the trip. Tourism can be a very price sensitive market. This has been caused by travel agencies competing for customers on price.

'In 1958, a two-week holiday to Spain cost the average woman 10 weeks' salary.

In 2006, a two-week holiday to Spain cost the average woman 10 days' salary.'
Source: *Nation on Film*, BBC, 2007

The most that you can charge for a trip is the maximum that the customer is willing to pay.

Fixed sum available

A lot of projects will have a specific fixed sum available. This is the total money that is available to run the project.

To keep to budget while having a fixed sum, it is important to divide the money into different key areas.

EVIDENCE ACTIVITY

This assessment will give you an opportunity to achieve the following grading criteria: P4 and M3.

1. Plan a travel and tourism project within financial constraints. (P4)

Plan a visit to a local visitor attraction in your area for yourself and the rest of your class. You have a budget of £25 per person to cover all your costs.

Your proposal should include:

- Objectives

- Timescales

- Financial breakdown

- Actions required

This should be in the form of a 10-minute presentation to your tutor.

2. Explain how a plan for a travel and tourism project enables the objectives to be met within the financial constraints. (M3)

As part of your proposal, you need to explain how you have managed the project in order to stay within the £25 per person budget. Consider how you can reduce entry cost (group bookings) and the cost implication of the transport that you have chosen and why you chose this method. This should be in the form of a written report.

2.4 Understanding how a travel and tourism organisation gains competitive advantage to achieve its aims

Every organisation needs to have a competitive advantage in order to compete successfully, so that customers choose their product rather than that of the competition. If the company is no different from the competition, then the customer has no reason to choose its product.

COMPETITIVE ADVANTAGE

A competitive advantage is something that an organisation offers that makes its products and services more appealing than that of the competition.

Example

In 2007, First Choice is advertising that their aircraft will have more leg room than any other standard seat for the summer.

Added value

Added value is when a company offers additional services to their normal range in order to give added value to the users. Many travel and tourism organisations use added value to increase the appeal of their products. This is particularly the case with visitor attractions. Added value may be in the form of a tour or a speaker or something that gives further insight into the attraction.

Example

Blue Reef Aquarium in Portsmouth offers speakers to school groups and it also has a specialist classroom to teach students about the animals in the aquarium. This is beneficial for school groups, as they have the opportunity to do some work about the sea life rather than just looking at it.

Total Quality Management

Total Quality Management (TQM) comes from the Japanese business practice of zero defects, no errors. It originated in the manufacturing industries such as car production. It has led to the reputation of reliability. It is a straightforward concept to apply on a production line that is manufacturing goods. This is less so when dealing with services. However, through vertical integration, tour operators control more elements of the product delivery chain in the package holiday. This increased control means that they can control the quality of every stage of the product delivery. It is worth noting that tour operators have not yet started to purchase the accommodation part of the package holiday.

Examples

Beaches Resort in the Caribbean not only provides accommodation, food and drink, but it also owns the beaches and offers sport facilities and entertainment facilities.

Key words

Vertical integration – an organisation that merges different parts of the service delivery chain

Training and staff development

One of the biggest day-to-day operating expenses for most travel and tourism organisations is the staff. The staff is the team that delivers the services that the customer pays to enjoy.

It only takes one bad service situation to affect the whole customer experience. A rude waiter could ruin a well-cooked romantic dinner, even in the most beautiful surroundings. This might not always be the fault of the staff. It is the management's responsibility to equip the staff with the skills and knowledge to provide good customer service. This is carried out through training and development. This also has the added benefit that staff members who feel that they are developing in their skills and training are more likely to stay with the organisation.

Example

Going Places send their staff on trips to destinations that they sell. These trips are called Familiarisation (Fam) Trips. It means that the staff can recommend the resort from personal experience.

Through training and development, it is possible to offer a higher standard of service to the customers with fewer errors and the prevention of problems.

Advertising

Promotion is the lifeblood of organisations. Without promotion, it difficult to impossible to find new customers. Promotion is not just used to encourage customers to buy the product, but also to reinforce the image of the brand. It is also used to explain the unique selling points of the product. Promotion also helps consumers feel confident that the product they are buying is the right one for them.

Pricing policies

How an organisation prices its products and services will affect how the consumer perceives them. There are a number of different methods that can be used to price products and services in the travel and tourism industry, depending on the type of product and service that is being sold.

> **Key words**
>
> Unique selling point – what makes the product or service different from that of the competition and what makes it stand out from the rest

Cost plus pricing

Restaurants, bars and nightclubs are not able to predict the number of customers they will have or what they are going to buy specifically. These companies need to have a pricing policy

that means that they can charge enough for the products to cover the production costs and also make a profit to cover the running expenses. In order to achieve this, they use cost plus pricing.

Example

If a fillet steak cost £3 to buy, the business knows that it needs to have a 70% margin to cover its running expenses. Therefore, the business must sell the steak for £10.00.

> **Key words**
>
> Margin – the percentage difference between the cost price and the selling price

Market skimming strategy

This is where the product is offered at a premium rate to ensure that the product remains exclusive.

Example

Some British Airways passengers pay a premium to travel First Class, rather than Europe Traveller or World Traveller Class. The cost difference is substantial, but First Class passengers are paying for a premium service, including a separate waiting lounge, larger seats etc. They are also paying for the status associated with being a First Class passenger.

Discount pricing

This is where discounts are offered on the prices. It could be used to encourage early uptake on sales or for specific groups at off-peak times.

Example

Airtours offers free children's places when you book a summer holiday early.

Thorpe Park offer discounted tickets for students, families with children, pensioners and group bookings.

Market penetration pricing

Market penetration pricing uses price to increase the market share. By reducing the price, the aim is to increase the number of consumers that will buy the product. This is often used when selling consumer goods, but it can also be used when a new product is being introduced to the market.

Variable pricing

Variable pricing is when you set different prices for different times. The demand for a resort changes throughout the year. In periods of high demand the price of the holiday will increase, and it will reduce in periods of low demand.

Table 2.5: Gite de Bretagne holiday home: Prices

Season	Low	Mid	High
Dates	06.01.07 – 06.04.07 03.11.07 – 21.12.07	07.04.07 – 29.06.07 01.09.07 – 02.11.07	30.06.07 – 31.08.07
1 Week rental	£400.00	£600.00	£850.00

Research tip

Collect a brochure from a local travel agency or use the Internet and select an example holiday or you could use the example below. Try plotting a graph of price against the time of year, so that you can show the variety in pricing.

> **Think** Why do you think that the highest price is at the time of year shown?

Competitive pricing

This pricing policy involves setting the prices to compete with the competition. Although you have to be aware of the prices charged by your direct competition in most organisations, this method is solely concerned with price. Using price as a competitive advantage has been successful for the low-cost airlines, e.g. easyJet and Ryanair, where they are selling a simplified service and price is the only really differentiator between companies.

Location

Location is an important part of the marketing mix. Customers will use a company that is more conveniently located if there is no perceivable difference in the product that is being offered. Location does not only include the business' location, but transport links and parking.

The Internet is increasingly being used to buy travel products and services. Location on the Internet, website name and location on search engine searches are becoming more and more significant.

Sales techniques

Sales techniques can also be used to give an organisation a competitive advantage. These methods include the following:

Up selling

This means moving the customer up the 'ladder' of products offered. This could include offering a range of different accommodation options when booking a package holiday e.g. offering a sea view room rather than just a standard room.

Additional services

This means a customer is offered extras as well as the product being sold. For example, tour representatives use the welcome speech on package holidays to sell excursions and trips. Travel agents will offer services such as foreign exchange and holiday insurance.

> **Key words**
> Differentiator – something that makes the business different from the competitor

AIMS

Both profit-making and non-profit-making organisations will have aims. These are expressed in the company's mission statement as the business' general intention. These will be identified in the Memorandum of Association for limited companies.

To make a profit

Profit-making organisations need to make a profit. This is so that the investors and owners can make a return on the money that they have invested into the organisation. Why invest in a business if you are not going to make money from that investment? It would be wiser financially to leave the money in the bank for the interest paid. Non-profit-making organisations also need to make money to operate or expand their products or services. However, this is not called profit as the money made will be reinvested in the organisation.

To be seen as environmentally friendly

The environment is becoming a more important issue as people are starting to see changes to the environment because of the behaviour of mankind. This includes global warming and environmental damage through industry. Tourism has had dramatic effects on some parts of the world with coastlines being built up with hotels and other tourism-related construction. The ecotourism

mantra of 'Take only photographs, leave only footprints' is becoming a more viable option. If no measures are taken, the environments that we travel to see will be systematically destroyed.

There are a number of organisations, both in the UK and abroad, that have a specific interest in the environment. These include the National Trust, National Parks and English Heritage.

As a greater number of consumers become more environmentally aware, businesses are changing their practices and aiming to be more environmentally friendly.

To improve product quality

Another aim of many organisations is the improvement of the quality of their products. This is not only to give a competitive advantage of having a better quality service, but also to keep up with consumer expectations. For a company to be perceived as giving excellence, they need to exceed the customer's expectations. As the customer's expectations will be set by their previous experience of the product, this means that the product or service constantly needs to improve in order to be excellent. This is sometimes known as creeping excellence. It affects both profit-making and non-profit-making organisations. Consumer expectations will constantly change due to experience, changes in technology, trends and fashion, and also because of the media.

Figure 2.9 & 2.10 Customer expectations of a modern, stylish hotel room will depend on current trends

CASE STUDY: RYANAIR

This press release was issued after comments by Ian Pearson, UK Environment Minister, about Ryanair.

RYANAIR — EUROPE'S GREENEST AIRLINE — RESPONDS TO FOOLISH COMMENTS OF UK ENVIRONMENT MINISTER

CELEBRATES WITH 5 MILLION FREE SEAT SALE

Ryanair, Europe's largest low fares airline, which is also Europe's greenest airline, today (Friday, 5th January 2007) rejected the foolish and ill-informed comments of UK Environment Minister, Ian Pearson.

Laughing off Mr Pearson's attack, Ryanair's CEO, Michael O'Leary said:

"Being attacked by Minister Pearson... is like "being savaged by a dead sheep". It is clear that Minister Pearson hasn't a clue what he's talking about.

1. The recent Stern Report confirmed that the airline industry accounts for just 1.6% of global greenhouse gas emissions. Airlines are neither the cause nor the solution to climate change.

2. Mr Pearson has nothing to say about road transport, which accounts for 18%, or the power generation industry, which accounts for over 25% of CO_2 emissions, despite the UK Government's abysmal record on tackling polluting power stations, many of which his own Government owns.

3. Ryanair is Europe's greenest airline. We have spent in excess of $10bn. acquiring a fleet of brand new Boeing aircraft, which have reduced our fuel consumption and CO_2 emissions by 50% per passenger kilometre.

4. Mr Pearson is a Minister of a Government, which has, like Scrooge, this Christmas doubled the air passenger tax on tickets from £5 to £10, grabbing another £1bn. in taxes without doing anything whatsoever to invest this money in the environment.

"Like most politicians, Minister Pearson talks a lot, but does little. Unlike politicians, Ryanair has spent over $10bn. to become Europe's greenest and cleanest airline, a fact recently recognised by the Dutch consumer organisation.

"At a time when aviation generates just 1.6% of greenhouse gases, isn't it time that Minister Pearson and other equally foolish politicians actually tackled the real causes of climate change, which are road transport and power generation?

"In the meantime, Ryanair will continue to be Europe's greenest airline while opposing these so-called "environmental taxes", which is just another way of greedy politicians grabbing more money from ordinary passengers while doing nothing at all for the environment. To celebrate, Ryanair are releasing 5 million free seats today and these seats can be booked on www.ryanair.com."

Source: www.ryanair.com

Example

Consumer expectations of holidays have changed dramatically over the years because of television programmes, such as *Holiday*. The range of services on a holiday has improved and changed. This can be seen just by looking at the range of products offered by Butlins, today compared to its hay-day in the 1950s.

> **Think** Speak to a family member about their experience on their first overseas holiday. Compare this to your first overseas holiday.

To be competitive

All organisations are in competition for customers, whether they are profit-making or non profit-making. Most consumers have a limited amount of disposable income. This means that the customer has to choose between the products of one company and another. All organisations need to make money to cover its costs and to develop and expand. A number of the aims we have looked at are used to be competitive. However, it could be said that to be competitive is only to follow the market leader. Many companies aim to be the market leader rather than just to compete.

Example

Emirates Airlines has invested heavily in new Airbus A380 aircraft, known as double-decker jumbos. This extra capacity on each aircraft will give Emirates the ability to offer all passengers a greater range in entertainment and relaxation facilities compared to its competitors.

Key words

Disposable income – money that a household has after all the bills and living essentials are paid for
Market leader – an organisation that is seen to be the best, most forward-thinking, adaptable or that gives a cutting-edge service

To support sustainable tourism

Tourism has to be sustainable for its long-term future. If tourism damages the area, then tourists will go elsewhere. If tourism has a negative impact on the environment and the indigenous population, then the long-term effects of this will lead to a loss of tourists.

Example

In the 19th century, tourists travelled to Africa to go on safaris and to shoot great beasts. The prize of having a wild beast head mounted on the wall was very fashionable in Victorian times. This has led to the near-extinction of a large number of animals in Africa. Today, people go on safari to shoot animals with cameras, and not rifles. The local governments have made a tremendous effort to protect these animals in game reserves and prevent poaching in natural environments.

EVIDENCE ACTIVITY

This activity will give you the opportunity to achieve the following grading criteria: P5, P6, M4 and D2.

Select one profit-making and one non-profit-making organisation from the travel and tourism industry. Check with your tutor that the organisations selected are appropriate.

1. Explain how the profit-making organisation seeks to gain a competitive advantage. (P5)

2. Explain how the non-profit-making organisation seeks to gain a competitive advantage. (P6)

3. Compare the methods the two organisations have chosen to use. (M4)

4. Suggest and justify other ways in which either one of your organisations could gain a competitive advantage. (D2)

The UK as a destination

unit 3

This unit looks at the reasons why the UK has great appeal to both inbound and domestic tourists. A working knowledge of the UK as a destination is crucial for a career in travel and tourism.

You will discover how to research and identify the key components of the UK's travel and tourism industry. You will also find out why the UK matches the needs of different customers and about the major trends and factors that are affecting the UK tourism markets.

By the end of this unit, you will:

3.1 Be able to use sources of reference to provide information on UK destinations; page 71

3.2 Know the location of the main UK gateways, tourist destinations and geographical features; page 75

3.3 Understand the appeal of UK destinations; page 85

3.4 Understand the needs of UK domestic and inbound tourism markets and the ways in which the UK meets those needs; page 88

3.5 Understand key trends and factors affecting the UK inbound and domestic tourism markets. page 96

So you want to be an...

Event Manager

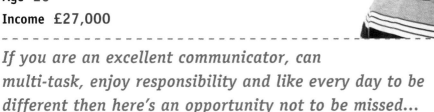

My name Jay Chatterjee
Age 20
Income £27,000

If you are an excellent communicator, can multi-task, enjoy responsibility and like every day to be different then here's an opportunity not to be missed...

Sum up your job for me?

I organise events all over the UK. They vary in size: from big international events in London or Manchester, to smaller regional events closer to where I live in Cumbria.

What can I expect to do as an Event Manager?

The job is really varied, and that's why I love it. In any one day you might have to manage the budget for an event, motivate staff, deal with clients, organise supplies and identify possible problems and solutions to them. Basically, everything about putting on an event is down to me.

How did you go about getting this job?

After leaving college I worked for 3 years as an assistant in a travel firm. I gained industry knowledge and this, coupled with my BTEC National Diploma, made me a strong candidate when I went for promotion.

What training have you had?

To be honest, apart from some training on the Project Costing System so that I can work out budgets, it's on the job experience that acts as the best form of training.

❝When you're busy the days just seem to fly by!❞

How many hours can I expect to work?

Ha. ha. Well, supposedly 38 hours a week, but at times it's closer to 50. In the run up to a big event you just don't know what problem might need sorting at 1am! Saying that, when you're busy the days just seem to fly by! I get great job satisfaction when an event I've organised is a success.

What skills should I have?

Being a competent IT user who is good with numbers is important. But basically, as long as you're confident in your ability to pick things up quickly, multitask, and communicate with lots of different people, you'll be fine.

What can I expect to earn?

I started on £24,000 and hope to earn at least £32,000 in the next couple of years. If I want to earn more than that then I'll need to move to a big company, possibly abroad. I'd love to work in New York one day.

So you're staying in the industry then?

I'd move on if I ever got bored, but there's not much chance of that because I'm so busy all the time. I love working with people and I can't ever see myself behind a desk full-time; I much prefer to be hands on!

Grading criteria

The table below shows what you need to do to gain a pass, merit or distinction in this part of the qualification. Make sure you refer back to it when you are completing work so you can judge whether you are meeting the criteria and what you need to do to fill in gaps in your knowledge or experience.

In this unit there are 5 evidence activities that give you an opportunity to demonstrate your achievement of the grading criteria:

page 75	P1
page 85	P2
page 86	P3, M1
page 95	P4, M2, D1
page 99	P5, M3, D2

To achieve a pass grade the evidence must show that the learner is able to...	To achieve a merit grade the evidence must show that, in addition to the pass criteria, the learner is able to...	To achieve a distinction grade the evidence must show that, in addition to the pass and merit criteria, the learner is able to...
P1 Use appropriate reference material to provide information on UK destinations	**M1** Analyse the appeal of destinations to domestic and inbound tourists	**D1** Evaluate the attraction of the UK for domestic and inbound visitors, making recommendations about how appeal to domestic and inbound tourism can be increased
P2 Locate gateways, tourist destinations and geographical features of the UK	**M2** Explain how four specific UK destinations can meet the needs of domestic and inbound tourist markets	
P3 Describe the features that attract tourists to three UK destinations	**M3** Analyse external and internal factors influencing recent key trends in the UK inbound and domestic markets	**D2** Evaluate the likely impacts of external and internal factors on the future of the UK inbound and domestic markets
P4 Describe the needs of the UK domestic and inbound tourism markets		
P5 Describe external and internal factors influencing recent key trends in the UK inbound and domestic market		

3.1 Using reference sources to provide information on UK destinations

REFERENCE MATERIALS

In order to provide accurate and timely information on UK destinations, you will need to know how to find and use reference materials. A great deal of material is freely available from the industry, but this is usually restricted to brochures and catalogues, which focus on the products and services of a business. Much of the information found in printed sources is also available on the Internet, although it is vital to make sure that you are using a reputable website and that you double-check any data for inaccuracies.

Key words

Reference materials – sources of information, for example, books, newspaper articles, websites etc

All the grading criteria for this unit specifically require you to list any reference materials you have used and how you have used them. You will find it useful to build up a list of useful reference materials, identifying where you found them (for example, noting down the website address, book title or name and date of newspaper and magazine articles).

Atlases

You will be familiar with paper-based atlases, particularly if you studied geography at GCSE. There are, however, some very useful interactive alternatives.

Think How up-to-date is the printed atlas you are using? Make sure that the UK regions and counties are labelled correctly.

Example

- www.nationalgeographic.com/maps – a map of the world with scrolling and zoom features. An advantage of this searchable atlas system is that you can print specific zoomed maps to help you identify the location of destinations.

- www.encarta.msn.com – select 'world atlas' from the home page. Microsoft's atlas uses a globe that you can click and zoom in on. The maps on this website look very similar to ones you will find in most atlases. You can also print any size of map and obtain directions from one location to another.

- www.earth.google.com – a mapping software with real satellite images of the world. Some areas have far more detailed photography than others. You will need to download the Google Earth software in order to use the system.

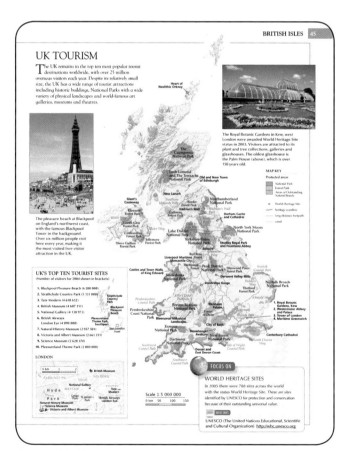

Figure 3.1 Paper-based atlases remain an important reference tool

Internet

The Internet can provide you with a broad range of reference materials. Not only are there many websites that cover all the different components of the UK travel and tourism industry, including transport, accommodation, regions, towns and attractions, but the Internet is also a valuable source for statistical data.

Example

Websites that are particularly useful for UK tourism include:

- www.visitbritain.com – this is the website of the British Tourist Authority. It has a search facility for accommodation, visitor attractions, events, flights and other forms of public transport. It also has useful practical information, including destination guides. There are up-to-date links to tourist information centres across the UK.

- www.culture.gov.uk – the Department of Culture, Media, and Sport is the government department with responsibility for tourism and the support of museums, galleries, the historic environment and other important historic and cultural aspects of the UK. The department is responsible for developing and implementing tourism policy and for supporting the tourism industry.

- www.visitlondon.com – this is the official website of the London Tourist Board. It has a search and booking facility for accommodation, attractions and events, as well as links to transport information.

Key words

Statistical data – facts and figures about fashions and trends in particular industries or on particular subjects

Research tip

For specific information about England, go to www.enjoyengland.com; for Scotland, go to www.visitscotland.com; for Wales, go to www.visitwales.com; and for Northern Ireland, go to www.discovernorthernireland.com.

Brochures

Your school or college library is likely to have a large selection of current travel brochures.

Research tip

It is possible to order specific brochures using services such as www.brochurebank.co.uk or www.travelbrochures.co.uk.

The value of travel brochures lies largely in the specific information they contain about travel to, features of and the accommodation at specific destinations. It is important to bear in mind that brochures are written to sell destinations to potential customers. They may ignore or play down negative aspects about the particular destination, such as travel time from airports, construction in the local area or poor weather conditions at certain times of the year.

Research tip

To compare the brochure description of accommodation and resorts with independent reviews, use www.holidaywatchdog.com.

Think Why might it not be wise to completely trust information contained in a brochure? What is the purpose of the brochure? What different means could you use to check the accuracy of the information provided in the brochures?

Statistical data

Organisations such as Star UK, Visit Britain and the Office of National Statistics provide useful statistical data:

- www.statistics.gov.uk – the Office of National Statistics is a government department and it is the principal provider of official statistics about the UK. It has some statistical data on travel and tourism. Information is divided into business, domestic, holiday and overseas tourism. It also has data on transport, the use of the travel trade and visitor expenditure.

- www.staruk.org.uk – this website provides summaries of key UK tourism facts and data, as well as links to official bodies involved in the UK tourism industry.

- www.caa.co.uk – the UK Civil Aviation Authority website includes UK airport and airline statistics.

- www.dft.gov.uk – the Department for Transport website provides statistics concerning all aspects of transport in the UK.

- www.naturalengland.org.uk – the leisure day visits survey can be found on this website. It is a large survey that reports the participation in leisure day visits.

- The UK tourism survey – this can be found on part of the Visit Britain website at www.tourismtrade.org.uk. This is a national consumer survey, focusing on domestic tourism.

Timetables

Transport timetables are not only a valuable source of information with regard to departure and arrival times, but they also provide useful data about routes and possible connections between different transport types. There are several different categories of timetables.

- Airline timetables – both international and domestic. Bear in mind that there are published departure and arrival times, but that real-time departure and arrival times can also be obtained, usually by using the departure airport or arrival airport's websites or customer service telephone numbers.

- Ferry timetables – there are a number of different water-based transport links between the UK and continental Europe, including car and passenger ferries, hovercraft and catamarans. Most have summer and winter timetables. They also have published timetables, but these are subject to change and can be checked on the operator's website, by phoning the contact numbers or by directly contacting the arrival or departure ports. There are also domestic water transport systems, linking the mainland with destinations including the Isle of Wight, the Scottish islands, and Northern Ireland.

- Train timetables – an online timetable, www.nationalrail.co.uk, gives published and live departure and arrival times for all services operated by every UK train operator. Another useful online source is www.transportdirect.info, which provides a comprehensive journey planner service, including trains, flights, road routes and coaches. Each individual train operator has their own website and links to all of these can be found at the National Rail website, along with information about their areas of operation.

- Coach timetables – the Guild of British Coach Operators, www.coach-tours.co.uk, has a database that can be searched by criteria including cities and areas, ports and airports, or by requirement, including airport transfers, excursions and holiday tours. One of the largest national and international coach companies is National Express at www.nationalexpress.com, where it is possible to plan a journey with a series of coach connections.

Destination guides

Destination guides mainly fall into two categories. The first are usually free and compiled either by the regional tourist board or destination tourist board in cooperation with local travel and tourism providers. The second category is made up by published destination guides produced by commercial publishers, including the AA, Footprint and Lonely Planet.

The Visit Britain website has comprehensive destination guides to all parts of the UK. Other independent websites, such as www.thistravel. co.uk, give independent destination guides and reviews, as does www.timeout.com, which is a well-respected London-based magazine, which also has a new edition that covers Manchester.

Other sources of reference

Travel trade press

The travel trade press provides a wide variety of up-to-date travel and tourism facts and figures, as well as highlighting key trends and factors affecting the industry. They are also valuable sources of information about career opportunities. The following is a list of the some of the main trade publications.

Newspapers

Sunday newspapers, including The Sunday Times, the Observer and the Telegraph all have dedicated travel sections. The Guardian newspaper (Monday to Saturday) has regular travel features, supported by travel.guardian.co.uk. The Observer replaces The Guardian on a Sunday with its own travel section called 'Escape'.

Most of the other daily newspapers, including the Mail and the Express, have their own dedicated travel sections seven days a week. Newspaper travel sections are useful for reviews of destinations, travel and tourism news and special offers on accommodation and transport.

Table 3.1 Travel trade publications

Publisher	Publications
Reed Business Information	Caterer and Hotelkeeper
The Journal of the Hotel and Catering International Management Association	
Travel Weekly	
Data Team	Conference & Exhibition Fact Finder
Haymarket Marketing Publications	Conference and Incentive Travel
Yandell Publishing	Group Leisure
ZeroTwoZero Communications	Hotel Analyst
William Reed Business Intelligence	Hotel Report
Leisure Report	
The Leisure Media Company	The Leisure Management Report
Leisure Opportunities	
Institute of Leisure and Amenity Management	Leisure Manager
CAT Publications	Meetings & Incentive Travel
Travelscope Publications	Travel GBI
United Business Media	Travel Trade Gazette

TV programmes

Television programmes that are relevant to the travel and tourism industry fall into three categories.

- Travel sales, for example, Sky Travel Shop (www.skytravel.co.uk) — these are essentially sales programmes with brief destination guides and details, but with a primary focus on telephone sales.

- Programmes with a travel and tourism element, such as Coast (www.open2.net/coast), which looked at the whole of the UK's coastline and featured many tourist destinations.

- Specific travel programmes, including Holiday, which ended in 2007, after 36 series.

EVIDENCE ACTIVITY

P1

Your local council's tourism unit has commissioned you to prepare a comprehensive investigation into the UK as a destination. Their view is that if they understand how it is structured then they can identify marketing opportunities and unique selling points for the area to attract more tourists. You will be expected to produce a comprehensive report for them. Before they commission the work they require you to prove your ability to use different sources of reference to compile your report.

1. Identify and list a range of reference materials that provide information on UK destinations (P1).

2. Prepare a bibliography of all books, articles and newspaper reports that provide relevant information on UK destinations (P1).

3.2 The location of the main UK gateways, tourist destinations and geographical features

GATEWAYS

Gateways are usually defined as entrances used by inbound tourists to the UK. Many of them are also used by domestic tourists, not only to visit overseas destinations, but also as a gateway to travel around the rest of the UK. The primary gateways in the UK are airports, seaports and the Channel Tunnel.

UK airports

Figure 3.2 In 2007 the number of terminal passengers in the UK reached an all-time high of 288 million

There are 33 international airports in the UK. Each airport has a unique location identifier, designated by the International Air Transport Association (www.iata.org), using three-letter location identifiers. The IATA code has various purposes, but it is specifically a coding system for passenger and cargo traffic. The code is used on tags attached to baggage and cargo, as well as on boarding passes and tickets to identify the departure and the intended destination airport.

Table 3.2 on page 76 shows the main international airports in the UK and their IATA codes. Until recently, many of them were regional airports that simply served other regional airports or used major international airports as their own gateway for outgoing domestic or incoming international tourists. Increasingly, however, these airports, such as East Midlands, Norwich, Bristol and Glasgow, are becoming international airports in their own right.

The busiest airport in the UK is Heathrow with 68 million terminal passengers in 2005, followed by Gatwick with 33 million passengers. On the basis of current data, it is estimated that the number of terminal passengers at UK airports will grow to 500 million by 2030.

The latest figures about passenger numbers in UK airports were published in 2005. They show that the number of terminal passengers had reached an all-time high of 228 million, compared to a figure in 1954 of just 4 million. The number of passenger kilometres flown by British airlines increased significantly in the period from 1985 to 2005, rising from 80 billion kilometres to 287 billion kilometres. Around 90% of all air passengers passing through UK airports were travelling internationally.

Table 3.2 IATA codes of the main international airports in the UK

Region	Airport	IATA code
London and East Anglia	Heathrow	LHR
	Gatwick	LGW
	London City	LCY
	Luton	LTN
	Stansted	STN
	Norwich	NWI
South	Bournemouth	BOH
	Kent	MSE
	Southampton	SOU
	Bristol	BRS
	Exeter	EXT
Midlands and Wales	Birmingham International	BHX
	Coventry	CWA
	Nottingham East Midlands	EMA
	Cardiff	CWL
North	Humberside	HUY
	Newcastle	NCL
	Durham Tees Valley	MME
	Blackpool	BLK
	Isle of Man	IOM
	Liverpool John Lennon	LPL
	Manchester	MAN
	Leeds Bradford	LBA
	Robin Hood Airport Doncaster Sheffield	DCS
Scotland	Aberdeen	ABZ
	Edinburgh	EDI
	Glasgow	GGW
	Inverness	INV
Northern Ireland	Belfast International	BFS
	Londonderry Airport	LDY
Channel Islands	Jersey	JER
	Guernsey	GCI

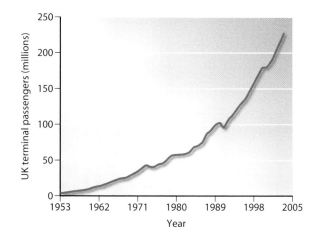

Figure 3.3 Numbers of UK terminal passengers 1953-2005. Source: Department for Transport

Key words

Terminal passengers – the number of people passing through the airport over a given period of time

Think As a result of the expansion of regional airports, many of them have reached their capacity. What are the problems in increasing this capacity using current infrastructure?

Research tip

To find out the airport codes of any airport in the world, visit www.world-airport-codes.com.

UK seaports

The seaports are dotted around the coastline, but those on the south coast are the main ones that provide vital links with mainland Europe. The primary links are to France, Belgium, Holland, Spain and Scandinavia. To the west, there are links across the Irish Sea to Northern Ireland and the Republic of Ireland. In the north of Scotland, there are also links to Scandinavia and Iceland, as well as the Orkneys.

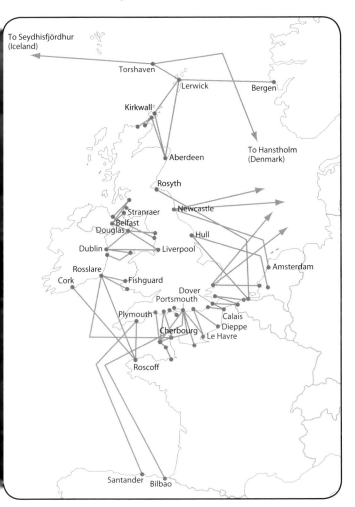

Figure 3.4 Ferry routes to and from the UK

Examples of some of the main transport connections include:

- Dover: to Calais, Boulogne and Dunkerque
- Larne: to Cairnryan and Troon in Scotland and Fleetwood in England
- Holyhead: to Dublin and Dun Laoghaire in the Republic of Ireland.

> **Think** Longer sea journeys are available between the UK and the USA or the Mediterranean. How would you find out about these forms of transport and the major ports used?

The Channel Tunnel

Commercial services started through the Channel Tunnel in May 1994. Since then, 195 million people have used the Channel Tunnel, using one of its two services:

- Eurotunnel Shuttle Service – these are trains onto which cars, camper vans, coaches, trucks and motorcycles drive to go through the Channel Tunnel. Approximately 188 million passengers have used this service.

- Eurostar trains – these operate from Waterloo and Ashford in Kent, connecting with Paris, Brussels, Lille, Avignon and Calais. Approximately 77 million passengers have used the Eurostar.

On average, 47,000 passengers used the Channel Tunnel on a normal day in 2006.

Table 3.3 Users of the Eurotunnel Shuttle Service and Eurostar, 2001-2006

Eurotunnel Shuttle Services				Eurostar
	Cars	Coaches	Estimated passenger numbers (in million)*	Passengers
2006	2,021,543	67,201	7.8	7,858,337
2005	2,047,166	77,267	8.2	7,454,497
2004	2,101,323	63,467	7.8	7,276,675
2003	2,278,999	71,942	8.5	6,314,795
2002	2,335,625	71,911	8.7	6,602,817
2001	2,529,757	75,402	9.3	6,947,135

*Estimated figures calculated on an average of 2.52 passengers per car and 38.75 passengers per coach.
Source: www.eurotunnel.com

Research tip

There is useful information about the Channel Tunnel on the corporate pages of Eurotunnel's website at www.eurotunnel.com. The official Eurostar website is www.eurostar.com. The section entitled 'About Eurostar' contains company information, press releases and information about career opportunities.

TOURIST DESTINATIONS

You will need to be able to identify the four capital cities of the different countries in the United Kingdom, the key coastal resorts, and towns and cities with a cultural or historical heritage.

Capital cities

The UK is made up of England, Scotland, Wales and Northern Ireland. Although the capital city of the United Kingdom is London, the other three countries also have their own capitals. City breaks are increasingly popular with domestic tourists. London is the most popular city destination, followed by Blackpool, Edinburgh and York. Belfast and Cardiff are also becoming increasingly popular tourist destinations.

Cardiff (Wales)

Cardiff (www.visitcardiff.com) is home to the Millennium Stadium and the National Assembly for Wales, which provides devolved government for Wales. Cardiff has an international airport and is connected to England by road with the M4 motorway. The number of tourists is increasing and there were 1.2 million tourist trips lasting for longer than one night in 2005. New attractions include the Millennium Centre, an arts venue that is home to seven different arts organisations, and the Millennium Stadium.

Edinburgh (Scotland)

Edinburgh (www.edinburgh.org) is home to the Scottish Parliament. It has its own international airport and is a major transport hub, connecting to the rest of Scotland and to England by road (the A1) and rail. There were an estimated 3.1 million trips tourist trips lasting longer than one night to Edinburgh in 2005. The city is well-known for its heritage, architecture and culture. Every year, it hosts the Edinburgh Festival, which is one of the largest arts festivals in the world.

Belfast (Northern Ireland)

Belfast (www.gotobelfast.com) has been the capital of Northern Ireland since 1921. It is home to the Northern Ireland Assembly, an elected body with legislative powers and responsibility for devolved government (which was suspended at the time of writing) and has two international airports, the George Best Belfast City Airport and the Belfast International Airport. The former mainly serves domestic flights and has some European connections. The main road route is the M2. Visitors are attracted by the city's history, culture and attractions, including the City Hall and Botanic Gardens. The city had 1 million tourist trips that lasted for more than one night in 2005.

London (England and UK)

London (www.visitlondon.com) is the premier tourist destination for both domestic and inbound tourists. In 2005, there were 24.5 million tourist trips that lasted for more than one night. Its tourist appeal is based on its history and heritage (for example, the Tower of London and Buckingham Palace), culture, shopping and nightlife. It is the largest city in Europe, with a population of over 14 million people and 300 different languages spoken. It is an international transport hub with a large port and five international airports. In terms of road transport, it is connected to the rest of the UK by eight motorways, including the M4 (west), M3 (southwest), M1 (north), M40 (northwest), M11 (north towards East Anglia), M23 (south) and the M20 (southeast).

Coastal resorts

The UK has 12,488 kilometres of coastline. The coastline ranges from heavily built-up ports and resort towns to uninhabited coastline. There are hundreds of coastal resorts; many of which have highly developed travel and tourism industries. UK residents take 26.7 million seaside holidays a year to UK seaside resorts. The top coastal resorts are Scarborough, Skegness, Bournemouth and Blackpool. Shorter trips are also made to the coast, which are not counted in the overall figure. In fact, 270 million day visits were made to the UK coast, generating £3.1 billion for the travel and tourism industry. Most of these were short trips of less than four hours.

Research tip

Online guides to the UK's coastal resorts include:

www.nwt.co.uk (North Wales)

www.gocoastal.co.uk

www.britishresorts.co.uk

www.totaltravel.co.uk.

Example

Gower Peninsula

The Gower Peninsula has the distinction of being the first ever UK government designated Area of Outstanding Natural Beauty. It is close to Wales' second city, Swansea. The surrounding landscape is made up of hills, valleys, beaches, woodland, marshes and caves. The beaches are famous for surfing. The quieter northern coastal area is popular with cyclists and horse riders. Many 'green travellers' are attracted to the area because Swansea has a fully integrated rural bus network.

Think What do you think is meant by the term 'green traveller'?

Use the Internet to find out whether the Gower Peninsula has ever received beach awards. If so, find out what was awarded and when.

Figure 3.5 UK coastal resorts

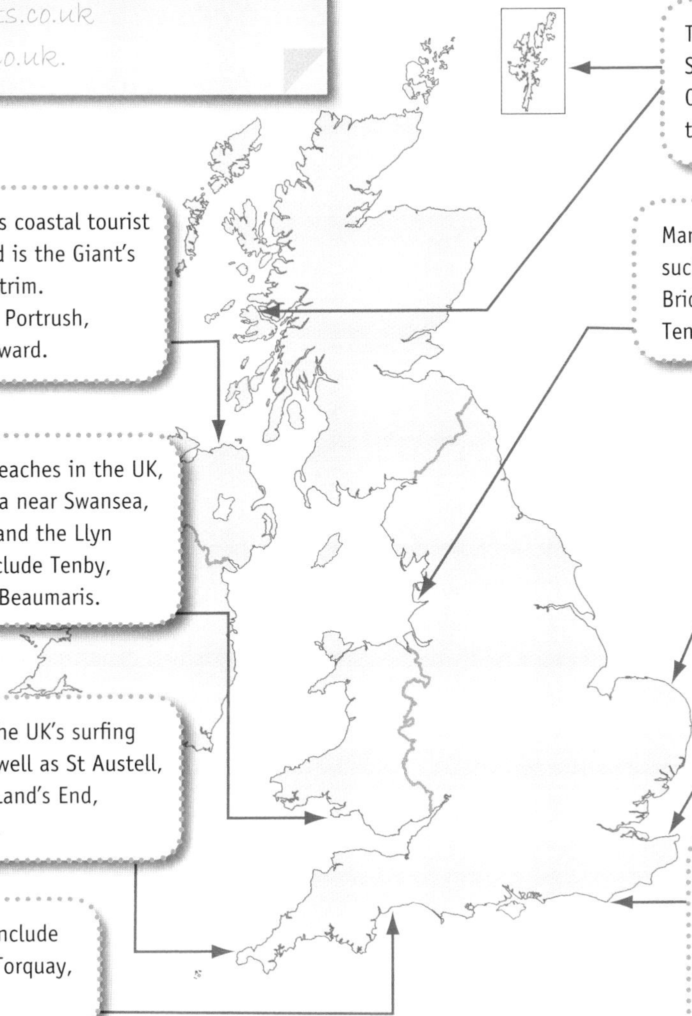

The main coastal resorts in Scotland are found in the Hebrides, Orkneys and Shetland Islands and the coast of Ayrshire.

One of the most famous coastal tourist attractions in the world is the Giant's Causeway in County Antrim. Popular resorts include Portrush, Ballycastle and Portsteward.

Many tourists visit northern resorts, such as Blackpool and Morecambe. Bridlington, Scarborough, Skegness, Tenby and Whitby are also popular.

Wales has some of the best beaches in the UK, including the Gower Peninsula near Swansea, St Bride's Bay, Cardigan Bay and the Llyn Peninsula. Popular resorts include Tenby, Aberystwyth, Llandudno and Beaumaris.

East Anglia's resorts include Aldeburgh, Hunstanton, Great Yarmouth, Clacton-on-Sea and Southwold.

Cornwall is home to the UK's surfing capital, Newquay, as well as St Austell, the Lizard Peninsula Land's End, Penzance and St Ives.

Kent's major resorts include Broadstairs, Herne Bay, Margate, Ramsgate and Whitstable.

Devon and Dorset's resorts include Bournemouth, Lyme Regis, Torquay, Torbay and Weymouth.

England's south coast seaside towns and resorts include Brighton, Eastbourne, Hastings, Rye, St Leonards and Bognor Regis.

Cultural and historical towns and cities

The UK has a long and complex history that stretches back by thousands of years. Each period or culture has left its mark on the UK's cities and landscape. Although many cites have important historical remains or features from several periods (London, for example), some cities are associated with particular periods.

Table 3.4 Historical towns and cities in the UK

Period	Town/city
Roman	Colchester, Chester, Bath
Viking	York
Medieval	York, Norwich, Exeter, Durham
Tudor and Stuart	Shrewsbury
Georgian	Bath, Cheltenham, Brighton
Industrial age	Ironbridge, Lisburn (Northern Ireland), Liverpool, Manchester, Leeds, Newcastle, Bristol

Many of these towns and cities are major tourist destinations, largely based on the appeal of their history, culture, attractions and architecture.

Research tip

There are many sites with information on historic towns and cities of Britain, including:

www.information-britain.co.uk

www.ashtav.org.uk

(The Association of Small Historic Towns and Villages of the UK)

www.english-heritage.org.uk.

CASE STUDY: BATH

Bath is a compact city, situated on the river Avon in Somerset and home to a population of around 85,000 people. It has a considerable number of attractions, including museums, galleries and gardens. The city itself is a World Heritage Site. The Romans first settled in the city 2,000 years ago, constructing the Roman Baths, which is the city's main tourist attraction today. Another historical attraction is the city's beautiful abbey, built in the 16th century. Bath's heyday was in the Georgian era when it was a popular spa town. It was during this period that the city's elegant Georgian architecture was developed, including the famous crescent of Georgian houses called the Royal Crescent. Purpose-built heritage attractions include the Museum of Costume, the Jane Austen Centre and the American Museum in Britain.

QUESTION

What other historical attractions are there in Bath? What information sources could you use to find out?

Figure 3.6 The Roman Baths

GEOGRAPHICAL FEATURES

It is not just man-made features that attract domestic or inbound tourists to the UK. Britain has a diverse landscape, with many rivers, mountain ranges and upland areas, lochs and lakes, and ancient woodland and forests. Many activities and attractions are found in the areas with these geographical features. Some tourists visit simply because of the appeal of the scenery, while others use the features of the area as part of their leisure activities, such as canoeing, walking and climbing.

Rivers

There are approximately 65,000 kilometres of natural waterways, which are more than three metres wide in the United Kingdom. There are, of course, many rivers in the UK and the most important is the river Thames. It is the deepest river in the country, over 336 kilometres long and it is used for a variety of tourist activities, including boating holidays, rowing and fishing. There is also a 184-mile long walking trail alongside the river. Rivers in upland areas, particularly Scotland and Wales, are used for adventure sports, such as kayaking or white-water rafting. The Norfolk Broads is a wetland and a very popular area for water-based tourism activities, including sailing, boating, rowing, canoeing, fishing, walking and bird-watching. It receives around two million visitors a year.

It is not just natural rivers that are used for tourism. The UK's canal network, formerly used for industry, is now mostly used for tourist activities. Canal boat holidays are a popular activity.

Mountain ranges and upland areas

The majority of the upland areas in the United Kingdom are now National Parks. They attract visitors for the beauty of their scenery and for the opportunities they afford for leisure activities, such as hill-walking and climbing. There are over 200 mountains and upland areas in England alone. Most are concentrated in the Lake District and the Pennines. Some of the most popular mountains for tourism activities are shown opposite.

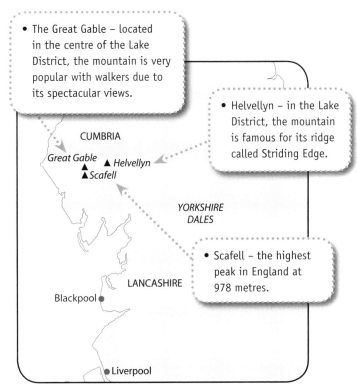

Figure 3.7 Mountains in England

Scotland has some of the most dramatic mountain scenery in the UK, including:

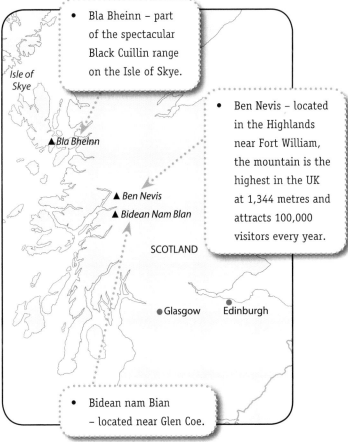

Figure 3.8 Mountains in Scotland

Wales has a number of mountains, including:

- The Glyderau range – near the village of Capel Curig in northern Snowdonia. It is very popular with climbers and walkers, with 5 peaks over 900 metres high.

- Cadair Idris – the second most popular mountain in Wales for climbers, despite only being the 19th highest in Wales. It is located near Dolgellau, at the southern end of Snowdonia.

- Snowdon – the tallest mountain in England and Wales at 1,085 metres in the Snowdonia National Park.

Figure 3.9 Mountains in Wales

In Northern Ireland, some of the most impres mountain ranges include:

- The Sperrin Mountains are in central Northern Ireland (www.sperrinstourism.com). They incorporate mountains, bog land and inland waterways.

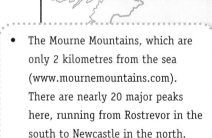

- The Mourne Mountains, which are only 2 kilometres from the sea (www.mournemountains.com). There are nearly 20 major peaks here, running from Rostrevor in the south to Newcastle in the north.

Figure 3.10 Mountains in Northern Ireland

Research tip

For more information on mountains in the UK, visit www.ukmountains.com and www.ukmountains.net.

National Parks

There are fourteen National Parks; nine in England, three in Wales and two in Scotland. National Parks cover 10% of the land area of England and Wales and 7.3% of Scotland.

Figure 3.11 UK National Parks
Source: www.nationalparks.gov.uk

National Park Authorities administer each of the National Parks. They are independent and funded by central government. They have two major roles:

- to conserve and enhance natural beauty, wildlife and cultural heritage

- to promote opportunities for the public to enjoy the parks.

The Norfolk Broads also has a responsibility to protect the area, so that its waterways remain navigable.

> **Think** Are there any other areas of the UK that you think should be protected as National Parks?

Islands

There are 6,100 islands around the coast of the United Kingdom; 291 of which are inhabited. The islands can be categorised as:

- English islands
- Welsh islands
- Scottish islands (of which there are several groups)
- other islands (which are not strictly a part of the United Kingdom. These include the Isle of Man and the Channel Islands).

English islands

The main islands off the coast of England are the Isle of Wight, Isles of Scilly, Lindisfarne and Lundy. There are in fact dozens more offshore and inshore islands than the main ones. Some of these no longer appear to be islands as they are so closely connected to the mainland.

Welsh islands

There are over 40 Welsh islands, but some of them are very small and uninhabited. Anglesey and Holy Island are the two largest islands and are popular with tourists. Caldey Island is home to a Cistercian monastery and is a popular destination for day-trippers, who can buy products made by the monks.

Scottish islands

There are several different groups of Scottish islands. The largest inhabited islands are Lewis and Harris in the Outer Hebrides. In total, there are 95 inhabited islands in Scotland, with a population of around 100,000 people. Many of the islands rely on travel and tourism to supplement their agriculture and fishing, as well as crafts work. They are well known for their remoteness, spectacular coastal and mountain scenery and pretty coastal towns.

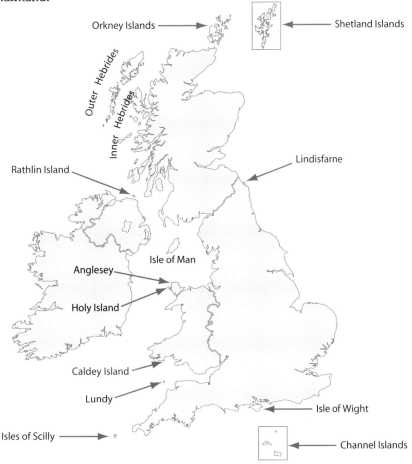

Figure 3.12 Major islands in the UK

Other islands (not part of the UK)

Rathlin Island lies 9 kilometres from Ballycastle in northeast Ireland and is only accessible by ferry.

The Isle of Man is in the Irish Sea, only 96 kilometres from the Lancashire coast. It has its own parliament and its capital is Douglas. The Isle of Man can be reached from England, Scotland, Ireland and Wales, either by ferry or from regional airports.

The Channel Islands are dependents of the UK and lie just off the coast of Normandy in France, giving them a distinctive history and culture that is different to the mainland. The five main inhabited islands are shown in the map below, although there are other smaller islands. There are direct flights from a number of regional airports in the UK, as well as a ferry operating out of Weymouth in southern England.

Bodies of water

The terms lake, loch and lough are used to describe any inland bodies of water, including all of the famous Scottish lochs, such as Ness and Lomond. The terms are also used to describe the Lake District in Cumbria, which is a National Park.

The largest loch in terms of area is Lomond, which is also the deepest. Loch Ness is a major tourist attraction, not only to see the Loch Ness monster, but also because it is surrounded by some of the most beautiful countryside in Scotland.

Lake Windermere in the Lake District is one of the most famous lakes in England. It is 19 kilometres long and the National Trust owns some of the shoreline. It is a major tourist attraction and there are over 10,000 boats registered to use the lake, including steamers and launches.

Research tip

A very useful description and mapping system of the lakes, lochs and loughs can be found on www.uklakes.net.

Woodland areas and forests

In the past, much of the UK was covered with woodland. According to the Forestry Commission, there are 2.8 million hectares of woodland in the UK; around 47% of this is in Scotland alone. There are a number of areas in the UK that are associated with dense and ancient woodland.

Some of the most popular forest areas for tourism activities include:

- Epping Forest (www.eppingforest.co.uk) in Essex, on the outskirts of London.

- Sherwood Forest (www.nottinghamshire.gov.uk) in Nottinghamshire. It attracts around 500,000 visitors a year. Famous for its connection with Robin Hood, Sherwood Forest is also home to one of the many Center Parcs across Europe (www.centerparcs.co.uk).

- The New Forest covers southwest Hampshire and part of south Wiltshire. It is both a National Park and a World Heritage Site. The forest covers 580 square kilometres, consisting of broadleaf woodland, heath land, grassland and wet heath land. The forest has over 240 kilometres of gravel tracks, making it an appealing destination for tourists interested in walking, biking or horse riding. Other attractions include the famous New Forest ponies, which roam freely through villages and by the roadside, and villages such as Bucklers Yard, a former Elizabethan ship yard, and Beaulieu, home to the National Motor Museum.

> **Think** Why do you think the New Forest has been designated as a World Heritage Site? What information sources could you use to find out?

Research tip

To find out more about woodland areas and forests, visit the website of the Forestry Commission at www.forestry.gov.uk.

EVIDENCE ACTIVITY

P2

As a further part of the selection process the tourism section at the council has given you a series of blank maps of the UK. You must identify and accurately locate a number of key features. Use this checklist to make sure that you have identified and located a sufficient number of them:

Table 3.5 Checklist of key features

Features	Number needed	Examples
Capital cities	4	London, Edinburgh, Cardiff, Belfast, and possibly St Helier in Jersey and St Peter Port in Guernsey
Coastal resorts	6	Blackpool, Great Yarmouth, Torquay, Southend-on-Sea, Scarborough, Rhyl
Historical and cultural cities and towns	6	Glasgow, York, Chester, Oxford, Cambridge, Exeter
Islands	6	Jersey, Guernsey, Isles of Scilly, Isle of Wight, Isle of Man, Hebrides and Orkneys
Lakes, loughs and lochs	6	Windermere, Loch Ness, Loch Lomond, Lough Neagh, Norfolk Broads, Bala Lake
National Parks	6	Brecon Beacons, Dartmoor, Exmoor, Snowdonia, Pembrokeshire coast, Cairngorms
Rivers	6	Thames, Severn, Clyde, Tyne, Foyle, Dee
Mountain ranges or upland areas	6	Snowdonia, Pennines, Chilterns, Peak District, Grampians, Yorkshire Moors
Woodland areas and forests	6	New Forest, Thetford Forest, Sherwood Forest, Royal Forest of Dean, Abernethy-Strathspey Forest, Ashdown Forest
Major airports	6	Belfast International (BFS), London Gatwick (LGW), London Heathrow (LHR), Cardiff (CWL), Glasgow (GLA), Manchester (MAN)
Seaports	6	Dover, Harwich, Belfast, Liverpool, Portsmouth, Southampton, Aberdeen

3.3 The appeal of UK destinations

In order to meet the grading criteria for this unit, you will be required to describe, analyse and evaluate the features that attract tourists to a number of different UK destinations. Each tourist destination has its own characteristic features, which will incorporate some or all of the following:

- natural appeal – its topography, including coastline, rivers, mountains, gorges and waterfalls.

- location – whether it is near to other tourist areas and close to gateways.

- transport links – both to the destination and within the destination, the variety of transport methods available, their convenience, ease of use and cost.

- attractions and nearby attractions – including man-made historical or modern attractions and the destination's overall educational and cultural appeal.

> **Key words**
> Topography – a location's detail, including its natural and human-made features

NATURAL APPEAL

An important part of the UK's appeal as a tourist destination lies in its natural appeal, particularly the variety of landscapes that can be found. Some areas have a natural appeal because of the attractiveness of the scenery. The type of scenery is often very different. For example, the Scottish islands are mountainous, rugged and windswept, while the Cotswolds may appeal to other visitors because of its more gentle rolling hills and cosy feel. For other visitors, it may not be so much the attractiveness of the scenery as the activities that are available that make a destination appealing (for example, Snowdonia attracts many walkers, while the coast around Torquay is popular with surfers). In other cases, it may be an actual physical feature of the landscape itself that becomes a tourist attraction, for example,

Cheddar Gorge in Somerset. For visitors, another factor that makes the UK appealing as a destination is its relatively small size, which means that many different types of landscape can be easily reached due to their close proximity to one another.

Research tip

The following websites give examples of regions with a particular natural appeal:

Coastlines – www.jurassiccoast.com

Rivers – www.waterscape.com

Mountains – www.snowdonia-wales.net

Gorges – www.cheddarcaves.co.uk

Waterfalls – www.ingletonwaterfallswalk.co.uk.

LOCATION

Location is an important factor in the UK's appeal as a tourist destination. Its proximity to the rest of Europe makes the UK appealing to European visitors. In terms of specific destinations, location can also be important in affecting a destination's appeal. Regions such as the Cotswolds, Lake District, Jurassic Coast, Yorkshire Dales and Scottish islands are popular because there are lots of different destinations within the region, meaning that tourists can travel between different destinations quickly and easily. Many of these regions are also near to major gateways. For example, the Cotswolds is only two hours from London and half an hour from Oxford.

TRANSPORT

For inbound visitors, there are many transport options available to reach the UK, and with the increase in low-cost travel, the UK is now directly accessible to visitors by air from 114 different nations. Transport within the UK is an important factor in determining destinations' appeal. Part of London's popularity as a destination lies in the fact that it is a transport hub, with road, rail and air links both overseas and to the rest of the UK.

Again the small size of the UK and the good transport links within it make most places easily accessible. Even National Parks such as the Lake District are near major roads (the M6) and railway links.

ATTRACTIONS

Having lots of attractions in the same area can make a destination more appealing, for example, one of the reasons why London is the most popular city to visit is due to the huge number of different attractions that can be found in the city. For families, a choice of attractions appealing to children can be particularly important in determining a destination's appeal. Traditional holiday resorts, such as Blackpool or Brighton, appeal to visitors looking for different sorts of entertainment and fun activities, while cities like Bath may appeal because of the range of historical or cultural attractions available.

EVIDENCE ACTIVITY

P3 – M1

The tourism information section want you to assemble information about the UK as a destination. You must prepare a verbal presentation using visual aids.

1. Select a capital city and describe how its location, transport routes, attractions and geographical features combine to attract tourists (P3).

2. Select a coastal resort and describe how its location, transport routes, attractions and geographical features combine to attract tourists. (P3)

3. Select a cultural or historical town or city and describe how its location, transport routes, attractions and geographical features combine to attract tourists. (P3)

The tourism section would also like a detailed analysis of transportation links, key attractions and the importance of the destination as a gateway to other areas.

4. Analyse the appeal of the three destinations for both domestic and inbound tourists. (M1)

CASE STUDY: DESTINATION APPEAL — DORSET AND DEVON COASTLINE

Figure 3.13 *Durdle Door*

Natural appeal

Part of the Dorset and east Devon coast is designated as being a World Heritage Site. The area, known as the Jurassic Coast, covers 150 kilometres of coastline.

The coast is appealing as a tourist destination for several distinctive features:

• The West Dorset cliffs, near Burton Bradstock, are the highest cliffs along the south coast of England.

• The cliffs around the town of Lyme Regis are famous for their fossils.

• Chesil Beach, the longest tombolo in Europe, is a 15-metre-high bank of pebbles running offshore for 29 kilometres between Portland and Bridport.

• The coastline near Swanage has several important geological coastal features including Lulworth Cove, Stair Hole (a roofless sea cave) and Durdle Door.

The appeal of the area is enhanced by activities and sites designed for schools, families with children and those interested in the cultural and historical heritage of the region.

Location

Some 30 gateway towns have been identified as providing access points to the coast and services for visitors. An example is the small town of Bridport, which has a tourist information centre and a museum. It has good transport links, with access to the A35. The town also acts as a hub for the Jurassic Coast bus service.

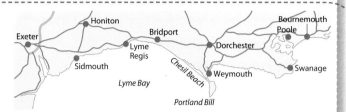

Figure 3.14 *The Jurassic Coast*

Transport

For domestic and inbound tourists, the regional airports at Exeter and Bournemouth provide access to the west and the south of the Jurassic coast. The area can also be accessed through a number of gateway towns, including Exeter, Bridport, Weymouth, Dorchester and Poole.

There is a Jurassic Coast bus service that connects Exeter and Poole with stop-offs along the coast, a southwest coastal path, boat trips, cycle routes and a rail network connecting the main gateway towns close to the coast. Many of the gateway towns also have visitor centres.

Attractions

The Jurassic Coast itself is not a man-made environment, but there are many built attractions along the coast and in the gateway towns.

• The town of Weymouth is a popular seaside resort, with attractions including Sandsfoot Castle, a sea life park and harbour area.

• Corfe Castle is a picturesque ruin near Swanage.

• Maiden Castle, near Dorchester, is a large Iron Age fort with embankments over 18 metres high.

• At Abbotsbury, there is a 600-year-old bird sanctuary (www.naturesouthwest.co.uk).

• At Wareham, there is a well-known ape rescue centre, Monkey World (www.monkeyworld.co.uk).

• In Exeter, there are museums, a medieval cathedral, Roman waterway and the nearby Crealy Adventure Park (www.crealy.co.uk).

• Close to Wool, another gateway town, there is the Bovington Tank Museum (www.tankmuseum.co.uk).

3.4 The needs of UK domestic and inbound tourism markets and the ways in which the UK meets those needs

DEFINITIONS

You will need to be able to identify, categorise and define certain travel and tourism terms, particularly when you are looking at the differing needs of domestic and inbound tourists.

Definition of domestic tourism

Domestic tourism is defined as visitors from the UK that visit another part of the UK. The UK domestic tourism market is significant. According to Star UK, UK residents took 151 million domestic overnight trips in the UK in 2005 and spent £26.4 billion.

Definition of inbound tourism

Inbound tourism is defined as tourism by visitors from outside the UK. The UK has a well-developed brand, which is recognised around the world. This brings in enormous numbers of inbound tourists. According to Visit Britain, in 2005 alone, over 29.97 million overseas visitors came to the UK, spending £14 billion.

DOMESTIC TOURISM MARKETS

There are a number of different domestic tourism markets, which the travel and tourism industry needs to provide for. Some of the main domestic tourism markets include:

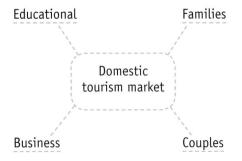

Educational   Families

Domestic tourism market

Business   Couples

Education

Many destinations and attractions routinely cater for school visits. On the Jurassic Coast (see case study on page 87), specific educational services are provided, including teacher training events, schools displays and outdoor education.

> **Research tip**
>
> For an example of how a number of different attractions and destinations deal with educational and school visits, look at www.museums.norfolk.gov.uk.

Families and groups

Domestic tourists are most likely to be in the 35–44 age group. They may be heads of families or part of an adult group visiting an area.

Business

There is a very complex and extensive network of businesses that provide a range of travel services for domestic business visitors. Typically, this would involve the booking of travel itself, the booking and organisation of venues, together with supplementary events, restaurant reservation and entertainment. UK business travellers will use one or more of the following services:

- flight, hotel, car and rail bookings
- conferences and corporate hospitality
- product launches and incentive travel.

> **Key words**
>
> Corporate hospitality – the entertaining of clients or customers by a business. It is often used by businesses to network with customers, for example, booking a box at a major sporting event
>
> Product launch – events designed to attract media and customer attention to the introduction of a new product or service
>
> Incentive travel – a reward given to an employee for exceptional work over a period of time

Couples

Couples and honeymooners usually want idyllic locations and hideaways. There are many destinations and accommodation providers in the UK that cater specifically for honeymooners, for example, www.scotland.org.uk/honeymoons.

DOMESTIC TOURIST NEEDS

Access to information

Domestic tourists still need to have access to information in order to plan trips. By far the most important information source for most domestic tourists is their previous experience, advice from friends and relatives and the Internet. Around 55% of UK homes are online and 58% of online users have made purchases using the Internet. Travel, accommodation and holidays are the most common purchases. People in the 25–44 age group are most likely to use the Internet in order to find out information and to purchase services and products.

Other sources of information include magazine and newspaper articles or tourism leaflets and brochures, which are freely available in a variety of locations, including restaurants, libraries and public buildings.

Table 3.6 Sources of information when choosing a holiday destination in England

Source of information	Usage (% of UK population
Previous experience	50%
Advice from friends and relatives	47%
The Internet	46%
Toursim brochures	27%
Travel agents	23%
Articles in newspaper/magazines	17%
Accomodation guides	15%
Television/radio programmes	11%
Advertisements in newspapers/magazines	10%
Television/radio advertisements	5%
Items in the post	4%

Source: VisitBritain

Accommodation

59% of people say that price is the primary consideration when choosing accommodation. Location is the second most important consideration at 49%. The Internet provides the primary source of information about accommodation, followed by previous experience and then advice from friends and relatives.

Table 3.7 Sources of information used to choose accommodation

Source of information	Usage (% of UK population
The Internet	49%
Previous experience	45%
Advice from friends/relatives	44%
Accommodation guides	37%
Tourism brochures	29%
Tourist information centres	23%
Roadside b&b, hotel or camping signs	12%
Articles in newspapers/magazines	9%
Advertisements in newspaers/magazines	9%
Television/radio programmes	3%
Television adveriesments	2%

Source: VisitBritain

Transport

Transport is an important requirement for domestic tourists. Only three in ten homes do not have a car, but congestion is set to grow by 65% by 2010.

The total number of domestic passenger kilometres travelled in 2005 was 797 billion kilometres; 388 billion kilometres were travelled by car. Rail travel accounted for just over 100 billion kilometres and bus and coach travel accounted for around 48 billion passenger kilometres.

Flying is an increasingly popular transport option for domestic tourists. In 2005, 25 million passengers travelled on domestic UK flights.

Research tip

The government department responsible for transport is the Department for Transport at www.dft.gov.uk. For public transport information, visit www.traveline.org.uk. Visit www.tfl.gov.uk for London transport.

Facilities

The facilities that domestic tourists may need will vary according to their circumstances. Many facilities in the travel and tourism industry describe themselves as being 'family friendly'. These include hotels that typically have children's menus, family suites and baby facilities.

Example

Park Resorts is a company offering 35 holiday parks in popular tourist locations around the UK. It actively promotes its family friendly facilities.

'Welcome to Park Resorts for a wide choice of 35 medium-sized Holiday Parks where you can enjoy the freedom of family self-catering holidays. We offer a range of quality self-catering caravan, lodge, bungalow, apartment and chalet holiday homes, all designed with your comfort in mind. Many of our Parks also welcome Touring Caravans and Tents.

Our Parks provide a wide range of on-Park facilities and leisure activities for all the family and great evening entertainment! What's on offer will vary by Park, so check out our website to see what suits you and your family best.

Look what's included at most of our Parks:
- *FREE Family Entertainment*
- *FREE Swimming Pools*
- *FREE Kids' Clubs for 5–11 and 12–16-year-olds*
- *FREE The Mix for 12–16-year-olds*
- *FREE Sports and Leisure facilities*
- *Plus comfortable accommodation and food choices'*

Source: www.park-resorts.com

Older and disabled domestic tourists may need additional services and support. They may require specialist accommodation and transport. There are several businesses and charities that deal with this aspect of the travel and tourism industry, for example, www.holidaycare.org.uk.

Example

The leading tour operator brand for older people is Saga Holidays (www.saga.co.uk). They provide fully catered and integrated holiday packages around the UK, including the Channel Islands and the Isles of Scilly.

Research tip

Other useful websites that specifically assist people with disabilities and older people to find accessible accommodation and other tourism services are:
www.tourismforall.org.uk
www.ageconcern.org.uk

Special events

There are a huge variety of special events that take place throughout the year in the UK. These range from music festivals to sports events, from carnivals to agricultural shows. Domestic tourists attending special events have specific needs in terms of booking and transport and accommodation (for example, many visitors would wish to stay near to the event).

Research tip

To see what special events are currently going on in Scotland, visit www.visithighlands.com and select 'highland 2007 or 2008'.
Here are some more useful links:
Festivals – www.efestivals.co.uk
Sports and arts events – www.whatsonwhen.com
Cultural events – www.entertaininglondon.com
Heritage events – www.english-heritage.org.uk

Exhibition centres are another useful source of information about specific events, including the National Exhibition Centre and the National Indoor Arena in Birmingham (www.necgroup.co.uk), and Earl's Court and Olympia in London at www.eco.co.uk.

Attractions

The largest and best-known attractions in the UK attract around 100 million domestic and overseas visitors each year. These attractions include museums, galleries and heritage sites. Some of them are mass-market, commercial leisure attractions, such as Blackpool Pleasure Beach.

Tourists visiting attractions also have specific needs in terms of transport and accommodation. They may also require information about the attraction (for example, opening hours, entrance fees) and its facilities (eating facilities, access for the elderly or disabled, activities for children).

Table 3.8 A sample of visitor attractions in Britain, and their popularity during 2006.

SITE	TOTAL VISITS	CHARGE/FREE	% change from 2005 +/-
Blackpool Pleasure Beach	5,730,000	F	-4%
Tate Modern	4,915,000	F	+21%
British Museum	4,837,878	F	+7%
The National Gallery	4,562,471	F	+9%
Natural History Museum	3,754,496	F	+22%
Science Museum	2,421,440	F	+19.8%
Victoria and Albert Museum (South Kensington)	2,372,919	F	+24%
Tower of London	2,084,468	C	+7.9%
St Paul's Cathedral	1,626,034	F/C	+17%
National Portrait Gallery	1,601,448	F	+4%
Tate Britain	1,597,000	F	-8%
National Maritime Museum	1,572,310	F	+3.7%
Kew Gardens	1,357,522	C	-10.4%
Edinburgh Castle	1,213,907	C	+2%
British Library	1,182,393	F	+6%
Chester Zoo	1,161,922	C	+6.7%
Eden Project	1,152,332	C	-2%
Canterbury Cathedral	1,047,380	F/C	-0.7%
Westminster Abbey	1,028,991	C	+0.1%
Roman Baths & Pump Room, Bath	986,720	C	+3%

Source: Alva

Figure 3.15 Blackpool Pleasure Beach

The website of Blackpool Pleasure Beach at www.blackpoolpleasurebeach.co.uk not only describes the rides, shows and restaurants in the town, but also has the facility to book accommodation and educational visits. There is also specific information about visitor facilities, including disability access, baby changing facilities, cash machines and parking.

Leisure activities

Recent research has shown that the average amount of time spent on leisure activities, including entertainment, culture, sports and outdoor activities, plus television and DVDs, is around three hours per person per day.

According to the Office of National Statistics, around three-quarters of adults take part in some kind of sports, games or physical activity. This includes walking, swimming, cycling and other sports such as snooker and pool. As far as the travel and tourism industry is concerned, leisure activities such as walking are the most significant.

Research tip

For a number of links to adventure activities and societies and associations, visit www.w-o-w.com.

Experiencing something new

The travel and tourism industry is always looking for new experiences and products that can keep the industry vibrant. New tourist experiences include:

- agro-tourism
- trekking
- cycling
- gourmet tourism
- extreme sports
- adventure holidays.

Key words

Agro-tourism – tourists spend time on farms in order to experience agricultural life and to see what goes into food production

Gourmet tourism – tourists either staying or visiting hotels and restaurants with a reputation for fine foods or learning how to cook and create gourmet dishes

Example

Ashburton Cookery School is located in Dartmoor National Park, 25 minutes from the South Devon coast. The cookery school offers courses ranging from one to five days. They also have themed cookery courses, such as fish and seafood, bakery and bread and Italian. The accommodation is in the school itself and the courses are run by experienced cooks who have been recognised for their specialist skills and knowledge.

Besides attracting individuals, adventure holidays can also appeal to businesses. Some visit outdoor adventure centres to take part in team-building activities. Another growing area of tourism is 'experience' tourism, where companies offer individual day or weekend experiences, such as driving fast cars, skydiving, parachuting, bungee jumping and falconry. An example of a company that offers this kind of experience is Direct Experiences (www.directexperiences.co.uk).

Think
Use the website www.ashburtoncookeryschool.co.uk to price a two-day French cookery course, including food and accommodation.

INBOUND TOURISM MARKETS

The UK has many appealing factors for inbound tourists, including its history, architecture, countryside and cultural traditions. There are many different reasons why overseas visitors come to the UK and this means that different types of tourist will have a particular range of needs. The main inbound tourism markets are business and leisure.

Leisure

There are a number of segments that are significant within the leisure market.

Business

There is a very broad range in terms of the types and purposes of overseas business visitors, including:

- individuals who are coming to work in the UK on a specific project, but are not going to be permanently based in the UK

- those with an official role, such as manning stands and exhibitions

- those who are travelling as a representative of an organisation in their own country

- entertainers, writers, consultants and those performing in the sports and arts

- individuals travelling to the UK on behalf of their own company

- coach drivers and couriers bringing groups on tour

- teachers travelling with school parties from overseas

- overseas lorry drivers

- individuals visiting trade fairs, exhibitions and conferences.

INBOUND TOURISM NEEDS

Inbound tourists have a range of needs. In the following case study, we will looking at the needs of overseas visitors from France and how the UK tourism industry helps to meet them.

CASE STUDY: FRENCH VISITORS

The information in this case study is taken from a report published by Visit Britain, available on its website at www.visitbritain.com.

Holiday-makers made up 34% of all visitors, business visitors accounted for 31% and visitors seeing friends and relatives made up 25%.

Market size

In 2004, the UK had an 11% market share of the 29.6 million French overseas tourist market, making it the second most popular outbound destination. There were around 3.3 million visits by French citizens in 2004 and total spending was an estimated £769 million.

Visiting trends

The most popular time for French holiday-makers to visit is between April and September, whereas VFR tourists are most likely to visit between September and December. 85% of all French tourists stayed in England for less than 8 nights. Many French return to England on a regular basis. In fact, in 2004, 79% of visitors had been to the UK within the last 10 years. 49% of French visitors were aged 35 or under.

Visitor destinations

Most French visitors stayed in England (77%). The top town for French visitors is London, followed by Brighton and Hove, Oxford, Birmingham and Manchester.

Perceptions of the UK as a tourist destination

A survey (the Anholt-GME Nation Brands index) conducted in 2005 showed that the history, heritage and culture of the UK were important factors for French visitors.

The survey showed that French visitors have a number of preconceived ideas about England in terms of the quality of experience that they expect to find.

Table 3.9

Strengths	Weaknesses
Close geographically	Expensive
An island culture	Terrible food
Its Europe without being European	Bad weather
History – colonial past means excellent museums and galleries	Not attractive, dull, melancholic
Educational – especially for the children	People are shy, cold and hidden or arrogant
Learn English – especially for the children	
Good for a weekend away	

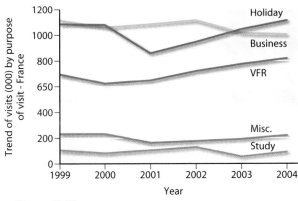

Figure 3.16

Local and national customs and traditions

French visitors ranked the UK second out of 24 countries for culture. They perceived the UK to be an exciting place for contemporary culture and ranked the UK in seventh place in terms of its heritage.

Special events

A large number of French tourists visited the UK to enjoy special events, including the Notting Hill Carnival, rugby and other sports events, live music concerts and the January sales in London.

Attractions

French visitors noted the following major attractions as being particularly significant to them:

- London's museums and galleries

- London's architecture

- sights associated with the Royal family

- castles and traditional English cottages

- the countryside, particularly the Cotswolds, Lake District and parts of Warwickshire (Shakespeare country)

- university towns

- historic towns such as Bath.

Accessibility

France has a close proximity to the UK and their citizens enjoy easy access to the UK, with 30 airports offering daily flights to the UK, frequent daily Eurostar departures and several sea routes. According to the latest figures in 2004, 38% of visitors from France travelled to England through the Channel Tunnel, 36% by air and 26% by sea. Trends suggest that the Eurostar service will continue to increase in popularity, particularly with the imminent opening of the high-speed link to King's Cross St Pancras in London.

Accommodation preferences

A large proportion of French visitors (43%) stayed as free guests with friends and relatives when visiting the UK. From those who stayed in paid accommodation, 16% stayed in hotels or guesthouses and 13% stayed in a rented house.

The following key quality issues were rated as being very important by French visitors:

- they expect to stay in mid-range accommodation, which includes bed and breakfasts

- younger travellers want youth hostels or university accommodation

- in hotels, they want the rooms to be functional, clean and good value with a private bathroom and toilet

- they consider food to be extremely important and expect bread and water with their meals and not to be rushed at meal times

- they will always compare food and drink quality with France

- they are often quite critical about service.

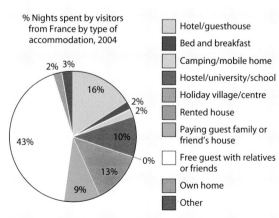

Figure 3.17 Accommodation preferences of French visitors

Access to information

The most common information source for French tourists who are planning and booking a trip is travel agents, with the Internet being the second most popular information source. Younger age groups (25–44) tend to use the Internet as their primary research tool.

Out of the 38% of respondents who said they preferred to use a brochure as their primary information source, 83% preferred a printed brochure, 12% preferred a downloaded version and 5% enjoyed both.

Table 3.10 Planning and booking a trip to the UK: Common information sources

Information source	When deciding on a destination	When planning an itinerary
Travel Agent	57%	52%
Internet	42%	37%
Brochure	38%	31%
Guidebook	38%	39%

Figures represent usage of information sources by French tourists

EVIDENCE ACTIVITY

P4 – M2 – D1

The tourism section would now like you to focus on the specific needs of the UK domestic and inbound tourism markets. This will help them match the needs against the potential of your local area. They do not want you to look at any of the same destinations that you considered for your last part of the job.

1. Describe the needs of domestic, business tourists (P4).

2. Describe the needs of domestic, family tourists (P4).

3. Describe the needs of inbound tourists from a selected European country (P4).

4. Describe the needs of selected non-European inbound tourists (P4).

5. Prepare a set of four illustrated guides to selected UK destinations, each of which specifically cater for the tourists described in 1-4 above (M2).

The council would also like some additional detail and evaluation on the four destinations, particularly looking at their special qualities and unique selling points.

6. Identify and evaluate each destination's special qualities and unique selling point (D1).

7. Identify any new developments, transport routes, initiatives or attractions that have led to an increase in the tourist markets in any or all of the four destinations (D1).

8. Make recommendations about how appeal to domestic and inbound tourism could be increased (D1).

3.5 Key trends and factors affecting the UK inbound and domestic tourism markets

KEY TRENDS

In recent years, the overall trend in terms of the number of inbound tourist visits has been on the increase.

Research tip

The trend tables and charts by country feature on the Visit Britain website allows you to create tables, pie charts and trend charts by region or country, purpose of visit, age, duration, gender and accommodation type.

Generating countries and regions

The United States is still the most significant overseas market, with 3,438,000 visits to the UK. France, Germany and the Republic of Ireland are very close behind.

Table 3.12 Top UK Inbound Markets 2005

Top 10 Visits 2005	% of all Visits	Top 10 Spend 2005	% of all Spend
USA 3.4 million	11%	USA £2,385 million	17%
France 3.3 million	11%	Germany £1,009 million	7%
Germany 3.3 million	11%	Irish Republic £894 million	6%
Irish Republic 2.8 million	9%	France £801 million	6%
Spain 1.8 million	6%	Spain £8704 million	5%
Netherlands 1.7 million	6%	Australia £644 million	5%
Italy 1.2 million	4%	Italy £558 million	4%
Belgium 1.1 million	4%	Netherlands £452 million	3%
Poland 1.0 million	3%	Canada £440 million	3%
Australia 0.9 million	3%	Poland £392 million	3%

Source: IPS 2005

There are a number of emerging markets for the UK. These are:

Table 3.13 Emerging markets in the UK

Emerging markets	Visits 2005	% Growth on 2004
Poland	1,041,000	97%
Hungary	274,000	46%
Russia	177,000	19%
Mexico	78,000	17%
South Korea	149,000	8%
India	272,000	7%
Czech Republic	292,000	6%
China	95,000	0%
Greece	199,000	-2%
Malaysia	86,000	-18%
Thailand	52,000	-22%

Source: VisitBritain

In terms of spending power, the USA is far ahead of all other groups of overseas visitors. Collectively, they spent £2.38 billion in the UK in 2005.

Example

Other countries whose tourists spend more than half a billion pounds annually are: Germany, Republic of Ireland, France, Spain, Australia and Italy.

Volume and value of domestic and inbound tourism

According to the latest figures from the International Passenger Survey, 30 million overseas visitors came to the UK in 2005, spending £14 billion. This was a record year in terms of both volume and value. Visits were up by 8% from 2004 and spending was also up by 8%. In the same year, the UK ranked fifth in the International Tourism Earnings League, behind the USA, Spain, France and Italy.

Length of stay and repeat visits

There is an increasing trend towards short breaks, rather than longer holidays. In 2005, breaks of one to three nights accounted for 43% of visitors to the UK. In 2004, 77% of inbound tourists had already visited the UK during the past ten years.

FACTORS INTERNAL TO THE UK

There are a number of significant trends that are having an impact on domestic tourism.

- As a country, the UK is shifting its spending from goods to services. There is a strong trend towards the pursuit of well-being, which includes travel and tourism.

- The UK has an ageing population, high divorce rates and many young adults are staying in education and at home later than ever before. This is affecting leisure consumption.

- As a result of concern over the environmental impact of travel, many individual tourists and organisations are shifting towards domestic tourism.

- Cities have become centres of leisure, rather than just work, leading to the development of urban tourism.

- Domestic tourists are more demanding and the travel and tourism industry has to cope with a wider range of tastes, preferences and requirements.

Key words

Urban tourism — focuses on cities and major towns as being the centres for tourist activities, including attractions and accommodation

Research tip

There is useful information about sustainable urban tourism worldwide at www.citymayors.com.

Think How might changing demographic trends affect leisure consumption?

Health, safety and security

There were concerns following the terrorist attacks in London and elsewhere in the world, which affected the travel and tourism industry as a whole. However, London and the rest of the UK are seen as a comparatively safe and secure environment in which to enjoy travel and tourism.

Currency strength

The strength of the British pound compared to other currencies, such as the Euro (the main currency of mainland Europe) and the Dollar (both the currency of the USA and the currency to which many other country's currencies are fixed), is very high, making it expensive for overseas travellers to visit the UK. Therefore the focus is on providing a quality service and experience to offset this disadvantage.

Accessibility

The development of regional airports and an integrated transport network is high on the list of priorities for the UK. This is allowing greater accessibility to areas of the UK that received relatively few tourists in the past.

Marketing campaigns

The UK as a whole, through organisations such as Visit Britain, which uses the England Quality Rose as its symbol for its marketing campaigns, is aggressively marketing and advertising Britain as a brand to the rest of the world. A major market research exercise was undertaken in eight overseas markets to see why tourists came to the UK. It was discovered that three words described the UK experience to tourists; these were 'depth', 'heart' and 'vitality'.

Think What do you think these three words actually say to inbound tourists?

FACTORS EXTERNAL TO THE UK

Economic conditions

As of 2007, unemployment in mainland Europe had fallen to around 7.5%, which should mean that more European tourists will be visiting the UK. US unemployment has risen slightly, but this may not have any immediate effect on the number of American tourists to the UK.

The exchange rate between the pound and overseas currencies remains a major concern. A strong pound makes the UK more expensive for inbound tourists. At the time of writing the pound is just short of two dollars to the pound.

Research tip

For up-to-date information on the exchange rate, use the BBC website at www.bbc.co.uk and select 'market data' and then 'currencies'.

Travel restrictions

The vast majority of European citizens do not require a visa in order to visit the UK. Whether a foreign individual needs a visa to visit the UK will depend on:

- their reason for visiting the country

- their country of nationality

- their current location.

The Home Office is responsible for passports and visas (www.ukvisas.gov.uk). The UK has 150 visa issuing offices around the world. From 2004 to 2005, they processed over 2.5 million visa applications, of which 81% were successful. US nationals do not need a visa to come to the UK.

New emerging markets

China is one of the many new emerging markets and up until October 2006, Chinese nationals had made over 140,000 visa applications to the British Embassy and consulates in China. Europe is a very popular holiday destination for Chinese people, but the UK lags behind France, Italy and Germany.

Research tip

For specific global intelligence reports, showing existing and emerging markets for the UK travel and tourism industry, visit www.tourismtrade.org and select 'market intelligence and research', then click on 'global intelligence reports'.

Research tip

For worldwide tourism market trends and indicators, visit the website of the World Tourism Organisation at www.world-tourism.org.

The USA is currently suffering from an economic recession. Because unemployment is relatively high, US consumers are spending less, causing more US businesses to close. In turn, this creates greater unemployment. As a result, this has also meant that the value of the dollar has fallen, compared to other currencies, making it more expensive for American tourists to consider overseas holidays.

Key words

Recession – this is a decline in general economic activity

On the other hand, the vast emerging market of China is set to become one of the primary sources of inbound tourists. Their global trade alone is worth $1.75 trillion. This means that income is being generated from overseas, making it possible for Chinese tourists to seriously consider visits to the UK, among other destinations. 2006 also saw the number of Internet broadband connections in China exceed 40 million.

Research tip

For up-to-date information on China, including travel services, visit www.chinatoday.com.

EVIDENCE ACTIVITY

P5 – M3 – D2

The final part of your commission from the local council is to describe to them the key factors that are influencing recent trends in the UK inbound and domestic tourism markets. You should present your findings in the form of an informal report, including an interpretation of statistical information.

1. Show the key trends in the UK inbound market over the last ten years (using at least three different sources of data) (P5).

2. Show the key trends in the UK domestic market over the last ten years (using at least three different sources of data) (P5).

3. Describe the key features of the trends you have identified in terms of internal and external factors (P5).

Ideally the council would like further analysis and a closer look at the internal and external factors.

4. Analyse a minimum of three external factors that are affecting the UK inbound and domestic markets (M3).

5. Analyse a minimum of three internal factors that are affecting the UK inbound and domestic markets (M3).

In order to have a view of the future, the council would like you to evaluate the likely impacts of these factors on the future of the UK inbound and domestic markets.

6. Evaluate the impact of a minimum of three external factors and comment on the likely impact on the future of UK tourism (D2).

7. Evaluate the impact of a minimum of three internal factors and comment on the likely impact on the future of UK tourism (D2).

Customer service in travel and tourism

This unit looks at the vital role of customer service in the travel and tourism industry. In order to achieve customer satisfaction, a good business reputation and repeat sales, customer service needs to be of the highest possible quality.

You will discover the key principles of customer service, how different customers will have different motivations and needs, and why it is important for businesses to adapt to different buyer behaviour.

You will also have to show your own ability to handle customer service situations either in real life or role-play situations.

By the end of this unit, you will:

4.1 Know the principles and benefits of good customer service in travel and tourism organisations   page 103

4.2 Understand how travel and tourism organisations adapt customer service to meet differing customer motivations
page 112

4.3 Be able to demonstrate customer service skills in travel and tourism situations   page 117

4.4 Be able to demonstrate selling skills appropriate to the travel and tourism industry   page 124

So you want to be a...

Customer Liaison Officer

My name Jerry Northover
Age 28
Income £28,000 + bonuses

Combine your people skills with your passion, and get out from behind that desk.

So, what do you do?

I run a yacht base on the south coast for my employer. I meet clients and ensure a smooth transition to departure, including debriefing, yacht handover and taxi transfers. Sometimes I even get to do a bit of sailing!

Any other responsibilities?

Welcoming the clients, boat and chart orientation, ensuring there are enough provisions and assisting navigation out of the dock are all down to me.

How did you get into it?

I've got a degree in Travel and Tourism and have a good knowledge of yachting. I can also speak French and German, which is handy for international clients. I found out about the job when they advertised in a national newspaper.

Are there not more exotic places you could go and work...

I quite fancied the jobs in Greece or Turkey, but I figured it was a good idea to start in England in case the job wasn't for me.

What training did you get?

Lots: health and safety, yacht training, navigation, customer service, a business administration short course and some management training. My company have been great and I've managed to get them to sponsor my MA in yacht management and servicing.

Are there any downsides? What about the hours?

Depends on the day; I usually have to be at my desk catching up with paperwork at around 7 in the morning. Yachts come in and out with the tide, so they decide your day. Sometimes I don't get away until 7 at night. When I go away as a trained crew member, I don't get away at all. In theory though it is a 40-hour week, but sometimes it's a 7 day week.

A job that you love – it must be badly paid?

Not at all; it's £28K plus about £4-5K in bonuses. You get extra commission for crewed voyages and for the number of departures and arrivals. You get extras for weekend work too. Abroad you get free accommodation and flights in and out of the UK every 6 weeks too. There's paid holiday as well.

What about the future?

I've applied to work out of Rhodes in Greece. Long-term I'd like to have my own business, chartering a couple of yachts out of a Mediterranean island. Heaven!

> **Long term I'd like to have...a couple of yachts**

Grading criteria

The table below shows what you need to do to gain a pass, merit or distinction in this part of the qualification. Make sure you refer back to it when you are completing work so you can judge whether you are meeting the criteria and what you need to do to fill in gaps in your knowledge or experience.

In this unit there are 2 evidence activities that give you an opportunity to demonstrate your achievement of the grading criteria:

page 117   P1–3, M1, D1

page 127   P4–6, M2–3, D2

To achieve a pass grade the evidence must show that the learner is able to...	To achieve a merit grade the evidence must show that, in addition to the pass criteria, the learner is able to...	To achieve a distinction grade the evidence must show that, in addition to the pass and merit criteria, the learner is able to...
P1 Describe how the principles of customer service and methods used to evaluate it are applied in two different travel and tourism organisations	**M1** Compare the service provided by two travel and tourism organisations, explaining how it meets the needs of different customer types	**D1** Evaluate the customer service provision in two organisations and make justified recommendations as to how improvements could be made to meet the needs of a wider range of customers
P2 Describe the benefits of good quality customer service and the consequences of poor service for two different travel and tourism organisations	**M2** Independently demonstrate skills in handling customer service situations effectively and dealing with complaints to the satisfaction of both the customer and the company	**D2** Consistently and confidently handle customer service situations (including a complaint and a sale), showing a thorough understanding of customer types, needs and wants in different situations
P3 Describe how differing buyer behaviour and motivations can influence the service provided by two travel and tourism organisations	**M3** Demonstrate effective selling skills to meet differing customer needs in different situations	
P4 Use customer service skills to provide service to customers in two different travel and tourism situations		
P5 Deal with two complaints (one of which must be in writing)		
P6 Demonstrate selling skills in a travel and tourism situation		

4.1 *Know the principles and benefits of good customer service in travel and tourism organisations*

PRINCIPLES

A level of customer service is constantly provided to travel and tourism customers in every interaction they have with someone working in the industry. We only tend to remember extremely good or bad customer service. Customer service can have a marked impact on the attitude of the customer. It can encourage them to be more inclined to use the business again and to tell others about their positive experience.

First impressions

It is said that people make snap judgements about people in the first three seconds when they meet them. People observe the attitude, mannerisms, body language and appearance. The first impression can either be very good or bad and it cannot be erased. It is an aspect of human nature for people to make these instant judgements.

An employee may not have even said a word. A good impression will make the customer more receptive and cooperative, while a bad impression may mean that the customer's attention can never be retrieved, no matter how much effort is put into doing so.

Good customer service therefore begins before any policies, procedures, organisational goals or even communication takes place.

> *Think* Think about the last time you visited a retail outlet. What was your initial impression of the employee that you dealt with? What were your instant judgements?

Company image

It is highly likely that a customer already has an impression of the image of the business before they even contact the organisation and have dealings with employees.

Company image is the way in which others perceive the business and its products and services. An image always needs to make sense. It must be believable and accurate, as well as being consistent. Any visual approaches or literature that can be read by customers should be matched by the way in which the employees actually handle customers.

A company's image is the sum total of all of its written materials, including elements such as logos. It is also the way in which the business deals with customers and others.

> **Key words**
> Logo – a sign, trademark or name that consists of letters or shapes that symbolise the organisation

It is evident that poor customer service can lead to a poor company image.

In many modern travel and tourism organisations, it is no longer the case that customers visit the premises. However, since this is a service-based industry, there are many businesses that routinely deal with customers on a daily basis. Customers therefore need to see an efficient and inviting business environment, and this means that the premises have to be designed not only as places of work, but also spaces where employees interact with customers.

Another major aspect of customers being given a first favourable impression of the business is efficiency. Efficiency extends to issues such as waiting time (either to speak to an employee face-to-face or when waiting in a queue on the telephone). Customers do not like to be kept waiting, but they accept the situation if it appears that the employees are working hard to see them as quickly as possible.

Speed and accuracy of service

Customers expect a quick and accurate service from businesses in the travel and tourism industry. They count on rapid information that can be relied upon in order for them to make decisions. Availability and pricing are perhaps the two most important considerations. Customers will expect to be provided with accurate information regarding the availability of hotel rooms, tickets to an entertainment event or seats on a particular flight, for example. They require to be given the correct information concerning prices. This will often mean that written, verbal or e-mailed confirmations will be sent out to the customer, either as an enquiry or a firm booking.

Products and services offered

In the modern fully integrated travel and tourism industry, it is now possible for tour operators, agents and other organisations to offer complete packages, ranges or variations to customers, so they act as a one-stop shop for purchasing services.

Many businesses will retain or create independent brand names for particular ranges of products and services. This helps customers to identify precisely what they are looking for and it allows the business to tailor-make the customer service provision to match that type of customer.

Key words

Brand name – a clear and recognisable logo and identity, so that the business helps the customer to recognise their product before those of competing businesses

Think How many tour operator brand names can you think of? Find out how many of them are actually owned by the same business.

Example

British Airways has very distinctive branding with its Union Jack colours that feature on advertisements, its website and, most recognisably, on the tails of its aircraft.

Figure 4.1 Instantly recognisable British Airways aircraft

Customer service policies

A customer service policy is a set of commitments made by a business to their customers. It will also set out the policies and procedures in order to achieve the desired level of customer service.

Our Commitment to quality & customer satisfaction

We strive to offer the best possible service to all of our customers and will make every endeavour to accommodate customer needs as practically as possible.

What you can expect from us:

Visitors
Our offices are open from 8.30am to 5.00pm Monday to Thursday and 8.30am to 4.30pm on Friday (except during Bank Holidays). Visitors are welcome; however it would be helpful to have received prior notification to ensure that the correct person is there to meet you.

Telephone
We aim to give a prompt and helpful response to all enquiries. If you are unable to contact us within normal office hours a voicemail service is available on all direct line numbers.

Figure 4.2 Example of a customer service policy from Teignbridge District Council

For many businesses, their customer service policies will begin with their mission statement. Middlesbrough Sport and Leisure, for example, has the mission statement: "To make more people more active". It provides leisure facilities across the whole of Middlesbrough from golf to athletics and from swimming to saunas.

A vital part of all customer service policies is setting minimum service delivery standards. It also means establishing comments and complaints procedures. It can extend to accessibility for the disabled and dealing with refunds.

Key words

Mission statement – the main purpose of the organisation and why it exists

Example

Service promises are standards that all customers can expect from the Middlesbrough Sport & Leisure Service. Some of the service promises are as follows:

- 'We will provide clean and safe equipment in good working order.
- We will try to answer all telephone calls within six rings.
- We will inspect toilet and changing facilities hourly and take remedial action where necessary.
- We will ensure that 80% of lockers are in operational order at any time.
- We will test our pool water at least three times daily to ensure customers' comfort and safety.'

Think What do you think is meant by the term 'remedial action'? How would the business manage promises 3, 4 and 5?

Teamwork

In order to maintain a high level of customer service, it is vital that employees work together as a team. They need to contribute towards customer service and to pick up from where other employees have left the situation. It should appear to be seamless, so that the customer is not disadvantaged by having different people deal with different parts of customer service.

Example

The Trafford Centre in Manchester (www.traffordcentre.co.uk) is a major retail, catering and leisure space, nine kilometres to the west of the city centre. It has a wide range of customer services and its employees are highly trained and well motivated. As part of their carefully structured selection process, teamwork is identified as being a vital aspect of customer service. The Trafford Centre has received an Investor in People award for recruitment and selection. Customer service training is undertaken by the English Tourist Board's 'Welcome to Excellence' programme.

INVESTORS IN PEOPLE

Figure 4.3 Investors in people logo

Research tip

For information on the 'Welcome to Excellence' initiative and national qualifications, visit www.welcometoexcellence.co.uk.

Effective communication

Communication is an essential part of delivering customer service. This could involve direct verbal or written communication with customers. Communication should be carried out in a professional, yet approachable manner at all times.

Communication is often referred to as a 'soft skill'. This is a skill that is learned gradually with experience, as well as being underpinned by specific training.

Meeting customer needs

Despite the development of the focus on customers and customer service, there are still some very bad examples of service practice. It is important for employees to adopt care principles in order to create a positive relationship with customers. Above all, they need to address the customer's specific needs at that time.

The customer may require basic assistance or information or they may have a more complex request or complaint. Regardless of the nature of the interaction, the employee needs to be in a position where he/she can fairly, reasonably and efficiently deal with the customer's requirements.

METHODS USED TO MONITOR AND EVALUATE SERVICE STANDARDS

Having established customer service policies and procedures, a travel and tourism organisation will need to make constant checks to ensure that employees are following the guidelines. This can be done in a number of different ways, all of which require an objective view of the interaction between the employee and the customer.

Mystery shoppers

There are several agencies in the UK (for example, www.mystery-shoppers.co.uk) that offer specific types of objective assessments of an employee's performance by providing information about the following:

- how the service received compared to the service that was expected

- how much the shopper trusts the business and their products and services

- how the customer service compares to that of competitors

- whether the last contact or transaction with the business has affected the customer's loyalty towards the business

- whether they feel valued as a customer

- whether they feel that they have been treated as an individual.

If the business is using an agency, then the mystery shopper will have been chosen to match the typical customer profile of the business. Alternatively, the business itself can use employees from other areas of the business to check the customer service performance levels.

Mystery shoppers can cover the following areas:

- covert video mystery shopping – the use of a covert video camera with a report and evaluation of customer service

- postal monitoring – using a home address to receive brochures and other promotional materials

- home addresses – used for personal visits by representatives of the business

- e-mail mystery shoppers – so that businesses can respond to enquiries made by the mystery shopper.

Questionnaires

Customer service questionnaires are clearly very useful in the travel and tourism industry.

A travel agent may ask the following customer service questions:

- whether the customer found the staff helpful and courteous

- whether the customer found the staff knowledgeable and efficient

- whether the staff showed an interest in the customer's needs

- whether the member of staff had a good telephone manner.

Observation

A mystery shopper can obviously observe the level of customer service being provided by a business. However, the customer service can also be witnessed by a supervisor or manager.

The day-to-day observation of customer service is an important part of a manager or supervisor's role, particularly when it means giving assistance and direction to employees in order to improve service standards or to congratulate them on good work. In some larger businesses, cameras are used to observe the interactions of employees and customers. In call centres, conversations can be recorded so as to monitor the employee's manner and level of service.

Quality criteria

There are several ways in which a business can monitor the customer service standards. These include the following:

- Value for money – is the customer of the opinion that they received an acceptable level of customer service in relation to the price of the product or service purchased or the overall value of the transaction?

- Reliability – was any information, advice or other aspect of the interaction unreliable or misleading? How much trust did the customer place in what the employee told them in response to questions?

- Staffing levels – was the customer seen in a timely manner and not forced to wait too long to receive assistance from an employee, either in a face-to-face or telephone situation? Were staffing levels reflected in the time in which it took for answers to be received if further information was necessary?

Monitoring methods

Having monitored customer service standards, it is important for the organisation to draw out as many themes or aspects as possible, including good practice and problems.

Customer surveys are formal methods of collecting feedback about the organisation's customer service. Before a customer survey is finalised, the business needs to be clear that decisions can be made on the basis of what is being asked, how it can be measured and whether it might be feasible to follow through on any suggestions made.

Many tour operators routinely use feedback methods, including questionnaires (often distributed on the aircraft on the return trip), follow-up telephone calls or letters and surveys sent to the customer's address after the holiday or visit.

Employee appraisals are now a highly common aspect of an organisation's routine in assessing current levels of customer service and employee expertise. Appraisals usually take place on either a six-monthly or yearly basis. The meeting between the employee (appraisee) and the supervisor or manager (appraiser) incorporates observation by the appraiser of the appraisee's performance in the period before the appraisal. It can also involve the appraisee identifying examples of good and bad customer service that they have provided. The purpose of an appraisal is to improve the levels of customer service by identifying areas of personal improvement required by each employee. It is the responsibility of the appraiser to then put any necessary training into place, monitor that training and re-test performance at the next appraisal meeting.

Research tip

For examples of performance appraisal forms, visit www.businessballs.com/performanceappraisals.htm.

BENEFITS OF GOOD SERVICE

The benefits of good customer service brings rewards to employees through job security and enjoyment of their work, to employers by means of a good company image as well as increased sales and profit, and to the customer by having their needs met and their expectations exceeded.

To the employee

For an employee, there is perhaps nothing worse than working in a chaotic environment where much of their time is taken up dealing with customer complaints, queries and problems. By working in an organisation that values high customer service standards, the employee can concentrate far more on the job itself, delivering excellent service to customers, rather than handling a continuous stream of complaints.

Job satisfaction is important as it not only means that the employee is happy in their work, but they also find it rewarding, challenging and it gives them the opportunity to expand their areas of skills and experience. It is vital for employees who are expected to deliver a high level of customer service to feel secure in their job role. Their jobs are unlikely to be at risk if they follow and exceed customer service policies and procedures. Employees that fail to give high levels of customer service may find themselves criticised during appraisals or, at worst, may face disciplinary procedures.

Given that appraisals are the basis upon which a business decides to award pay increases due to the employee having met targets, pay raises are a natural result of the continued delivery of good quality customer service. Some businesses will also use Employee of the Month awards or will reward employees that have been singled out for particular praise by customers for exceeding any expectation they may have had about customer service.

> **Key words**
>
> Job satisfaction – a measure of how happy an employee is with their job
> Disciplinary procedures – steps taken to reprimand an employee for bad behaviour or poor performance

Research tip

For more guidance on disciplinary procedures, visit www.direct.gov.uk. Select 'Employment' and find 'Resolving workplace disputes' under the 'Employees' sub-menu.

To the employer

The first major advantage for an employer in providing high levels of customer service is the hope that it will bring higher sales and, consequently, higher profits. Sales and therefore profits tend to come from customers who use the same business on a regular basis, such as always booking summer holidays with the same company. Providing good customer service means ensuring that the customer remains loyal to the business.

The general principle is that 80% of profits come from 20% of customers. This 20% is the most loyal and the most profitable, and good customer service goes a long way to ensure that they remain this way.

The media and the general public will always respond negatively to stories featuring a travel and tourism business that has provided less than excellent service. The reverse is the case when a good customer service story can be passed on to other potential customers and to the media. Many customers respond in a positive manner to real life examples of good customer relations.

Many businesses spend an unnecessary amount of time and money on dealing with complaints that could easily have been avoided if customer service standards had been maintained. By setting minimum levels of service, complaints are reduced in number and seriousness, therefore freeing up employees' time to concentrate on positive relationships and sales.

Having a good and solid reputation for delivering high customer service levels can give a business an advantage over its competitors. This can be on a number of different levels. Not only will their sales and profits be higher, but they will also be spending less time and money dealing with problems and have positive news and views about them.

To the customer

A customer contacts an organisation in the travel and tourism industry in order to receive guidance, advice, services or products. Every time that contact is made, the employees working for the business need to identify the customer's specific needs. This means that the needs are likely to be different in each situation, and they are more or less demanding or complex. High levels of customer service work to ensure that the business exceeds expectations, regardless of whatever kind of response the customer required. This leaves the customer with a strong and positive impression of the business and a greater likelihood to use the business on another occasion, as well as to recommend it to others.

As we have already seen, customer loyalty is important to a business. It is also important to customers as it puts them in a position where they can rely on the fact that they will receive good service from a business without taking the risk of dealing with another organisation. This mutual dependency between the business and the customer is important for both sides. For the business, it means sales, profits and recommendations made by the customer to others. For the customer, it means a predictable and high level of service with an organisation that has a strong grasp of their needs and requirements.

Figure 4.4 The National Maritime Museum

Example

Customer service is important to the National Maritime Museum because there would not be a business without customers. Excellent customer service results in higher visitor numbers and greater customer diversity, increased sales, survival in terms of competition, satisfied customers and greater job satisfaction for staff, and repeat business and customer loyalty.

Think The museum's own feedback suggests that 94% of all visitors would recommend the museum to others. Why is this important?

CONSEQUENCES OF POOR SERVICE

As far as a business is concerned, the consequences of poor service can range from financial problems to difficulties with employees, from negative media coverage to a loss of reputation and the possibility that it may be subjected to legal action.

Financial

Just as a business can enjoy increased sales and profits through ensuring minimum customer service levels, a weaker grasp of this important concept may lead to possible financial problems. If fewer customers are attracted to the business as a result of their knowledge of poor service levels, sales will be reduced. Equally, existing customers may seek products and services elsewhere, leading to even more loss of sales. Ultimately, sales produce profit once the business' costs have been taken into account. If a business has fewer sales, but still has high costs, it becomes even harder to make a profit.

Reputation as an employer

Many individuals that work in the travel and tourism industry have chosen this area for career progression. The employees with the most potential will look for organisations that have a good reputation as an employer. This will be a company that has a good standing with their customers and employees that are satisfied, secure and well-paid, which means that they are motivated.

Businesses that do not have a good reputation, and that are perhaps handling an enormous number of complaints and problems, will inevitably have low employee morale. Employees will feel under pressure, depressed and are likely to be looking elsewhere for work. The first employees to leave will be the best ones. In any case, this will lead to a high staff turnover, meaning that an increasing number of employees are inexperienced and immediately put under pressure by problems caused by poor customer service.

Key words

Staff turnover – the number of employees joining and leaving the organisation over a given period of time. The higher the percentage, the higher the staff turnover

Repeat business

As already mentioned, most businesses will find that 80% of their sales and profits come from the most loyal 20% of their customers. These are repeat customers, purchasing products and services time after time. The remaining 20% of sales and profits come from the other 80% of customers. Many of these are one-off customers that only ever purchase once and then move on to another organisation.

The goal of all businesses is to turn these customers that shift from one organisation to another into loyal customers who will give them additional repeat business, sales and profits.

Adverse publicity and reputation

In a highly competitive market such as the travel and tourism industry, even a hint of a problem, complaint or difficult situation can be considered to be adverse (negative) publicity. This will give all competitors a temporary advantage over the business until the situation is resolved and publicised.

Adverse publicity can drive customers away or make them reluctant to commit to using the business' services. This is often a state of affairs that continues far beyond the time period in which the problem existed.

Naturally, issues such as adverse publicity affect the reputation of a business. Poor customer service is one of the prime examples of complaints and negative word-of-mouth from customers or individuals that have had dealings with the business. Turning around a poor reputation is incredibly difficult to achieve, as well as being extremely expensive.

Legal

Like all businesses, organisations in the travel and tourism industry are bound by a number of laws that govern aspects of their activities, from the use of data, the way in which they describe their services, how they handle certain groups of customers, and the level of health and safety provided, etc.

Although this is by no means a comprehensive list, the following need to be taken into account with regard to poor customer service levels and the potential risk of breaking the law.

- Data protection. A business routinely collects data about its customers and stores this data in order to better serve those individuals by targeting them with selected marketing communications. Businesses must not misuse this data, or they will find themselves in breach of the Data Protection Act (1998).

- The equality of the treatment of customers is of paramount importance, not to mention the fact that it may result in illegal actions. The Disability Discrimination Act (1995 and 2005) makes it specifically illegal for operators of any transport to discriminate against disabled people. This also extends to the access of any goods, facilities and services.

- Many organisations in the travel and tourism industry are criticised for the way in which they describe their products and services. They must not apply any false or misleading descriptions to anything they sell, including brochures and other written materials, as well as verbal statements made by employees. The descriptions of products or services being sold must match the characteristics of the product or service. It is a criminal offence to provide a false or misleading statement under the Trades Description Act (1968).

- For businesses that routinely deal with customers on their own premises, health and safety is another primary customer service concern. Under the Health and Safety at Work Act (1974), all commercial premises must comply with the act. This includes travel agencies, airports and visitor attractions.

Research tip

For information on the Data Protection Act, visit the website of the Information Commissioner's Office at www.ico.gov.uk.
For information on the Disability Discrimination Act, visit www.direct.gov.uk.
For information on the Trades Descriptions Act, visit the website of the Department of Trade and Industry at www.dti.gov.uk.
For information on the Health and Safety At Work Act, visit the website of the Health and Safety Executive at www.hse.gov.uk.

4.2 Understand how travel and tourism organisations adapt customer service to meet differing customer motivations

CUSTOMER TYPES

Customers have a much greater choice of travel and tourism organisations and processes than they have ever had before. This means that there is not only great competition between similar organisations that offer a broadly similar range of products and services, but there are also customer preferences in terms of the way in which they want to buy and interact with the business.

Broadly speaking, we can identify customer service interactions in terms of individuals or groups, but this is far more complex than it may first appear.

Individuals

Individuals as customers can be split into two distinct groups: those looking for leisure-based products and services and those at leisure while using them, or business customers.

The level of customer service required for either customer type is high, but leisure-based individuals can be best described as being the consumer market. In other words, this is the direct-to-customer sale market, as opposed to individuals, whose bookings may be made by a third party on their behalf.

Leisure individuals will require face-to-face customer service assistance. Business customers may require customer service when the product or service is being used, such as interactions with staff in a hotel or at the check-in desk of an airline.

Groups

Although it may be a specific individual who makes a group booking, once the group itself begins to interact with the business, such as on an aircraft, in a hotel or at an attraction, particular members of the group may have specific customer service requirements and motivations. It should not be assumed that all group members have the same motivations and needs.

Specific needs

Many retail outlets, attractions, transport hubs and other organisations in the travel and tourism industry have already begun to adapt their facilities in order to cater for those with disabilities as a result of legislation. This extends beyond simple access and often requires internal changes to premises and layout. For example, doors may need to be widened and internal lifts constructed. Additionally, staff may have to be trained in order to learn how to lift and assist the less mobile.

Figure 4.5 Customer using shop mobility

Other customers may have specific needs due to medical conditions. For example, those who have breathing difficulties may need alternative means of moving around the premises. Some theme parks have electric golf carts that can be used by those with walking difficulties. Airlines may also have to deal with people that have specific phobias. There are millions of people who have a fear of flying. Some of these have been triggered off by specific events, while others have the phobia largely due to claustrophobia.

Key words

Claustrophobia – fear of being in an enclosed space

Customers with cultural and language needs

In a multicultural society, all travel and tourism organisations should expect to encounter customers whose ability to speak English is either limited or non-existent. Unfortunately, only a handful of businesses offer foreign language speaking services beyond many of the more obvious European languages, such as French or German. However, many attractions, such as museums and theme parks, have signage in multiple languages and language options on portable commentary devices.

For different cultures and religions, there are specific dietary requirements and other aspects of their normal daily routine that do not necessarily accord with standard customer service policies. It is important to identify any possible problems that current procedures would cause in dealing with these customers with different cultural and language backgrounds.

CASE STUDY: DEFINING DIFFERENT TYPES OF CUSTOMERS

The fundamental customer service that the National Maritime Museum provides is access to its historical buildings and unique collections for everyone. As a result, the museum has a very wide range of customer needs and types.

The museum provides products and services to a wide range of customers. On any given day, museum staff may deal with:

• people wishing to research their family history

• ship model-makers requiring advice

• film companies wanting to use the buildings as a location for an advert or television drama

• tourists looking for a fun day out

• foreign tourists wanting to experience British history

• school groups investigating the museum to help with their studies.

QUESTIONS

The museum collects information about its different types of customers in four ways: data from the computerised admission tills, customer comments, focus group feedback and exit surveys. Briefly explain what you think these four methods mean.

CUSTOMER NEEDS

In an increasingly integrated market where travel agencies are owned by tour operators that, in turn, own airlines, the natural commercial inclination is for the travel agent to sell products and services that provide the business as a whole with a greater profit. This means that they will inevitably favour selling products and services provided by their own group, or tour operators that offer the better level of commission to the travel agency.

However, businesses need to be aware of the fact that they need to sell a broad range of products and services in order to match customer needs. If they don't do this, then they run the risk of the customer purchasing them from a competitor.

Key words

Commission – a percentage of the value of the sale, which is paid to the selling agent by the tour operator, airline or attraction

Products and services

The primary role of any employee that has direct contact with customers is to identify the specific needs of the customer and then to match them with the available products and services on offer. This is not always a straightforward situation. Dates, for example, may be mentioned, as will ideal travelling times. Specific interests may be highlighted, as will any particular constraints. It is the role of the employee to match and meet, and often exceed, the expectations and needs of the customer. This is a skill that is acquired gradually with experience.

Stated or implied

A stated need may be a precise day when the customer wishes to fly, watch a musical, book a meal in a restaurant or visit an attraction. Stated needs are explicit and usually cannot be moved. Therefore, it is the role of the employee to find a way of ensuring that these explicit needs are fulfilled.

Implied needs may not necessarily be stated, but they can be interpreted from the conversation with the customer. For example, if two adults want to travel to a resort and they have children, then a quiet resort with little or no facilities or transport would not necessarily be ideal for them. Implied needs are therefore aspects of the customer's needs that have to be taken into consideration, even though the customer may not have explicitly stated them.

Un-stated and anticipated

Un-stated needs are basically assumptions that are made by the customer. For example, if a hotel has a swimming pool, then the customer expects that it will be in operation. There may also be an un-stated expectation that there is a resort representative and someone to meet them at the airport to transfer them to the accommodation. Another customer's un-stated need may be to trust any descriptions or promises that have been made by the business in relation to the service or product that is being offered for sale.

Anticipated needs are often difficult to distinguish from un-stated needs. There is always an anticipation that the quality of the product or service will at least be at the level promised or that it should exceed this level.

Example

If the customer has booked a four-star, all-inclusive hotel, then there is an anticipated need or expectation that the food will be of a good quality and that the hotel facilities will be superior.

BUYER BEHAVIOUR

Businesses in all industries spend a great deal of time and effort trying to predict buyer behaviour. There are many internal and external factors that can influence the frequency, quantity and quality of customers for particular products and services. Buyer behaviour seeks to measure the current buying trends, and then to predict how those trends might be translated into behaviour in the future.

For the travel and tourism industry, which can be described as seasonal in some respects, buyer behaviour, or at least the prediction of behaviour, is of vital importance as it will determine the level of commitment of a tour operator, for example. This will influence the tour operator's purchase of airline seats, contracts signed with hotels and the recruitment of call centre and resort-based staff.

Push and pull factors

Push factors, or push marketing, are really an old-fashioned way of pushing products and services towards customers by creating interest in products, services and brands. The business will already have a range of products and services that it has to sell to potential customers. It begins with the products and services and offers them as they are to potential customers by using price cuts, promotions and advertising in order to generate sales.

Pull factors, or pull marketing, try to identify the specific needs of different customer groups, and then the business designs products and services to match these needs. There are, of course, a number of different additional factors that affect buying behaviour outside the normal commercial area of advertising and promotion.

Weather is a primary consideration. In fact, weather influences customer buying behaviour, whether they are considering an attraction in the northeast of England or an archaeological site in Egypt.

Customers have access to far more information than they did in the past. This means it is possible for them to identify ideal visiting times, either to an overseas location or to an attraction in the UK. Almost everything that the resort, attraction or country attempts to do to encourage 'out of season' visits is likely to be met with limited success.

A customer's budget for travel and tourism products has a strong influence on their buying behaviour. There are certain psychological price points beyond which they will not venture. Seeing what they perceive to be unnecessary additional expenses, such as under occupancy, added to their holiday price totals, also influences them heavily. The travel and tourism business is notorious for having headline low prices, whereas in reality, availability is low and there are hidden costs that are added at the last minute before the final booking confirmation.

Travel motivators

Identifying the key travel motivators of the client is another important aspect of customer service. This is a mix of the customer's background, their reason for choosing particular products or services and the purpose for which the service is being purchased.

The first two aspects of travel motivation are related to class and social status. We readily associate certain resorts and attractions with particular classes of individuals.

Table 4.1 Office for National Statistics classification of employment types

Number	Socio-economic classification
1	higher managerial and professional occupations
2	lower managerial and professional occupations
3	intermediate occupations
4	small employers and own account workers
5	lower supervisory and technical occupations
6	semi-routine occupations
7	routine occupations
8	long-term unemployed

Source: Office for National Statistics

This kind of approach has overtaken the traditional working, middle and upper class classifications. It is far more useful in terms of categorising British customers by class and social status. It is also possible to see that these two factors have a direct influence on individuals' consumption of travel and tourism products.

Think The Office of National Statistics produces several different types of occupational, social class and socio-economic classifications. How could a travel and tourism organisation use these classifications to identify customer needs and buying behaviour?

The three most common purposes for travel are leisure, business and visiting friends and relatives. The leisure group can be considered to be the mass market, which would include package holidays and family visits to attractions. Cost may be a consideration. Business travellers, on the other hand, are likely to be less concerned about price and more concerned with quality and convenience. Finally, those visiting friends and relatives are more likely to be concerned with the convenience of travel and may not be influenced or interested in accommodation or attractions at their destination.

All customers are influenced by the media to some degree. Businesses can use the media in two specific ways.

- To use public relations to encourage the media to run positive features and news about their business, products and services. This will be considered editorial content and more likely to be believed than advertising.

- The placing of advertising in targeted magazines and newspapers to match the specific customer types. (This is done by comparing the readership profiles of the media with the customer profiles created by the business.)

The final key travel motivator is for customers to seek a business that is able to cater for all of their needs with the minimum level of personal input required from themselves. They want relaxation and to be happy in the knowledge that everything has been organised for them by a professional business with employees showing high levels of customer service and understanding.

EVIDENCE ACTIVITY

P1 –3, M1, D1

You work for a travel and tourism organisation that does not have a specialised customer service function. Recently there have been a number of complaints and there are no policies and procedures in place in order to deal with them, or to monitor their conclusions. Your employer has asked you to prepare a written report, beginning with an investigation into two different travel and tourism organisations.

1. Describe the key principles of good customer service. (P1)

2. Describe the two organisations' customer service policies, mission statements and how they monitor their service standards. (P1)

3. Clearly state which type of research method you have used and why it was chosen. (P1)

4. Describe the benefits of good quality customer service in both organisations. (P2)

5. Describe the consequences of poor customer service in both organisations .(P2)

6. Describe how different buyer behaviour and motivation influences customer service provided by the two organisations. (P3)

The employer would like you to make a comparison between the two organisations.

7. Compare the service provided by your two chosen travel and tourism organisations. (M1)

8. Explain how the customer service provision meets the needs of different customer types. (M1)

Finally your employer would like you to evaluate the customer service and make justified recommendations, so that the business can create its own policies and procedures.

9. Evaluate the customer service provision in your two chosen organisations. (D1)

10. Make justified recommendations as to how the two organisations' customer service could be improved to meet the requirements of a range of customers. (D1)

4.3 Be able to demonstrate customer service skills in travel and tourism situations

CUSTOMER SERVICE SKILLS

The face, or frontline, of any travel and tourism business will be its employees. They may interact with customers in face-to-face situations, on the telephone, by e-mail or in writing. For many customers, the only real measure or opinion that they may form about the business will be as a result of their interactions with employees. It is therefore important for employees to have a fully rounded range of customer service skills.

Creating a welcome

Different organisations will prefer different styles of greeting or addressing customers. Some prefer a more formal approach and expect the employee to refer to the customer as sir or madam, or to address them personally as Mr, Mrs, Ms or Miss. Other businesses prefer a more informal approach, greeting customers by the employee stating their first name and asking how they can be of assistance.

The first few seconds of any interaction are vitally important as these will set the tone of the conversation and it may make the customer more or less willing to interact.

Building rapport

Having met or greeted a customer, it is then important to put them at their ease and to discover precisely what it is that they want. Building a rapport means encouraging the customer to be comfortable and unthreatened by the interaction, so that they are prepared to exchange views and information. In this way, whatever the situation, the employee can be clear about the customer's needs.

Effective listening

At least half of any conversation with a customer should involve the employee actively or effectively listening to them. Effective listening goes beyond actually hearing and understanding what they are saying and needs to involve encouragement that makes it clear to the customer that the employee is listening and has understood what is being said. This can be done by verbal confirmations, such as yes or no, or nodding and smiling to show agreement.

Everybody's listening ability fluctuates. The employee may appear bored, disinterested, distracted or in a hurry. It is important never to interrupt and to focus on the customer and what they are saying. It is always a valuable tool to write down notes if the situation is complicated. It is also important to keep an open mind until the conversation has finished and not to jump to any conclusions. To confirm to the customer that the employee has been listening, it is a wise course of action to repeat the key parts of the conversation back to them.

Questioning

Having listened to a customer, the employee may still be unaware of their exact needs. Not all customers are able to be clear and it is the role of the employee to find out precisely what they want. The employee should:

- ask questions one at a time to avoid confusion

- ask questions in a logical order

- try to avoid personal or direct questions

- recognise that there is a difference between questioning and interrogation, and not bully the customer into answering

- try to ask open questions as these will give the customer the maximum opportunity to give a fuller answer

- ask follow-up questions if necessary when specific information is required

- be tactful when asking difficult questions.

Developing a dialogue

Once a customer has been placed at their ease and appreciates that the employee is listening and understanding their needs, a more open dialogue or conversation can take place. This means that the customer is more likely to reveal precise details of their needs, so it becomes an easier task for the employee to help them. A confrontational interaction or a one-way interaction is not a conversation or a dialogue. It serves neither the employee nor the customer with any useful purpose.

Non-verbal communication

Non-verbal communication is only relevant to face-to-face customer service situations. In fact, a face-to-face communication is a mixture of verbal or spoken skills and non-verbal or body language skills.

It is important to use both of these elements to reinforce one another. It is also a valuable skill to learn about other people's body language and what messages are unconsciously being portrayed.

Body language really falls into four major categories.

- Facial expressions – such as a smile that makes a major difference when welcoming a customer. Eyebrows tend to move upwards when someone does not believe something and eyes can widen if someone is surprised and narrow when someone is angry.

- Gestures – many people use their head and hands to reinforce understanding or what they are saying. We shake our heads when we disagree and nod them when we agree. It is also intimidating to point at someone. It is important to remember that gestures can often mean something very different if used by people from other cultures.

- Posture – this is the way in which someone sits or stands. Sitting in a comfortable position in a chair, perhaps with the ankles crossed, gives the impression of being relaxed and confident. Sitting on the edge of a seat shows nervousness. Standing upright, with the head held high gives the impression of confidence, whereas slumped shoulders show a lack of confidence.

- Eye contact – it is important to maintain eye contact with the customer involved in the conversation. However, it is important not to appear to be staring at them. Eye contact shows that the employee is giving the customer their full attention.

Personal presentation

Many businesses in the travel and tourism have strict dress codes, which often involve wearing a uniform. The idea is not only to promote the business, but also to present a consistent employee image. Most organisations will have clear guidelines and rules about grooming, hygiene and cleanliness of clothing.

The key point behind any rules on personal presentation is to ensure that a consistent, professional image is presented to the customer. This may extend to hairstyles, the wearing of jewellery, make-up and visible tattoos.

Figure 4.6 Airline staff in uniform

Communication skills

There are three basic ways in which communication will normally take place between an employee and a customers.

- Face-to-face – where the employee has contact with a customer, for example at a reception desk, in a retail environment or on an aircraft.

- Telephone conversation – where the customer may be booking or purchasing a product or service, following up a booking, making a complaint or calling for additional information.

- Written communication – this can take the form of an e-mail or a more formal letter, perhaps a response to a query from a customer or a booking confirmation.

Identifying, meeting and exceeding customer needs

We have already seen that it is the key role of customer service to begin by precisely identifying the needs of the customer. The next stage is to identify how these needs can be met from the available products, services and procedures. This matching process is important and is completely reliant upon the employee's ability to have correctly established the needs. If this has not taken place, then the likelihood is that the customer's needs will not be met.

Customers expect their basic needs to be met. However much can be gained by using the personal contact with the customer to make them feel valued. This could mean promising to call back at a particular time and fulfilling that obligation, offering an incentive to the customer, or reassuring the customer that every part of their enquiry will be handled personally by that employee.

This involves appearing to 'go the extra mile' in order to exceed customer needs and make them delighted with the service that they have received.

Key words

Incentive – a reward, gift, promise or extra that is not usually included in the package and is used to encourage or thank the customer

RANGE OF SITUATIONS

Customer service situations tend to fall into four different areas:

- customers requesting information, such as flight details

- customers seeking advice, such as visa requirements

- customers with more complex requests, such as flight upgrades

- customers with complaints, such as delayed flights or poor quality service.

Requesting information

Customers requesting information is one of the most common situations and employees should have this information readily to hand. Typically, an initial enquiry regarding products or services from a customer will focus on details of flights, journeys, entrance fees and possible costs.

Since many systems are now computerised, employees should be able to access this information with a few keystrokes and, if necessary, print off a hard copy, giving the customer a chance to view the information, particularly if the encounter is a face-to-face situation.

Seeking advice

Advice on visas and health requirements may require the employee to carry out more research, particularly if they are not familiar with the rules governing particular countries. Many travel and tourism businesses offer visa services, such as Kuoni (www.kuoni.co.uk). They can advise on how to obtain visas, their costs and application times.

Similar advice may be necessary regarding health and safety abroad. The UK has agreements with many European countries, so that both of the countries' nationals can make use of publicly funded healthcare. However, many countries' healthcare does not conform to British health

and safety standards. The most common source of information is available from the Department of Health and called *Health Advice for Travellers*.

Research tip

For further information on health advice for travellers, visit the website of the Department of Health at www.dh.gov.uk. Look for 'Policy and guidance' and then select 'Health advice for travellers'.

Complex requests

More complex requests may involve the employee having to liaise with airlines, transfer companies and other external organisations. In the case of airport assistance, if the traveller has mobility problems, for example, this is usually dealt with directly by the departure and arrival airports.

Example

Bristol International Airport offers special assistance to its customers including Braille signs, lifts to all floors and special assistance points throughout the terminal.

Research tip

Find out more about the special assistance services offered at www.bristolairport.co.uk.

Priority seating and flight upgrades are usually handled at the check-in desks, although priority seating can be booked in advance. Priority seating is usually only allocated to those with disabilities, medical problems or people travelling with very young children.

Flight upgrades may take place when there has been overbooking on an aircraft and it is necessary to move some customers from economy into business class, for example. This will usually be made available to frequent flyers or those with special requirements.

Key words

Economy – basic grade seating and services on an aircraft

Business class – seating and services on an aircraft of a higher quality and price than economy

Frequent flyers – many airlines have special clubs or loyalty schemes for customers who regularly use their services. Frequent flyers that have travelled a certain amount of mileage may be entitled to automatic upgrades

Complaints

Complaints are often the most difficult customer service situations, as the customer may already be angry and aggressive because they have either experienced a flight delay or poor quality service. The key points to remember are:

- that the customer is angry with the organisation and not with the employee personally

- that the employee should try to remain calm, be sympathetic and interested

- the employee should suggest that any face-to-face conversation take place in a less public arena

- the employee should listen and take notes if necessary

- the employee should try not to do or say anything to make the matter worse

- the employee needs to find out exactly what the customer wants them to do

- the employee should check with a supervisor or manager before making any promises and then do what has been agreed as quickly as possible.

Research tip

Finding the complaints procedures for major tour operators is very difficult. They are quite well hidden on their websites. To find the My Travel complaints procedure at www.mytravel.com, scroll to the bottom of the homepage and select 'Help and FAQS'. A link to a brief statement on complaints can be found here.

Think Why do you think that companies deliberately make their complaints procedure hard to find? Ask your family and friends if they have ever made a complaint to a tour operator or airline. What was the procedure that they had to follow?

BUSINESS SKILLS

Each travel and tourism organisation will have its own methods and procedures for the completion of documentation or the use of information technology. This is a basic difference between paper-based or electronic-based document completions.

Completion of documentation and use of IT

Some travel and tourism businesses use completely automated and computerised booking and reservation systems. The system is an integrated one that can confirm customer details and then send any necessary confirmations, either by e-mail or by text. They can also generate letters that will have to be manually completed for posting.

Most document completion requires some form of human input. Businesses will usually have a range of pro-forma blank documents, such as forms, flight tickets and invoices, which can be partly completed using information technology and partly completed by hand.

Key words

Pro-forma – these are ready printed, single part or multi-part documents, which may need to be completed by an employee by hand

Document completion requirements will very much depend on the type of business involved and the customer service situation. They will invariably involve situations where a sale is being processed or a complex request or complaint is being dealt with. Many organisations use computerised reservation systems, which handle the entire booking process.

Research tip

There are four market leaders in computer reservation systems.
Galileo at www.galileo.se
Worldspan at www.worldspan.com
Sabre at www.sabre-holdings.com
Amadeus at www.amadeus.com.

Think What do you think are the advantages and disadvantages of computerised booking systems?

COMPLAINT HANDLING

Customer care means meeting customer needs and this also extends to difficult situations, such as handling complaints. It is important to be able to deal effectively with customers in every type of situation.

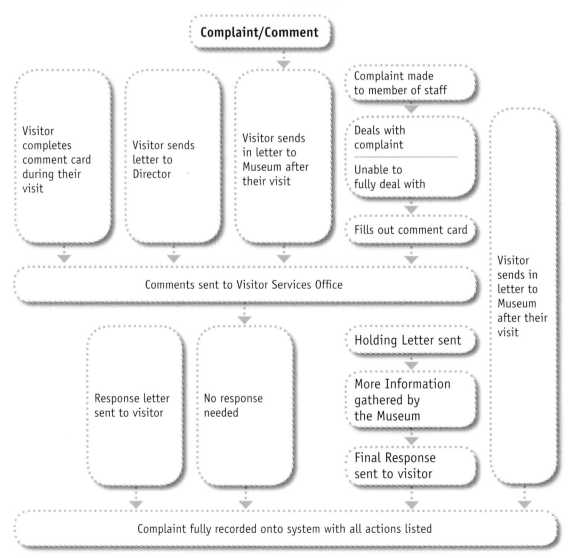

Figure 4.7 Complaint handling flow chart for a museum

Listening

The first and most important stage is to actively listen to the complaint and to give a suitable response, such as 'I'm glad you've brought this to our attention' or 'I'm sorry you have a problem' or 'I'm sure we can sort this out'. At this stage, it is important not to acknowledge that the organisation has actually done anything wrong. All that has been agreed is that there is a problem and that it will be looked at and dealt with.

Questioning

As already mentioned, it is important for the employee to establish precisely what is wrong and how the customer perceived it to have come about. This may involve asking additional questions in order to clarify and confirm key points and particularly identify any other member of the organisation who may have been involved. They may be able to provide valuable insights into the root cause of the complaint.

Empathising

It is important for the employee to show understanding and be positive, while reassuring the customer that, whatever the nature of their complaint, it will be taken seriously and that the employee will actively seek a solution to the situation.

Understanding the problem

Before the employee can actively undertake any role in dealing with the complaint, he/she has to be absolutely sure that they understand the situation. It is also important for the employee to appreciate what the customer feels to be an ideal resolution of the matter. Skilled questioning techniques can help the employee to understand the problem. Above all, the employee needs to get to a point where they fully understand the complexity of the situation and can then take positive steps to deal with it.

Taking control of the situation

Sometimes customers will be very awkward and angry, but it is important for the employee to remain calm and attempt to take control of the situation. It is important for the employee to listen to the facts, rather than how the customer is putting it across. A calm and unhurried approach, together with signs that the employee empathises with the customer, will go a long way to diffuse the situation.

Agreeing solutions

The customer must be given a realistic expectation of what the employee can deliver. It is important for the employee to build in 'slippage' time. This means telling the customer that it will take slightly longer to sort out the situation than it usually will, just in case additional problems are encountered. In this way, when the employee returns quicker than promised with a solution, the customer will be impressed and their expectations will have been exceeded.

Only solutions that comply with the company's policies and procedures can be agreed and this will usually mean checking with a supervisor or manager before offering a positive solution to the situation.

Follow-up

If the employee has to break a promise to a customer, then they must feedback the reason to the customer and be up-front and honest about why they have failed to deliver a solution.

If the employee has done what they have agreed to do, then this will result in a guaranteed happy customer. It is important to check with the customer that they are happy once the solution has been put into place. An opportunity to talk to them, even by e-mail, will give the customer an opportunity to feedback and confirm that they were satisfied with the solution and that the problem is now over.

4.4 Be able to demonstrate selling skills appropriate to the travel and tourism industry

STAGES OF SELLING

Selling is a key part of customer service and it actually extends beyond convincing a customer to purchase a particular product or service. Showing good selling skills can mean building a long-term relationship with a customer and projecting a strong image and reputation for the business.

Building rapport

It is important to establish a favourable impression from the beginning. This involves being sincere and welcoming. The selling process, or indeed the product or service itself, may have been sold a dozen times already that day, but it is a personal experience for the customer. This means that it is important to focus on good communication and the effective use of body language.

Establishing customer needs and expectations

It is important to quickly establish precisely what the customer needs and what their expectations may be. This can be done in the following way:

- Begin with open questions to acquire as much information as possible. These questions should begin with words such as 'what', 'why' and 'how'.

- Use leading questions that can help to narrow down the customer's needs. Ask questions such as 'Where have you already been?' and 'What did you like about it?'

- Finally, move onto closed questions, so that you can obtain specific information and confirm points, such as 'Are you looking for a beach holiday?'

Features and benefits

Having established the customer's needs and expectations, it is now the role of the employee to match a product or service to the needs and expectations. The employee will select the most suitable ones and focus on a small number of features or benefits that will directly appeal to the customer. For example, if the customer has said that they like beach holidays, the employee could tell them that this resort has an even better and quieter beach only five minutes away from the main resort.

Overcoming objections

Customers may not want to commit immediately and they may wish to put off making a decision. An employee with good selling skills will be able to overcome these objections and find something positive in the product or service that directly overcomes the objections. For example, if the customer does not want to walk to the nearest beach, the employee could tell them that the hotel has a free minibus shuttle service that runs all day between the hotel and the beachfront.

Closing the sale

Once the customer has agreed that the product or service matches their needs and expectations, it is now the role of the employee to turn it into a positive sale. It may be necessary for the employee to re-emphasise some of the points and to reassure the customer that they can buy in confidence and that the product or service will be precisely as has been described during their conversation.

Completing documentation

It may be necessary to immediately book and reserve the product or service, perhaps using a computerised reservation system. Alternatively, a deposit can be taken from the customer, which may require the completion of pro-forma documents.

As documentation is completed, the employee needs to confirm each stage of the process with the customer and provide them with any necessary copies in line with company procedures.

AFTER-SALES SERVICE

A customer service relationship between the employee and the customer does not end when the sale has been completed. There may be an ongoing dialogue and an opportunity for the employee to make additional sales or make amendments to the original booking. This is known as after-sales service and it is an integral, but often neglected, area of customer service.

Many businesses are content with having made a sale and having established a firm commitment using a contract, which guarantees full payment for the product or service from the customer. However, effective after-sales service continues the relationship between the business and the customer and helps to ensure extra sales and a long-lasting relationship.

Example

Although the National Maritime Museum is free for general visits, it still needs to generate income from many of their products and services. Effective marketing is important, but so are 'selling skills'. There are a number of ways in which the museum staff can encourage customers to buy products and services, including:

- raising awareness of products and services
- understanding customers' needs and expectations
- telephone information
- face-to-face communication
- use of the website.

Think Briefly explain how you think the museum could generate a sale from each of the five points.

Research tip

www.londonnights.com is a discount booking service for London hotels. The website contains very clear after-sales service procedures on the website. From the homepage select 'Site map' and then 'After-sales service'.

Pre-departure

Before departure there may be an opportunity to sell additional products and services to the customer. A travel agent will routinely send out a booking confirmation to the customer. Later on, they will also send out a payment request for the balance a number of days before the holiday or visit. Much nearer to the departure date, they will also send out any necessary tickets or vouchers for the customer to present at the check-in desk and at the hotel. Each communication offers an opportunity to sell additional products and services. These could include:

- travel insurance
- currency exchange
- car hire
- excursions
- car parking and/or overnight hotel accommodation at the airport
- additional baggage allowance
- flight upgrades
- priority boarding.

Many of these additional sales opportunities are actually taken by a business during an online booking process.

Research tip

Test one of the major tour operators by following a booking procedure and see how many additional services are offered before booking confirmation and payment is required. Good examples are Olympic Holidays (www.olympicholidays.co.uk) and Fly Drive Florida holidays, incorporating visits to the theme parks, such as www.firstchoice.co.uk/florida.

Research tip

Find out more about passenger rights by looking at the EU portal europa. eu.int/comm/transport/air/rights/index_en.htm.

Customers can also be the driving force behind changes, amendments and cancellations. Personal circumstances may dictate this. Many businesses in the travel and tourism industry have published refund scales, depending on the time that the cancellation is made in relation to the departure time.

Post departure

In continuing an ongoing dialogue with customers through after-sales service, it is possible to establish a relationship with them that improves the possibility of them making bookings in the future. Businesses will establish databases on all of their customers and routinely send out information and offers in order to encourage future bookings.

There may also be the need to make changes or even cancellations. The reasons for this may be driven either by the business or by the customer themselves. For example, if a flight is cancelled or there is a problem with accommodation in the resort, then amendments may have to be made by the selling business. Suitable alternatives will have to be found and offered to the customer. In the event of flight cancellations that offer no opportunity to book an alternative suitable flight, the business may have to offer a full refund. However, it would be more inclined to offer an alternative holiday at a reduced rate in order not to lose the sale.

Immediately after using products and services, the business may send out a questionnaire that entitles the customer to a discount for a future booking if they fill it out and return it.

There may be issues arising from the actual departure that may result in a complaint or a problem. Typically, these will be issues such as lost property. If luggage is lost *en route*, then this may be the responsibility of the airline, but the booking agent will usually work as a point of contact between the customer and the airline itself. Any assistance, even in situations that are not the direct responsibility of the selling business, can help to firm up a longer-lasting relationship and can be considered to be integral parts of after-sales service.

Example

Due to new European Union legislation passed in 2005, air passengers within the EU now have more rights if their flights are cancelled, they are denied boarding due to overbooking or they are obliged to suffer long delays.

Think What do you think passengers are entitled to if their flight is delayed for a long time?

EVIDENCE ACTIVITY

P4 – 6, M2 – 3, D2

Having prepared a report on the principles and benefits of good customer service, your employer now wants you to demonstrate customer service skills in a number of different situations. These demonstrations are to be recorded, so that the good practice can be shown to other employees once the policies and procedures have been written. In the role of a travel agent, carry out the following tasks.

1. Research and feedback to a customer the results of the following request:

A family of four, children aged 5 and 13, wish to fly from the nearest regional airport and spend one night in Paris and then fly on to Rome, where they will spend three nights. They then wish to return via Madrid (two nights) and Paris (one night). They require information and pricing on flights, accommodation and transfers. (P4)

2. Research and feedback to a customer the results of the following request:

Visa and health requirements, as well as any other relevant advice, for a couple in their late forties wishing to fly to and backpack across Mali. (P4)

3. Deal with the following complaint in a face-to-face situation:

A customer of an airline, due to a family crisis, was unable to check-in to the flight that they had booked. They telephoned the airline, but after waiting for 25 minutes, had to ring off. They left a message explaining the situation and requesting a refund or transfer of ticket. Company policy requires that cancellations are dealt with on the spot and due to the circumstances a refund and transfer cannot be offered. The best that can be done is to offer the customer a 50% discount if they re-book their flight. (P5)

4. You have received an email from an irate customer who has sent the message via an Internet Café in Egypt. Unfortunately, the customer's husband was taken ill abroad and required hospital treatment. To their horror they discovered the travel insurance that you sold them is not recognised by the medical centre and that they have already had to pay £3,000 in treatment fees. The customer will also require an air ambulance to bring him back to the UK and his wife wants you to organise this immediately and pay all the costs. Having checked the insurance booking details, the customer declined non-emergency treatment cover, which appears to be the problem. The best you can do is to refer them to the insurance company. (P5)

5. Independently demonstrate your skills in handling customer service situations in concluding complaints to the satisfaction of both the customer and the business in the situations described in 3 and 4. (M2)

In order to see customer service in its true context, your employer also wants you to demonstrate how it can be incorporated into the sales process. In order to do this, your employer has created a typical situation:

6. A single parent father and his young son (6 years) have a budget of £1,000 for a fortnight's holiday in July. The customer wants a child-friendly, quiet beach resort within 3.5 to 5 hours flight time of the regional airport. Identify at least three options, outline the features and benefits, overcome any objections, close the sale and complete the documentation. (P6)

7. The customer does not have any travel insurance and has not yet arranged car parking at the airport. Try to secure these extra sales as part of your after-sales service. (P6)

8. When the customer returns to England his child's favourite toy, was left or lost on the aircraft. Initial enquiries have not located it. Contact the airline and feedback their comments to your customer. (P6)

Demonstrate effective selling skills and a high level of product knowledge in the above scenarios, mentioning key features and benefits. (M3)

Demonstrate a consistently high level of performance in all of the customer service and complaints situations and show a high level of confidence in your sales knowledge and technique. (D2)

The European travel market

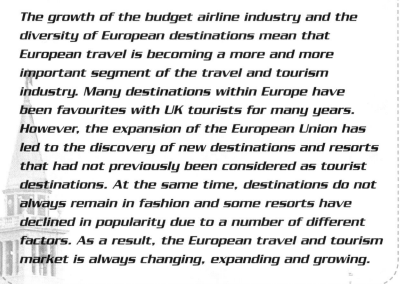

unit 7

The growth of the budget airline industry and the diversity of European destinations mean that European travel is becoming a more and more important segment of the travel and tourism industry. Many destinations within Europe have been favourites with UK tourists for many years. However, the expansion of the European Union has led to the discovery of new destinations and resorts that had not previously been considered as tourist destinations. At the same time, destinations do not always remain in fashion and some resorts have declined in popularity due to a number of different factors. As a result, the European travel and tourism market is always changing, expanding and growing.

In this unit, you will learn about:

So you want to be a...

Tour Manager

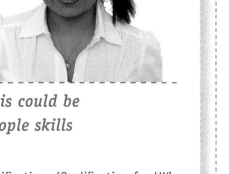

My name Denise Awali
Age 26
Income £15,000

If you like the idea of being paid to travel, then this could be the job for you. A flare for languages and great people skills could help you to land this exciting role.

What does a Tour Manager do?

I organise and accompany customers on package tours.

What are your day to day responsibilities?

I make sure the travel arrangements run according to plan, and that the accommodation, meals and service meet customers' expectations. During the journey I'll give a commentary on the places we visit and sell excursions. I liaise with hotels, restaurants, coach companies and tourist attractions, and keep records. I stay with the group all the time - I never know when I'll be needed to give advice or deal with emergencies.

How did you get into the job?

I have a BTEC National Diploma in Travel and Tourism; you also need a good standard of general education, experience of working with people, an interest in geography or history, and foreign languages. It helps to have worked abroad.

What training have you had?

I had a two-week induction course to familiarise me with company policies and procedures, customer service techniques and our main destinations. My company also helped me start studying for my Blue Badge qualification. (Qualification for UK's professional, registered tourist guides.)

What are the hours like?

I spend 30 weeks a year on tour and I'm on call 24 hours a day when I'm with a group. I'm the first up and last to bed!

It sounds like a demanding job, what skills do you need?

You should be able to get on with people regardless of their ages or backgrounds. You need to be a good communicator: confident and outgoing, but also polite and tactful. It also helps to be organised, smart and tidy, and energetic!

> **I enjoy that every day is different and I get paid to travel!**

What's the pay like?

I started on £12,000 three years ago. The pay varies between companies – the top rate's about £18,000. I can earn commission on the excursions I sell and I get free accommodation and meals for the duration of the tour.

What are your plans for the future?

I enjoy the fact that every day is different and I get paid to travel, so I want to continue doing this type of work. Eventually, I would like to move into long haul tours and travel to more exotic destinations like China and India.

Grading criteria

The table below shows what you need to do to gain a pass, merit or distinction in this part of the qualification. Make sure you refer back to it when you are completing work so you can judge whether you are meeting the criteria and what you need to do to fill in gaps in your knowledge or experience.

In this unit there are four evidence activities that give you an opportunity to demonstrate your acheivement of the grading criteria:

page 138   P1

page 146   P2, M1

page 150   P3, M2, D1

page 154   P4, M3, D2

To achieve a pass grade, the evidence must show that the learner is able to...	To achieve a merit grade, the evidence must show that, in addition to the pass criteria, the learner is able to...	To achieve a distinction grade, the evidence must show that, in addition to the pass and merit criteria, the learner is able to...
P1 Identify and locate countries, gateways and key leisure destinations within the European travel market	**M1** Explain how different factors influence the appeal of specific leisure destinations for different types of customer	**D1** Recommend how a European destination could increase its appeal for different types of customers
P2 Describe factors that contribute to the appeal of leisure destinations within the European travel market	**M2** Explain how specific European destinations meet the needs of different customer types	**D2** Evaluate the effects of current factors on the European travel market in the future
P3 Describe, with examples of destinations, European leisure experiences and their appeal to customer types	**M3** Analyse factors that shape development of the European travel market	
P4 Describe the development of the European travel market and its destinations and identify factors that have contributed to this		

7.1 *Key facts about European destinations*

COUNTRIES

European countries

There are 49 countries that are considered part of the continent of Europe. Some of these countries, such as the UK, Germany and France are major tourist-generating countries. Not all European countries are large tourist-receiving countries, but overall Europe receives over 400 million tourists each year and the World Tourism Organisation expects this figure to rise to over 600 million each year by 2020. Many European destinations are well known, but currently smaller European countries, like Lithuania, Slovenia and the Ukraine, are not popular tourist destinations. The largest country in Europe is Russia and some of the smallest countries include Andorra, Monaco and the Vatican City, which is a separate state inside the Italian capital of Rome.

Key words

Tourist-generating country – a country from which a large number of tourists originate. A country from which many people travel overseas on holiday

Tourist-receiving country – a country which receives a large number of tourists or visitors. A large number of people visit this country for their holiday

The European Union

Many of the countries in Europe have chosen to join the European Union (EU). The European Union is a group of European countries who work together to help each other with economic, social and trade agreements. The European Union countries provide aid to poorer areas to promote regeneration and economic growth.

Example

The European Union helps fund projects that will promote tourism in a region. The Eden Project in Cornwall was given £26 million by the European Union in order to provide jobs and attract tourists to that area of the country.

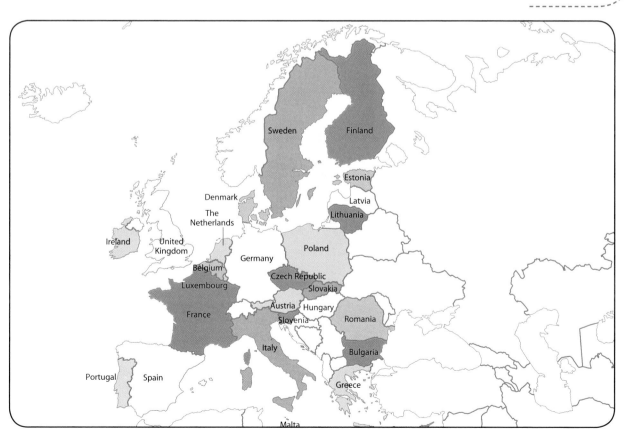

Figure 7.1 Countries in the European Union

European Union countries help to promote tourism in other European Union countries by running specific marketing campaigns. The European Union has also developed the Package Travel Regulations, which are the regulations and legislation governing the tour operations industry and which apply to the sale of package holidays throughout all European Union countries. These regulations are studied in more detail in Unit 1, Investigating Travel and Tourism and in Unit 12, Tour Operations.

> **Think** Which European countries do you think are tourist-generating areas? Which are large tourist-receiving areas?

Example

Countries that are currently members of the European Union are:

Austria	Latvia
Belgium	Lithuania
Bulgaria	Luxembourg
Cyprus	The Netherlands
Czech Republic	Malta
Denmark	Poland
Estonia	Portugal
Finland	Romania
Germany	Slovakia
Greece	Slovenia
Hungary	Spain
Ireland/Eire	Sweden
Italy	United Kingdom

Research tip

More information about the European Union and its current members can be found on the European Union website: www.europa.eu.

Eurozone countries

Figure 7.2 The Euro

Eurozone countries are those within the European Union who have chosen to use the Euro as their currency. The Euro was introduced in 12 countries in 2002. Countries in the European Union can choose whether they want to use the Euro or keep their existing currency. Some countries, for example, Denmark and the UK, have chosen not to join the Eurozone so far. For tourists, visiting countries that use the Euro makes travelling easier and more convenient. They can compare prices between countries and do not need to organise and pay for currency exchange when travelling within the Eurozone. Some countries that are not in the Eurozone will still accept Euros and give tourists change in the local currency.

Example

Countries that use the Euro € are:

Austria	Ireland/Eire
Belgium	Italy
Finland	Luxembourg
France	The Netherlands
Greece	Portugal
Germany	Spain

> **Think** Why do you think that some European countries have decided to not use the Euro as their currency?

Research tip

The current exchange rate for the Euro and other European countries can be found at the currency exchange website www.xe.com.

Research tip

An up-to-date list of the countries that accept Schengen visas and further information can be found at www.eurovisa.info, which is the official website for Schengen visa applications.

Schengen countries

Tourists who do not have a passport from a European Union country are usually required to have a visa to enter European Union countries. In order to make it easier for people to travel between different countries in the European Union, visiting tourists can apply for a Schengen visa.

A Schengen visa allows the passport and visa holder to travel to any or all of the European Union states that are part of the Schengen Agreement without having to apply for separate visas for each country they visit. A Schengen visa normally lasts for 6 months and allows travel for 90 days during that 6-month period.

One of the main uses for Schengen visas in the tourism industry is for tourists from non-European countries, who book cruises around the Mediterranean. As these cruises involve stopping at many different countries, including the Greek Islands, mainland Italy and Spain, travel is easier with only one visa requirement.

Example

Countries that currently accept Schengen visas are:

Austria	Italy
Belgium	Luxembourg
Denmark	Norway
Finland	The Netherlands
France	Portugal
Germany	Spain
Greece	Sweden
Iceland	

GATEWAYS

A gateway is not the final destination or resort in which the tourist is staying, but it is their first arrival point. Gateways are not always airports. They can also be ferry or train terminals. For example, many people arrive in the UK through the gateways of Heathrow or Gatwick airports. Tourists can then travel on to their final destination with a connecting flight to a local or regional airport or by using another form of transport.

Key airports and their IATA codes

IATA stands for the International Air Transport Association. Each gateway airport around the world is given an individual IATA three letter code that identifies it. This code appears on baggage labels, flight and travel tickets, and on the arrival and departure boards at airports.

Key words

Gateway – a point of access into a country or region, usually an airport or sea port, although it may also be a border crossing or railway station

IATA three letter code – the individual three letter code that identifies each airport throughout the world

Example

Here are some of the most commonly used IATA codes, the gateway name and the nearby resorts in Europe.

Resort	IATA code	Airport destination
Acharavi	CFU	Corfu, Greece
Afandou	Rho	Rhodes, Greece
Alanya	AYT	Turkey
Alcudia	PMI	Majorca, Spain
Algarve	FAO	Portugal
Amalfi	NAP	Italy
Ayia Napa	PFO	Cyprus
Benidorm	ALC	Spain
Costa del Sol	AGP	Spain
Golden Bay	MLA	Malta
Kokini Hani	HER	Crete, Greece
La Caleta	TFS	Tenerife, Spain
Lido de Jesolo	VCE	Italy
Los Pocillos	ACE	Lanzarote, Spain
Marbella	AGP	Spain
Marmaris	DLM	Turkey
Playa Balito	LPA	Gran Canaria, Spain
Rabac	PUY	Croatia
Rimini	BLO	Italy
San Antonio	IBZ	Ibiza, Spain

Eurostar/Eurotunnel

The Eurostar is a fast non-stop train service that goes under the English Channel between the UK and France. Boarding points in the UK include London Waterloo train station and the Eurostar terminal at Ashford, Kent. In 2007, a new boarding point is due to open at London King's Cross, enabling passengers to connect to rail services to the north of the UK. The direct fast train goes to a range of large cities within France, including Paris, Calais and Lille, and also to Brussels in Belgium. Eurostar also run direct trains to Disneyland Paris and in the winter months they run the Ski Train, which is a non-stop train from the UK directly to resorts in the French Alps.

Eurotunnel is also known as the Channel Tunnel – a non-stop freight train between Folkestone on the south coast of England and Calais in France. Drivers drive their car, camper van, coach or caravan onto the freight train and remain in their vehicles while the train travels through the tunnel to arrive in France. The journey takes approximately 35 minutes.

Reservations for both Eurostar and Eurotunnel should be made in advance, either by a travel agent or telephone or on the Internet. Details of the vehicle will need to be provided when booking a place on the Eurotunnel.

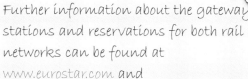

Research tip

Further information about the gateway stations and reservations for both rail networks can be found at www.eurostar.com and www.eurotunnel.com.

Figure 7.3 Eurostar routes and terminals

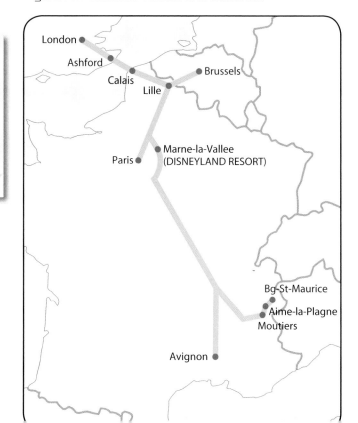

European ports

Some of the major ports that are used for travel out of the UK are Dover, Portsmouth, Harwich, Newcastle and Hull. These ports are used by tourists who choose to travel by ferry instead of by air or rail.

These may be people on self-drive holidays who wish to take their own car, caravan or camper van over to Ireland, continental Europe or Scandinavia, or by people who wish to connect with public transport once overseas. One of the main reasons why people choose to travel to Europe by sea as opposed to using Eurotunnel is that the ferry is often cheaper. However, journeys by ferry are normally slower than Eurotunnel. Some ferries that travel longer distances, for example between Hull and Rotterdam and Zeebrugge, have accommodation, entertainment and food and drink outlets onboard. Not all sea transport is by ferry and some routes like Poole to Cherbourg in France are serviced by high-speed catamarans.

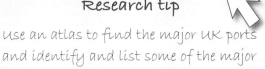

Research tip

Use an atlas to find the major UK ports and identify and list some of the major routes across Europe.

LEISURE DESTINATIONS

The wide range of destinations in Europe means that there is somewhere to suit all different tourist requirements. The wide variety of physical landscapes in Europe means many different types of destinations are available to tourists, from the mountain ranges of the Alps to the islands of the Mediterranean.

Europe's destinations can be categorised into five main destination types. However, some destinations may fall under more than one category and appeal to a number of different tourists, so bear in mind that it may not be possible to categorise all tourist destinations into only one type.

- seaside resorts

- winter sports resorts

- countryside areas

- cities

- cruise regions.

> **Think** Can you identify three European destinations for each of the different destination types listed above?

Seaside resorts

Europe, particularly the area around the Mediterranean Sea, has a large number of seaside resorts that attract both overseas and domestic tourists. The majority of seaside resorts are in the south of the Mediterranean where the climate is the most suitable with hot, dry summers. The wide range of seaside resorts means that there is a resort to suit all types of customers. Travel agents have to be careful to not make assumptions about customers' preferences, for example, that young people want a busy resort with lots of nightlife or that elderly couples are looking for quieter destinations. Travel agent staff should ask the customer questions in order to establish their needs and requirements and match these to the destination choice.

Some seaside resorts, for example, the coasts of Turkey and Greece, are only open during the summer season from May to September. However, many of the mainland resorts, in particular, those in Spain and Portugal, are open throughout the year for both winter sun and summer holidays.

At destinations that are open year-round, the customer type and types of entertainment on offer change throughout the year to cater to the different types of customers who visit during different seasons.

Example

Benidorm on the Costa Blanca in Spain is renowned for its busy nightlife during the summer months and its more gentle afternoon entertainment and tea dances during the winter when customers are generally older and possibly retired.

Key words

Summer season resort – a resort that is open to tourists from May to September
Winter sun resort – a sunny destination that attracts visitors during the winter months of October to April

Think Find a UK tour operator's main summer sun brochure and examine the range of different seaside resorts on offer. Plot these destinations and resorts on a blank map of Europe and locate each resort's gateway airport.

Winter sports resorts

There are a large number of ski resorts throughout Europe that are only open during the winter months. Some ski resorts in Russia and Norway also offer winter sports in the summer. Newspapers often report that winter sports resorts in Europe are in decline due to global warming.

Most traditional ski resorts are found in Switzerland, France, Italy or Austria. Newer resorts are also developing in countries such as Bulgaria and Romania.

Today, most resorts offer skiing and snowboarding, and off-piste or heli-skiing for the more adventurous. A wider range of winter sports and activities is normally available in the Scandinavian resorts, where customers can almost always be guaranteed snow. Alternative activities can include sledding with huskies, cross-country skiing, reindeer rides and bobsleighing. Many resorts offer private and group skiing lessons and resorts with gentler slopes will also offer a range of children's classes. One important consideration when booking a ski holiday is to match the skiing ability of the customers to the difficulty levels of the slopes in each resort.

One of the most appealing parts of a ski resort is the après ski activities on offer to customers. The evening entertainment can range from discos and organised bar crawls in lively resorts like Andorra to the saunas and steam rooms and roof-top bars in Norway. Matching both the skiing ability of the customer and their preferences for après ski entertainment to the correct resort is one of the most important aspects of booking a ski holiday.

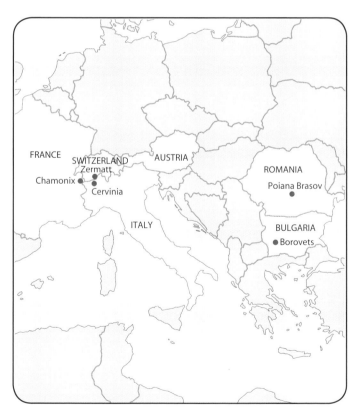

Figure 7.4 Some of Europe's winter sports resorts

Countryside resorts

Countryside resorts are sometimes called lakes and mountains resorts. Often these places are ski resorts during the winter and lakes and mountains, or countryside resorts, during the summer. Therefore, they are open to tourists all year round.

Other countryside destinations are open throughout the year regardless of the weather. These destinations are often based in or near small cities, towns or villages on the shores of lakes that are surrounded by mountains or on the edge of National Parks in areas of particular beauty, such as the Black Forest in Germany. Examples of lakes and mountain resorts include Lake Garda in northern Italy and Lake Lucerne in Switzerland.

These types of resorts attract tourists due to their spectacular scenery or for the opportunities they offer for wildlife watching, hiking or walking in the mountains and forests, or boating and lake trips. Some countryside resorts offer activity holidays that focus on walking, climbing and other outdoor pursuits like rafting, canoeing or paragliding. For example, Interlaken in Switzerland advertises itself as an adventure sport location.

Figure 7.5 Adventure sports in Switzerland

Cities

Over the last few years, the number of people taking short city breaks has increased due to the growth of low-cost airlines, which now offer cheap flights to many European cities. Europe has a diverse range of cities that have different appeals as tourism destinations. Many cities are historical or cultural destinations. Each European capital or major city has a particular heritage or attraction (or many attractions) for tourists, varying from connections with important past historical events, famous art or architecture or a connection with a famous person in history. Rome and Paris are both cities famous for their museums, art galleries, architecture and historical buildings. Some cities are also popular due to the entertainment or cultural events they offer. Cities like Berlin and Moscow are famous for past historical events and are important city break destinations.

Many eastern European cities like Riga and Prague attract stag and hen groups who take advantage of the cheap flights, food and drink to celebrate overseas.

There are some cities that are renowned for shopping or their local markets. Tour operators offer specific shopping breaks to the local Christmas markets in Germany and Austria or wine tours of the champagne producing areas in France.

Research tip

The European Union elect a cultural city every year. Use the Internet to find out which city is the European City of Culture this year. Explore the historical and cultural attractions that the city has to offer and consider which types of customers might like to visit the city.

Cruise areas

The cruise sector has been increasing in popularity over the last few years and European cruise destinations attract a wide range of tourists both from the UK, overseas and especially the North American market.

Cruises allow tourists to visit a number of interesting ports and tourist attractions in one holiday in a similar way to an organised coach tour. During the summer months, the cruise industry is focused mainly in the Mediterranean with major ports like Naples, Genoa and Athens acting as embarkation or joining cities. These ships will cruise for 8, 11 or 14-day itineraries during which time they will visit a number of different ports that offer tourists opportunities to visit leisure destinations and the chance of see important historical or cultural sites.

During the winter months, the cruise ships change their routes and some sail around the Canary Islands and northern Africa. These journeys often form part of a 'cruise and stay' winter holiday based around the Canary Islands.

In addition to the general interest Mediterranean cruises, there are also more specialist cruise ships and holidays available. These can vary from river cruises along the River Danube or smaller cruise liners that travel through the Norwegian fjords or around the Orkneys. These ships may be wildlife or history orientated. They are often accompanied by a guest lecturer who is a specialist in the subject or destinations being visited.

More information about cruises can be found in Unit 10, Investigating the Cruise Sector.

Key words

Embarkation – when a passenger joins a cruise ship, normally at a major port at the start of a cruise

EVIDENCE ACTIVITY

P1

For this activity, you will need an atlas and at least two blank maps of Europe.

1 Use a blank map of Europe to identify the following:
   - three winter sun destinations
   - three summer sun destinations
   - three lakes and mountains/countryside resorts
   - three European cities that are major tourist destinations
   - three areas that are popular with cruise ships.

   Try to space out the destinations and resorts you have chosen around Europe and do not concentrate on one particular country. (P1)

2 Now identify the gateway airport or port for each of the resorts that you have identified. Remember to list the three letter IATA codes next to each airport. (P1)

3 Finally, use another blank map to identify:
   - Eurotunnel and Channel Tunnel routes and terminals
   - three major European rivers that are used for the tourism industry
   - the different seas and oceans in Europe. (P1)

7.2 *Factors determining the appeal of leisure destinations in the European travel market*

The appeal of a tourist destination is all of the factors that cause tourists to choose that particular destination over any other destination on offer. Customers consider many different factors when selecting a holiday destination. Although price may be one of these factors, a number of other important features will also influence their decision. These include:

- accessibility
- geographical features
- attractions
- local culture
- economy/economic factors.

ACCESSIBILITY

Transport options

When considering the accessibility of a destination, a potential tourist will consider the different forms of transportation available to and within the resort. The main forms of transport that tourists can choose to the gateway include flying, sea transport or rail transport.

The accessibility of the departing airport or gateway may be an important factor in destination choice. Some UK tourists choose to travel from local or regional airports like Bristol, Cardiff and Edinburgh and this narrows the number and choice of destinations that can be reached by direct flights. Flights from some UK regional airports are more expensive than flights from larger national airports. This additional cost must be weighed up by the customers against the difficulties of getting to one of the UK's major airports. Travelling to a large UK airport may involve travel by rail or road and, in some cases, overnight accommodation in an airport hotel is required before an early morning departure. Flights departing during the night are often cheaper than daytime flights. However, families with small children may prefer to pay the additional cost for the convenience of a daytime flight.

Journey time

Journey time will be a factor for some tourists, depending on the length of their trip and how easy it is for them to travel. For example, families with young children may want to limit the time they spend travelling, or tourists booking short breaks may not want to spend a large proportion of their holiday travelling.

Tourists who are booking independent holidays will also consider the transportation available in the resort when they have arrived. These could include the availability and cost of car hire and the reliability and ease of use of public transport. This may also be an important factor for tourists on self-drive or flight-only holidays.

Transfer time

Tourists who are booking a package holiday may consider the transfer time from the airport to the resort and the method of transport used by the tour operator. This could be a coach or taxi and may involve waiting for other customers to arrive before the coach departs from the airport. These small delays and the transfer time add to the overall journey time, and so some customers may choose to book a private transfer either by taxi or pre-booked private car.

> **Key words**
> --
> Accessibility – the ease of getting to a destination
> Transfer – the journey from the gateway airport to the resort or final destination

GEOGRAPHICAL FEATURES

The geographical features, also known as topography, are the resort's surrounding area and scenery. Geographical features that will affect a tourist's decision to visit a place also include the climate, mountains, beaches and coastline.

Seas and coastline

Two of the most important geographical features of many European seaside resorts are the beach and coastline. A dirty, crowded beach will not attract many tourists, but a beach that is clean and offers a wide variety of facilities, including sports and food and drink outlets, is a great attraction to tourists, and in particular for families with children. Beaches that are particularly popular with tourists are those that slope gently into the water without any sudden drops and those that have golden sand as opposed to pebbles or small stones. Good examples of beach resorts are Lido de Jesolo in Italy and Antalya in Turkey. European beaches can earn the Blue Flag beach award, which is given to beaches that meet high standards in a number of different categories. These include disabled access, cleanliness, water quality and the number of lifeguards.

Research tip

A list of current Blue Flag beaches can be found at www.blueflag.org.

Europe's oceans and seas are not themselves an attraction for many tourists, but the resorts located on the coasts are popular and the warm temperature of the southern seas, such as the Mediterranean and the Adriatic, draw many tourists to the nearby beach resorts. Some of the wildlife in the seas and oceans do attract tourists. For example, whale and dolphin watching is popular in the Canaries or North Sea. Wreck dives are available in Malta and Gozo. Other ways in which the seas of Europe are used for tourism include fishing, sailing and boating holidays.

Mountain ranges

The majority of mountain ranges in Europe have been turned into winter sports resorts and summer walking or activity resorts. These destinations often offer tourists a range of difficulty levels for both skiing and hiking. Mountain resorts with famous mountains that are suitable for climbing normally offer accompanied or guided climbs to climbers with different abilities.

In many mountain resorts, the tourists do not need to be able to climb or hike to the top of the mountains and the spectacular views can be accessed by cable car or funicular. Some mountain resorts try to offer a range of other activities, which will appeal to tourists who are not focused on one type of sport, as this widens their appeal and increases the number of people who might choose to visit.

Key words

Funicular – also known as funicular railway, it consists of two cars joined by a cable, for transporting people up and down steep slopes

Inland waterways

Inland lakes, waterways, canals and rivers provide many opportunities for tourists to enjoy nature. This can be in the form of organised tours or guided river cruises along popular rivers like the River Elbe or daily lake excursions across the local lake, visiting nearby beauty spots and secluded restaurants. These are the typical types of boat trips on offer in many Italian and Swiss lake resorts on Lake Lugano and Lake Maggiore.

Rivers also offer tourists a range of independent holidays like river boating or canal boating. This could be a one day excursion or a full self-catering week or two-week long holiday. Rivers and canyons are also used for adventure sports and often feature as excursions involving white-water rafting or canyoning. Occasionally these adventure sports are available as a special interest holiday, for example, kayaking in the Scottish lochs.

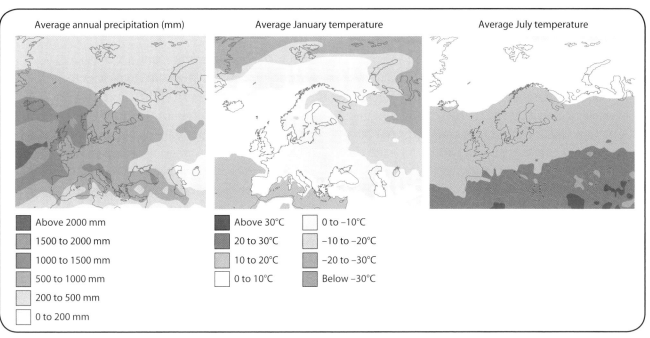

Figure 7.6 European climate

Temperature and precipitation

Climate can also affect travel arrangements. Occasionally airports may be closed and flights delayed or cancelled due to very poor weather conditions, extreme temperatures or sleet and snow.

The temperature within Europe varies greatly. The northern Scandinavian countries and Russia have a cold, dry climate, making winter sports an important form of tourism. The wetter, colder climate of the United Kingdom and Ireland means that tourists visit mainly during the summer months. Further south, there are the warmer climates of southern Italy, Turkey and Greece, attracting a large number of visitors over the summer months.

The differences of temperature across Europe can lead to some confusion among customers. Therefore, when booking holidays for departure during the winter months, care should be taken before booking to check the customer's expectations of the temperature. Assumptions about temperature should not be made. In many southern European destinations like Spain and Italy, temperatures are often not as high during the winter as expected. Therefore, a customer expecting sunshine and hot weather may be disappointed.

Some of the winter sun destinations like the Canary Islands, Malta and Cyprus are guaranteed sun for most of the year. However, this does not always mean that temperatures will be high. Global warming is also affecting the temperatures of some European resorts (particularly winter sports destinations).

Research tip

Up-to-date information sources like the World Travel Guide should be checked (either a paper copy or online at www.worldtravelguide.net).

ATTRACTIONS

Visitor attractions can be divided into two categories, natural and built. A built visitor attraction is one that has been built by people, for example, a stately home, theme park or museum. A natural visitor attraction is one that is not man-made and occurs naturally in nature, for example, a beautiful view, forest, waterfall or cave.

Natural attractions

Natural visitor attractions are either a geographical feature within the local scenery or may be a specific feature that tourists wish to visit. Natural attractions can range from National Parks and World Heritage Sites, which have been officially designated as areas of natural beauty, to scenic attractions or viewing points, which have become tourist attractions, like Wookey Caves near Bristol and the viewing point across the Aletsch Glacier in Switzerland, which is the highest viewing point in Europe. Northern Europe is particularly well known for its natural attractions, including a number of large waterfalls, geysers, fjords and the Northern Lights, which can be seen during the winter months.

> ***Think*** What are the most popular attractions near to where you live? Are they built attractions or natural attractions?

Built attractions

Built attractions are often, but not always, historical buildings. These include places like Buckingham Palace or the Eiffel Tower, which attract tourists because of their historical significance and importance as national icons. Other types of built visitor attractions have a cultural purpose or have been built specifically for the leisure or tourism industry, like the Hermitage Museum in St. Petersburg, theatres, concert halls and art galleries such as the Louvre in Paris. Theme parks are another type of built attraction. These can range from the smaller single ride attractions to larger multi-ride theme parks.

Example

An example of a small single ride attraction is the virtual reality Time Machine in Cyprus that tells the country's history. Examples of large multi-ride parks include Alton Towers, Disneyland Paris and PortAventura in Spain.

The term 'built attraction' also covers the variety of leisure activities that are built to entertain and provide facilities for tourists. This includes the bars and restaurants available for tourists and the different types of evening entertainment on offer, such as cabarets, casinos and nightclubs. Sporting and leisure facilities like water parks and amusement arcades are also regarded as built attractions.

Figure 7.7 Theme parks are a built attraction

CULTURAL

There are a wide range of different cultures across Europe. Cultures vary in terms of way of life, traditional cuisine, religion and the celebration of special occasions.

Lifestyle

The way of life at the tourist destination may be different and more relaxed than in the UK or tourist generating area. For example, in Spain and Italy, shops are often closed during the afternoon for a siesta and are open later in the evening. The pace of life is generally slower and more relaxed.

Food and drink

Different areas of Europe are famous for different varieties of food and drink, for example, pasta in Italy and vodka in Russia. Visitors may be encouraged to experience local dishes and try the locally produced drink. Local foods and drink are often cheaper than tourist menus and eating at local restaurants offers the opportunity to experience local culture and meet the people who live there.

Religions

The predominant religion in most countries is Christianity, although different denominations of Christianity dominate in different areas (for example, Greek Orthodox in Greece and Roman Catholic in Italy). Traditional religious cultures may shape how local people dress, eat and often behave. Tourists should respect the local culture and religion and this will sometimes affect what is considered to be the appropriate way to behave. For example, in Turkey, where the predominant religion is Islam and most of the local population are Muslims, tourists are asked to follow the local way of life and to cover their shoulders and knees when walking around the local markets. Sometimes it is possible to visit local churches, mosques and synagogues and this offers the opportunity to learn more about the local religion and host population's way of life.

Research tip

Choose a European country that has not been covered on this page and use books and the Internet to find out about its lifestyle, food and drink and religion.

Cultural events

Many of the traditional festivals across Europe are spectacular and colourful. Often these are local festivals that have grown into larger visitor and tourist attractions over time and now attract both domestic and international visitors. These festivals can vary in size from small events to well-known and publicised attractions like the Passion Play in Oberammergau in Germany.

Some of the more famous attractions include the masked carnival in Venice in Italy and the beer festival in Munich in Germany.

Music and film festivals occur throughout Europe and provide attractions for younger tourists or tourists looking for a cultural experience. Over the years, film festivals in Cannes and Locarno and the music festivals in places like Glastonbury have become established attractions with a number of return visitors.

Large regular sporting events are also a tourist attraction and, in some cases, they have become one of the highlights of the destination's tourist calendar. An example of this is the Grand Prix race in the streets of Monaco, which attracts a large number of tourists who are not specifically interested in either the destination or sport, but visit because of the social aspects. Popular sports like football and rugby have their own dedicated fan base that travel to a destination for international games in order to support their local or international team.

Key words

Culture – a people's way of life, local customs and historic traditions

Host population – the local people who live in the tourist-receiving area

ECONOMIC

The economic conditions of both the tourist destination and the tourist's own country are important factors in determining the choice of destination. Global, European and local economic factors, interest rates and the level of tax that people have to pay in their own country have an impact on the amount of disposable or free income that customers have available to spend on their holiday. This has a direct impact on their destination choice with cheaper destinations and cheaper hotels being appealing to more tourists when economic conditions are difficult.

Availability of low-cost travel options

The rise in low-cost airlines and the number of cheap flights has increased the number of people who can afford to travel overseas independently.

Rates of exchange

Another economic factor that affects the number of tourists who travel to a destination is the rate of exchange between different currencies. If the rate of exchange is good for the UK Pound Sterling, then more people will travel to the foreign destination as their money will buy more of the local currency and go further. This can

lead to a tourist feeling that a destination is good or bad value for money, and in turn affects the number of visits and return visits.

Example

The exchange rate for the Euro has varied from a low in May 2000, when €1 was worth £0.57, to a high in May 2003, when €1 was worth £0.72. This means that in May 2000, €100 was worth the equivalent of £57, but in 2003 it was worth the equivalent of £72.

> **Think** What is the current exchange rate for the Euro? Is it better value for money today than in 2000 or 2003?

Cost of staying at a destination and value for money

The cost of staying at a destination, which includes the price of accommodation per night, food, drink and the entrance prices of visitor attractions and tours, needs to be taken into account when choosing a destination. When economic conditions in the tourist generating country are poor, tourist receiving countries that have a cheap standard of living will become more attractive to tourists.

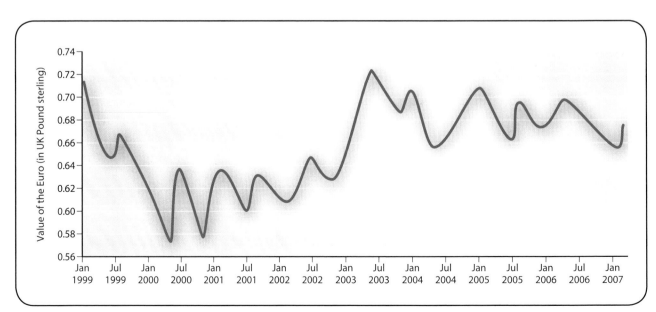

Figure 7.8 Graph showing rate of exchange of Sterling to Euro from Jan 1999 – Jan 2007

CASE STUDY: PRAGUE

Figure 7.9 A view of the historic city centre

Prague is easily accessible from the UK with a range of low-cost budget and scheduled flights from different UK airports. Its short flight time (just under 2 hours) and the fact that no visas are required for tourists with UK passports make it a popular choice for short city breaks. Local transport from the airport to the city centre is cheap and regular, and tourists also have the option of taxis or booking an organised transfer.

Situated in central Europe, the surrounding area is hilly and picturesque. Prague is situated on the banks of the River Vltava and has a varied climate, bracing cold temperatures during the winter when snow is common and warmer temperatures during the summer.

Prague offers its tourists a range of different attractions. The historic city centre features the castle, (a UNESCO World Heritage Site) and the medieval bridge over the river. Tourists who venture outside the city can visit Terezin, the former concentration camp, and Bohemia, a lake and woodland area that is famous for walking, forests and the production of crystal.

In addition to its traditional crystal, the Czech Republic offers a large selection of gifts and shopping opportunities including wooden folk carvings, hand-embroidered clothing and pottery. Prague's nightlife offers a choice of activities including small traditional taverns, casinos, bars and a five storey nightclub on the river bank.

Traditional food and drink includes bramborák, a potato pancake, and local beers and sparkling wines from the Bohemia and Moravia regions. Official events, such as the annual Spring Music Festival and the Christmas markets, are advertised by the Prague Tourist Board. Other unofficial events like impromptu concerts are advertised by flyers and poster throughout the streets.

Traditionally a catholic country and, for many years, a communist country, dress is conservative and tourists wishing to visit the churches and cathedrals should ensure that they dress respectfully. Although the city has low crime rates, care should be taken when visiting the central Wenceslas Square in the dark.

Prague is considered to be a cheap break by UK tourists. The cost of living is lower and the exchange rate between the Czech Koruna and the UK Sterling is currently good. The cost of accommodation, food and drink is therefore favourable and money can be withdrawn directly from ATM machines throughout the city.

QUESTION

Why do you think the following types of tourists might be interested in visiting Prague on a city break?

• an older couple
• a family
• a stag party
• school groups on an educational tour.

EVIDENCE ACTIVITY

P2 – M1

1   Choose three different European leisure destinations from the list of different destination types below. Describe the different activities and appeal factors that each of the selected destinations offer to their customers.
   • city
   • seaside resort
   • winter sports resort
   • countryside areas
   • cruise areas. (P2)

2   Identify the different customer types who might visit each of the selected destinations. Explore what factors particularly appeal to the customers you have identified for each destination. (M1)

Figure 7.10 A summer sun destination

7.3 Market segmentation in the European travel market by leisure experience

As you will have already realised, some European tourist destinations can be classified as either winter or summer destinations or they are destinations that are visited for a special activity or event. This is called market segmentation and each destination attracts a particular customer type. Market segmentation within a destination can be identified in two different ways.

1) By the destination type itself. This is called destination segmentation.

2) By the specific customer type who visits the destination. This is called customer segmentation.

> ### Key words
> Market segmentation – the way in which travel companies or destinations split the potential market in order to focus on meeting the needs of a particular type of customer

LEISURE EXPERIENCE

Summer sun destinations

Summer sun destinations are resorts and destinations that are only open for tourists during the summer months. These include the majority of the Greek and Turkish coastal and island resorts, the Balearic Islands and some of the smaller mainland and other island resorts. These destinations offer a range of facilities during the summer months and attract a large number of tourists. However, they do not have sufficient attractions or good enough weather to appeal to tourists during the winter months of October to April. Therefore, hotels, bars and other resort facilities are closed during the winter season and reopen each summer. Tour operators will only offer these destinations to customers in their summer brochures.

Winter sun destinations

Winter sun destinations are normally summer sun resorts that are also open during the winter months. This is mainly due to their better climate during the winter months and the wider range of activities they offer. These resorts change their tourist market during the winter months, offering long stay holidays that may be one, two or three months long. These long stay holidays appeal to older customers who are retired and want to escape the colder weather of Britain during the winter. Some examples of long stay winter sun resorts are Cyprus and Malta, which are offered to tourists throughout the year.

Activity and adventure destinations

Some destinations attract tourists who are interested in a particular sport or activity, for example, several resorts in the Algarve in Portugal attract golfers and the mountain resorts of Switzerland, Austria, Italy and France attract people who are serious climbers. Activity resorts often offer a range of different activities that will appeal to more active families and couples, as well as to the single sports enthusiast. This ensures that families and couples who are not all sports enthusiasts will also find the destination appealing and find plenty to do when they get there. The weather may be a deciding factor in the range of activities that a resort is able to offer.

Example

Specialist travel agents, such as Footloose Adventure Travel, sell both organised and individually tailored activity holidays. Some of the organised holidays they sell include walking and yoga holidays in France, biking and walking holidays in Spain, family activity holidays in French Alpine resorts, and activity holidays that include a variety of activities, for example, diving, biking, trekking, canyoning, rafting, kayaking and paragliding.

Cultural and historical destinations

Cultural destinations like Madrid, Vienna and Venice often attract visitors who are on educational or study tours, in addition to people who are interested in learning about the past or who wish to see a specific historical or cultural attraction, such as the First World War battlefields in France. Traditionally, cultural and historic attractions appeal mainly to the older market, however the increase in low-cost airlines has meant that many of these cities are now accessible to more people in the UK. These places have also recently become a popular short city break destination with younger people and they are often used by schools and colleges for educational visits.

Example

NST provide specialist travel services to educational organisations, including schools, universities and religious groups. It offers both pre-planned and tailor-made visits to countries around the world, including many European countries and places as far away as China, India and Mexico. It can arrange group discounts for travel and accommodation and they provide their own specialist guides for some tours. They also own a number of outdoor activity centres in the UK and abroad.

Cruise destinations

Cruises are becoming an increasingly popular way to visit many different destinations during one holiday. The ports and resorts that cruise ships stop at are normally also winter or summer sun destinations, and the majority also have a particular historical or cultural attraction that is of interest to short day visitors. For example, Naples is a popular stop due to its proximity to the ancient Roman city of Pompeii. Larger European cities that also have large ports, many hotels and a busy gateway airport are often used for the embarkation and disembarkation of passengers. These cities include Barcelona, Athens and Istanbul. River and coastal cruises attract tourists with a particular interest in the features, cities and towns found in that particular area.

The cruise market has recently been changing. The traditional older rich market is less evident on many of the ships and the image of cruising has altered with the increase of single nationality ships attracting families. An example of this is the Thomson Spirit that offers British food, entertainment by British television stars and has a British crew. Cheaper ships, such as EasyCruise, that overnight in ports near to resorts with a vibrant nightlife, has also led to an increase in the number of younger people booking cruises. The traditional cruise market is more evident on the special interest and smaller ships that continue to appeal to older, wealthier customers.

Example

P&O Cruises have five different ships offering a range of cruises, from two night weekend breaks to world voyages. The company appeals to a broader range of customers by marketing three different types of cruise experience: 'contemporary and innovative', 'original and authentic', and 'traditional and intimate'. It also offers family-friendly and child-free cruises.

Tours

In a similar way to cruises, tours can allow tourists to visit a number of different destinations in one holiday. The majority of tours are by coach and are accompanied by a tour guide. Accompanied and organised rail tours do exist across Europe and are particularly popular in Switzerland. Coach tours are popular with people who do not like to fly and also appeal to older travellers who prefer to have all aspects of their holiday organised for them.

Example

Epsom Coaches is a bus and coach operator. It operates over 80 vehicles and offers a variety of tours, from day excursions within the UK to month-long holidays in Europe. In 2007, some of the European holiday tours it offered were trips to the Dutch bulb fields, Iceland, the Norwegian islands, Moscow and St. Petersburg, and the Amalfi coast.

Customers who do not like organised tours may consider backpacking or travelling independently by rail or car across Europe. This allows them to stop where they like for as long as they like, and tourists can chose their own itinerary and book accommodation on arrival at the resort. Independent travel allows the customer the freedom of choice in making their own travel arrangements, and therefore appeals to tourists who feel confident about travelling or are young and adventurous.

Research tip

Visit www.raileurope.co.uk and www.eurorailways.com to find out further information about Europe's railways and the wide range of rail passes that are available.

Key words

Itinerary – the customer's proposed route of travel

Event and business destinations

Some destinations will only attract tourists because a specific event brings them there. This could be a wedding, business trip, conference, exhibition or specific sporting event.

Other places sell themselves on their business and conference facilities and advertise themselves as business destinations. These resorts do not try to attract leisure tourists and focus solely on business trade. These destinations are normally close to busy gateway airports that allow businessmen and women easy access to their meetings throughout Europe. Some, like Amsterdam and Brussels, attract both business and leisure tourists.

CUSTOMER TYPE

Generally different types of customers prefer different types of resorts, but these generalisations do not always apply to every customer. Therefore, it is important to ask the customer questions when they are booking to clearly establish their holiday needs and requirements. Some of the questions you could ask include finding out about the types of excursions and tours they want to go on, how long they plan to spend at the beach and pool, if they are looking for children's facilities and if they prefer to travel independently or with a group.

Couples

Couples can be in any age group and therefore do not always like the same type of resort. Young couples who may be on a tight budget could be looking for cheaper destinations with lively nightlife and bars, and they are more likely to make their own independent travel arrangements using the Internet. Other young couples who are inexperienced overseas travellers may prefer to book an organised tour or package holiday.

In comparison, older couples whose children may have grown up and left home are known as 'empty nesters' and normally have more money to spend on their holiday. They may be interested in historical or cultural destinations or possibly a cruise or tour. Some older couples prefer the security of an organised tour or cruise and like to travel with a tour guide. Others prefer to visit beach destinations that they are familiar with and have visited before, or they choose long-stay winter holiday destinations with suitable entertainment.

Key words

Independent travel – travel that is not organised in advance by a travel agent. Customers make their own travel arrangements.

Figure 7.11 Familiies with young children may look for different holiday destinations than a couple

Families

Families with young children look for destinations that offer a range of children's facilities, children's clubs and good beaches, in addition to suitable visitor attractions like water parks. Many families travel on a budget and look for destinations that are cheap. For example, package holidays to sunny Mediterranean resorts like Menorca, the Costa del Sol and the French Riviera are often popular family choices. When the children become older, the family's choice of destination often changes and their destination choice becomes more focused on shops, bars and larger theme parks. Destinations appealing to teenagers usually have a wide range of different leisure activities like sports, cinemas and shops. Destinations appealing to families try to offer a wide variety of attractions and different facilities for all ages.

Singles

Single travellers often chose activity holidays where they can meet other people with similar interests. These could include walking tours or cultural holidays. Some single travellers prefer to travel with specialist singles tour operators, and therefore their destination choice is limited to the destinations offered by that particular tour operator. Solo is a tour operator that offers specialist single holidays.

EVIDENCE ACTIVITY

P3 – M2 – D1

1 Using your knowledge of European geography and destination appeal, choose three appropriate destinations for each of the following customers. Use different destinations from those studied in the previous assessment activities:

- a family with two small children aged 5 and 7. They are on a budget and want a destination with children's facilities and a good beach
- a couple aged 22 and 26 who want to combine a beach holiday with some culture and history
- an older couple who are looking for a weekend break. They are interested in history and culture and do not have any budget restrictions
- a mixed group of couples, all aged around 35. The men are interested in activities like walking and adventure sports. The majority of the women, however, are looking for a more relaxing holiday with some shopping and a range of facilities
- a single older woman who would like to visit many different destinations while meeting other people with similar interests. (P3)

2 Now you have named three appropriate destinations or resorts for the customer types listed above, select the destination or resort that you think would be best for their holiday and explain why this destination or resort would be best for their holiday. (M2)

3 Choose one of the destinations you have explored in Question 2 and research its current target market. Now consider how this destination can expand its target markets and attract different types of tourists. Use your knowledge of the travel and tourism industry to justify your recommendations. (D1)

7.4 Factors affecting the development of the European travel market

Destinations will either grow or decline in popularity over time. The reasons for a destination's sudden growth in popularity can often be traced to one of a number of different factors. These could range from an increase in the number of arrival flights to a large public sporting event, which helps to publicise the destination and introduce it to a new audience.

However, the specific reason for a destination's decline is harder to pinpoint and may be due to a combination of different factors.

Example

Since hosting the 1992 Olympics, the Spanish city of Barcelona has enjoyed a boom in tourism. As part of the preparations to host the games, huge amounts of money were invested in improving the transport infrastructure (including a new airport and ring road), amenities and in regenerating the port area. In 1991, tourism was worth less than 2% of the city's GDP. By 2002, this had risen to 12.5%.

DEVELOPMENT

Butler's Destination Product Life Cycle

In 1980, Richard Butler designed the Destination Product Life Cycle, which is based on the Product Life Cycle you may have seen in Unit 5, Marketing Travel and Tourism Products and Services. He applied the Product Life Cycle to tourist destinations to show their growth and decline, charting the different stages of a resort's development.

Butler identified seven different stages of tourism development within a tourist destination. Not all destinations will follow all of the stages of the Destination Product Life Cycle. Some resorts may never fully develop and others may never enter the decline stage of the Destination Product Life Cycle.

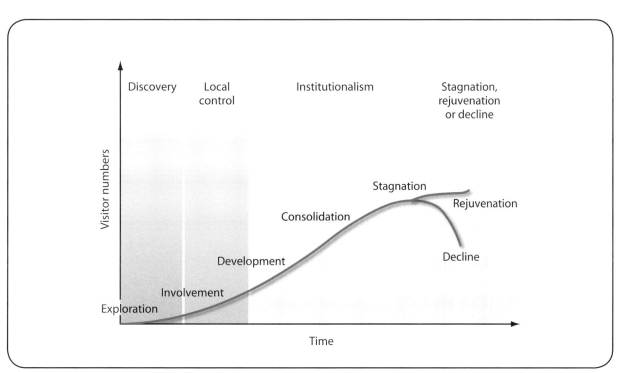

Figure 7.12 Butler's Destination Product Lifecycle

Stage 1 – Exploration

The first stage is called Exploration. This is when the destination is visited by a small number of adventurous tourists. Tourist facilities are not developed and the visiting tourists stay in local accommodation and use the local facilities of restaurants and bars. No special attractions are built for tourists to use.

Stage 2 – Involvement

After Exploration, the second stage is called Involvement. This is when a larger number of tourists begin to visit the destination. The local community start to get involved with trying to attract tourists, possibly by marketing or advertising the destination's facilities or attractions. Some hotels, restaurants and attractions are built or opened to accommodate tourists.

Stage 3 – Development

The third stage called Development can be seen in many destinations where they are building a large number of new facilities for tourists. During the Development stage, tourist visitor numbers are increasing and the local population enjoy the additional money that tourists bring to the destination. Better tourist facilities are built in order to attract more tourists.

Stage 4 – Consolidation

The fourth stage is Consolidation. This is when the number of arriving tourists does not grow significantly and the tourism industry and destination are both stable and less building work is evident. Large numbers of tourists are visiting the resort and the accommodation is full to capacity with no empty rooms. As the numbers of arriving tourists are not growing, additional hotels and facilities should not be built.

Stage 5 – Stagnation

The fifth stage is called Stagnation. This happens when the destination is no longer as fashionable or popular as it was. Many tourists have already visited the destination and do not want to make a return visit. The destination possibly no longer appeals to tourists. This may be due to excessive building work that has destroyed the natural beauty and original natural attractions of the destination, a change of destination image or a change to the economic conditions that may have made the destination expensive to visitors.

Stage 6 – Decline

After Stagnation, the destination goes into Decline. The visitor numbers drop, hotels are empty and the facilities built for tourists are not filled to capacity. The destination begins to lose money and local people who rely on the tourist industry for their jobs may become unemployed.

Stage 7 – Rejuvenation

Following Decline, a destination will try to regain its market share and encourage tourists to visit. The destination may choose to market itself to different types of visitors or age group, or it may decide to become a special interest or activity destination. The destination hopes to attract new and different tourists by changing its appeal and facilities.

If this is successful then the destination will enter Butler's seventh stage of the Destination Product Life Cycle called Rejuvenation. If the destination does not succeed in changing its market share and regaining tourists, then it will continue to decline and become less and less popular.

Reasons for destination growth

A number of different factors cause a destination to begin the Destination Product Life Cycle.

- **Growth of leisure travel**
  The availability of cheap flights has fuelled the growth of short or weekend breaks. Specialist holidays, such as activity holidays, are also becoming more popular. This opens up opportunities for destinations to promote themselves to new markets. Countries offering new activities or historical or cultural events, which have not been well advertised in the past, can also expect an increase in the number of tourists who visit. This may follow a destination's decision to change their target market in response to a decline in tourist numbers and may be the result of a regeneration campaign to reposition the destination to a different target market.

- **New products and services**
  In recent years, an increasingly important factor has been the way that new areas, which had not been easily accessible before, are targeted by low-cost airlines as a new and profitable route. When a low-cost airline opens a new route to a destination, it has a direct impact on the number of arriving visitors. These destinations often start at the involvement stage of the Destination Product Life Cycle as they had not been tourists receiving areas in the past and are undeveloped as tourist destinations.

- **Political factors**
  Changing political circumstances can open up new countries or regions to tourism. Since the collapse of Communism in the early 1990s and the opening-up of the borders between eastern and western Europe, many eastern European countries such as the Czech Republic, Hungary and Poland have experienced a massive growth in tourism. Countries that have joined the European Union or Eurozone have also experienced increased numbers of tourists due to the ease of travel and lack of difficulty with currency exchange.

- **Economic factors**
  Increases in disposable income in tourism generating countries, such as the UK, over the past few years have enabled more people to take trips abroad and to go on more holidays.

  A result of this increased disposable income and the greater availability of cheap flights is that increasing numbers of people own second homes abroad. By the end of 2006, 800,000 Britons owned second homes abroad, which is an increase of 45% since July 2004.

> **Think** Consider the case study of Faliraki on page 154 and identify the different stages of the Destination Product Life Cycle. Consider the factors that led to the resort's development and decline.

Example

Bulgaria is one of Europe's fastest growing tourist destinations. Its appeal as a tourist destination lies in its varied scenery of beaches and mountains, meaning it can offer both summer beach holidays and winter ski holidays. It is also very affordable to visit. Between 2000 and 2004, the number of overseas visitors increased by nearly 50% to 4.6 million.

CASE STUDY: FALIRAKI

The island of Rhodes contains the Colossus of Rhodes, which is one of the Seven Wonders of the World and a World Heritage Site. Tourism is the island's primary source of income and the main source of employment for the island's population. One of the oldest and largest resorts is Faliraki. The resort appealed to tourists interested in a beach holiday with easy access to many cultural and historical sites.

In the mid 1990s, it was a popular family tourist resort. With its beautiful six-kilometre long beach, UK tour operators sold the island to families by offering three-star hotels and children's clubs, and by advertising the diverse range of facilities available, including water sports, the nearby historic town of Rhodes and varied nightlife, which appealed to both families and couples who were looking for a beach resort with a cultural aspect.

Faliraki gained notoriety when it was shown on ITV1's controversial 'Club Reps' series. The aspects of partying and nightlife shown on the programme led to an increase in the number of younger single tourists visiting who were looking for a holiday based around partying and nightlife. This increase in the number of youth holidays and youth specialist tour operators lead to the destination becoming an important venue in the Mediterranean club scene.

An increase in drunken behaviour caused families and couples to complain to their tour operators and this resulted in bad publicity for both the island and resort. Increases in crime led to some tour operators advising tourists not to walk alone at night.

As the destination's image declined, traditional tourist numbers dropped and the destination became even more reliant on the youth market. An attempt by the Greek police to control young tourists' behaviour only fuelled the resort's bad reputation. The young market moved on to newer and more exciting (and less well policed) destinations, spurred on by the banning by the police of popular youth activities like bar crawls. UK youth tour operators, such as Club 18-30 and Escapades, cancelled their Rhodes programmes and moved to other up-and-coming destinations elsewhere.

The resort and island are currently left without a target market and are in the process of trying to redefine their market and re-attract their original traditional family and couples market.

Figure 7.13

Reasons for destination decline

The reasons for destination decline are often very specific to a particular destination. However, some of the reasons may be as follows.

- The destination or country becomes politically unstable and people feel that it would be dangerous to visit.

- A resort, destination or country receives a lot of bad publicity on the television or in the press, and the traditional image of the destination is damaged.

- A destination may have relied on one nationality or market segment for their visitors, and a change to the economic conditions in the tourist generating region means that potential tourists may have less disposable income to spend on holidays and no longer visit. This causes a drop in visitor numbers. With no other tourists or target market, the destination goes into decline and the destination must re-segment to a new audience in order to avoid decline and enter rejuvenation.

- Other more exciting, newer destinations are perceived by the tourist to be more appealing.

- The large number of tourists and built attractions have spoilt the original features of the destination and it is now no longer considered to have the original natural appeal that it once had. Built visitor attractions may be crowded or in bad repair due to visitor numbers, and the destination and attractions do not have the same appeal that they did in the past.

- Low-cost carriers or airlines change their routes and the destination is no longer a cheap and easy option for visiting tourists.

A case study on a declining destination can be found on page 154. More information on the impacts of tourism development can be found in Unit 11, Sustainable Tourism Development.

EVIDENCE ACTIVITY

P4 – M3 – D2

1 Identify two developing destinations in Europe and explain the factors that you think have led to their recent development. Which stage of Butler's model do you think these destinations are at? (P4)

2 Identify two declining destinations in Europe and explain the factors that you think have led to their decline. Place these two destinations on Butler's model. (P4)

3 Consider how different trends and fashions within the travel and tourism industry are affecting the growth and decline of destinations. Relate these factors to one declining and one developing destination. (M3)

4 Evaluate how a range of different factors, social trends and political issues are affecting the rise and decline of european tourist destinations. Use a range of different examples to show how current events can impact on a destination's current and future popularity. (D2)

Long-haul travel destinations

unit 8

Working in the travel and tourism industry means that you will be asked to give advice about destinations you have never visited. In some cases, customers may have been saving for years before booking their dream holiday, and they trust you as a travel expert to make the correct recommendations and send them on a trip of a lifetime. Not all customers know a lot about many long-haul countries and so they will rely on your knowledge and expertise. Getting it right and ensuring that the customers return happy is one of the most fulfilling parts of working in the industry. This unit aims to give you an overview of many of the issues and challenges that are important when planning an exotic long-haul holiday.

In this unit, you will learn about:

So you want to be a...

Reservations Consultant

My name Hannah Davies

Age 32

Income £17,000 plus commission

If you've got a flair for selling, a good telephone manner and an eye for detail, then read on...

What do you do?

I help customers plan and book their trip. My company offers trips to many long-haul destinations but my speciality is Australasia.

What does a typical day involve?

I deal with customer queries; giving advice on their choice of airline or any stopover cities. I look for the most appropriate accommodation to fit their specific requests and explain the different tours on offer. Once the travel plans are finalised I make the reservations.

What sort of person would make a good reservations consultant?

The job is about selling holidays so you need good selling and telephone skills. The ability to research information is important as you have to do a lot in order to create the best holiday for customers. You need to be able to communicate with different types of people.

How did you find your current job?

I have a BTEC National Diploma in Travel and Tourism, which was a first step. I knew I wanted to work for my company so when I was at college I did work experience with them which lead to a full time position. I had a day-long interview, including a presentation selling my favourite holiday and a role play using the telephone.

What training have you had?

I began by shadowing other consultants, listening to how they conducted telephone calls and watching how they interacted with customers. I also attended the company's induction course which included sessions on telephone technique and selling.

Are there any perks of the job?

Last year I was sent to Australia on an educational visit to improve my knowledge of what I'm selling and next year they are planning to send me to New Zealand.

> **Last year I was sent to Australia...**

What are the hours like?

I work a 37 hour week in shifts. I work 8 am to 3pm or 3pm to 9pm.

What about the pay?

The pay is about £17,000 but it gets better as you gain more experience. I earn commission on each holiday and tour I sell, which can add a lot to my salary.

Where do you go from here?

I would like to manage a team of sales staff, which involves setting targets and motivating the team to reach them. I'd also have to monitor service quality and deal with difficult customer enquiries.

Grading criteria

The table below shows what you need to do to gain a pass, merit or distinction in this part of the qualification. Make sure you refer back to it when you are completing work so you can judge whether you are meeting the criteria and what you need to do to fill in gaps in your knowledge or experience.

In this unit there are four evidence activities that give you an opportunity to demonstrate your acheivement of the grading criteria:

page 160	P1
page 170	P1, P2, M1, D1
page 176	P3, M2, D2
page 178	P4, M3

To achieve a pass grade the evidence must show that the learner is able to...	To achieve a merit grade the evidence must show that, in addition to the pass criteria, the learner is able to...	To achieve a distinction grade the evidence must show that, in addition to the pass and merit criteria, the learner is able to...
P1 Identify and locate continents, major long-haul tourist receiving areas, countries and destinations of the world using appropriate reference sources	**M1** Explain in detail why different long-haul destinations attract visitors with different motivations, and how travel factors can influence choice of destination	**D1** Assess the success of long-haul destinations in meeting the needs of different types of visitors, and make feasible recommendations as to how a destination could minimise the effects of the factors that negatively affect its popularity
P2 Select and describe different types of holidays offered by long-haul destinations for different types of customers identifying both travel and motivating factors	**M2** Assess the significance of the key features that influence the appeal of a selected long-haul destination	**D2** Evaluate how the selected destination could capitalise on its facilities in order to influence its future development
P3 Describe the features that contribute to the appeal of a selected long-haul destination	**M3** Independently plan a detailed multicentre tour, clearly justifying selections for the chosen visitor profile	
P4 Plan a multi-centre long-haul tour to meet a given client brief, showing references used		

8.1 *Location of major long-haul destinations worldwide*

Figure 8.1 Examples of some long-haul travel destinations

DESTINATION RANGE

Long-haul destinations are destinations, resorts and cities that have a flight time of over six hours from the UK. Some of the main long-haul destination areas are shown on the map and include the Caribbean, North and South America, most of Africa, the Middle East and Australasia. This is not a complete list of all long-haul destinations as destinations that appeal to more adventurous tourists, for example, Brunei, are often being developed by smaller specialist tour operators. Therefore, extensive research needs to be undertaken before advising a customer that a specific long-haul destination is not available for tourists.

The six-hour flight time means the majority of the countries that are not in Europe, northern Africa and the closer parts of the Middle East are classified as long-haul destinations. Due to the large number of countries that could be classified as long-haul, the industry tends to concentrate on or offer the opportunity to visit particular areas of the world that specifically appeal to tourists.

Some of the busiest long-haul destinations are the Maldives, Thailand, Dubai, the USA, Sri Lanka, China, Hong Kong, Mauritius, Singapore, Malaysia, India, Australia, Barbados, St Lucia, Antigua, Cuba, Tanzania, Mexico, New Zealand and Bali.

> ***Think*** Use a blank world map and an atlas to mark the destinations listed in the previous paragraph on a map. Name the continents in which these destinations can be found.

Research tip

Research is very important in long-haul travel, as the destinations are often very different from European resorts that the customers may have visited before. A wide range of sources should be used to ensure that all the relevant information is given to the tourist.

REFERENCE SOURCES

Primary sources of information are first-hand sources or knowledge about a destination. These would be gained from a visit either on holiday or by attending a travel agents or a tour operator's educational tour to a destination. Secondary sources of information are those that have been published, such as guide books. Although many people who work in the travel industry are often well-travelled, a range of secondary sources will need to be used when researching long-haul destinations.

The large number of destinations on offer means that no travel agent could have visited all of them. Therefore, some travel agents and tour operators employ specialist reservation staff who focus on a specific area of the world and deal only with bookings and reservations for that area. Secondary sources can be divided into paper resources and electronic media resources.

Paper-based resources

A paper-based atlas is one of the first places to look for information about a destination's location, time zone, airport and features. Tour operator's travel brochures often provide information about excursions and details about specific hotels. Where available, leaflets and tourist office guides will also provide general destination information. Guidebooks, for example, the Globetrotter guides normally offer a historical overview of a destination, as well as specific information about local customs and traditions. Travel agents' gazetteers are a set of guides that provide detailed information about a resort, hotel or destination.

Another good source of paper-based information about long-haul destinations are the supplements published in national newspapers and the travel guides that are published in travel industry specific papers, such as the Travel Trade Gazette (TTG). These provide an overview of a destination's facilities and are often accompanied by a range of photos, which display the best features and attractions within a destination or hotel.

Electronic formats

Travel guides, such as the World Travel Guide, are now available in both paper and online formats and provide lots of information about all aspects of a destination, including details on international and internal travel, rail and public transport information, accommodation, climate, health issues, visitor attractions and lists of public holidays. The web site for the World Travel Guides is www.wtg-online.com.

Other websites on the Internet can also provide detailed travel information. Care should be taken, however, to check that these are reliable tourist information sources or government sites and not personal websites. The best online resources are often the destination or country tourist board websites, which you can find either by using the WTG guide or through a search engine.

Some destinations and resorts also publish DVDs and television programmes concentrating on holiday destinations, which can offer an overview of a tourist's destination, resort or hotel.

EVIDENCE ACTIVITY

P1

Use a blank map to locate some more popular long-haul destinations. Make sure that you include the following:

New York, Las Vegas, Bangkok, Miami, Toronto, Boston, Hong Kong, Brazil, Thailand, the USA, Canada and South Africa. (P1)

8.2 *Nature of long-haul travel factors affecting customer choice*

A wide number of different factors affect the customer's choice of destination. Customers will take into account many different factors when choosing their holiday. These include their budget, the type of destination they want to visit, their choice of accommodation, their motivation or reason for the visit, and other important practical factors about their proposed trip, for example, the climate, safety and security of the destination.

DEFINITION OF LONG-HAUL

The definition of a long-haul destination as having a flight time over six hours means that some destinations that might appeal to a long-haul tourist as exotic, for example, Morocco or Jordan, are not actually classified as long-haul. These destinations are considered to be medium-haul and do not form part of this unit.

NATURE OF LONG-HAUL TRAVEL

The majority of long-haul holidays are organised by specialist long-haul tour operators and there is less independently organised travel. Some long-haul tour operators specialise in a particular area of the world, while others are more general and cover the main long-haul destinations. The tour operator's name, image and reputation can strongly influence the customer's choice of who they travel with and where they travel to.

Long-haul travel is often thought to be an expensive and specialist holiday with customers viewing the trip as a luxury tourism product. While some long-haul holidays can be cheaper than a holiday in the UK or Europe, there is also a section of the long-haul travel market that is extremely exclusive. This involves the creation of individual private tailor-made holidays on a customer-by-customer basis. These tailor-made itineraries can include travel by private jet, personal guides, individual transfers and accommodation in small boutique hotels.

Holiday brochures for long-haul destinations fall into two different categories. The first type of brochures are the ones offered by independent specialist long-haul tour operators. These tour operators focus either on long-haul in general or a specific destination or product.

The second type of long-haul holiday brochures available to tourists are those printed by mass market tour operators like Thomson or First Choice. These mass market tour operators offer a limited range of long-haul resorts and destinations.

Example

Kuoni is a leading long-haul tour operator that offers a range of holidays, tours and cruises to destinations around the world. Silverbird only offers holidays to the Far East and therefore it is a specialist in that area of the world.

Specialist independent tour operators are considered to be more knowledgeable and offer more unusual holidays than mass market tour operators who generally offer long-haul destinations at cheaper prices. Some customers choose to book a long-haul holiday with a specific tour operator as they feel the name and reputation of the tour operator may increase their social status. Although some customers are interested in the tour operator with which they will be travelling, others take into account factors like the price, the activities and facilities on offer at the destination. More information about the different types of tour operators can be found in Unit 12: Tour Operations

Key words

Tour operator – an organisation that puts together an inclusive holiday for sale to the public
Tailor-made – a holiday arrangement designed especially for a particular client

DESTINATION TYPE

Long-haul countries provide a wide range and variety of different destination types. These destinations attract many different types of customers. Therefore, it is important to establish a customer's needs in advance of booking to make sure that they enjoy their holiday.

Cities

Some cities, like New York, are popular destinations for a holiday. Cities that are easily accessible from the UK, either in terms of the flight time or the number of flights per day, are popular with customers looking for a short break or weekend getaway. These long-haul city destinations offer a range of shopping, culture and sightseeing opportunities. Most also offer a wide range of accommodation that may range from youth hostels to five-star city centre hotels, bars and restaurants, which are suitable for different budgets.

Coastal or seaside

Coastal or seaside destinations that are classified as long-haul destinations are often a stretch of beach or coast, which has been developed into a tourist destination. Accommodation and tourist facilities have been built along or around the coast and a seaside destination has been created. Tourists are attracted by the ease of access and beautiful beach or coastline, and the range of facilities on offer. These destinations often appeal to families. A major coastal resort is the resort of Cancun in Mexico, which is a beach resort that offers a range of different accommodation and lively nightlife.

Purpose-built

There are a large number of purpose-built destinations in the Caribbean, Indian Ocean and Far East. These are generally large gated or fenced hotels that offer tourists all the facilities they require within the hotel complex. Many purpose-built resorts have shops, private beaches and a range of on-site entertainment, restaurants and bars. Purpose-built resorts are mainly four or five-star complexes. However, there are some three-star resorts that are used by the mass market tour operators.

Customers often book purpose-built resorts as they are looking for secure accommodation that offers a range of facilities. These resorts are often all inclusive and appeal to a wide range of customers. All-inclusive resorts are especially popular with people who are budget conscious as food, drink and many of the facilities, like water sports, are included in the price.

Natural

Natural long-haul destinations are places where the scenery and wildlife are the main attractions. Some destinations, such as Niagara Falls or the Grand Canyon, may be famous for a specific viewpoint or photo opportunity. Others, like safari destinations, in Tanzania, for example, may attract tourists due to the opportunities to watch wildlife. Destinations like the rainforests of Panama and the Amazon River offer tourists the chance to experience a different landscape or natural vegetation. Some of these natural destinations require lengthy and difficult journeys and may only offer basic accommodation. These factors may deter some customers from booking this type of destination, and should be discussed with the customer before proceeding with the booking.

Example

Niagara Falls is a typical example of a tourist resort that has been established around a natural attraction. With an extensive range of hotels and entertainment venues, there is also the famous Maid of the Mist boat ride to see the Falls up close.

Historical or cultural

Visits to historical and cultural long-haul destinations offer the tourist the opportunity to discover an ancient civilisation, such as the Incas in Peru, or to visit important historical monuments or museums. Again, some of these destinations can only be reached by long journeys or treks. However, some tour operators offer a range of different types of transportation, such as donkeys, horses or jeeps, which opens up the experience to different types of people. Important historical monuments often have better transportation links and tourist accommodation, and facilities will have been built in the surrounding area.

> **Think** Other than the examples already given in the text, name three long-haul cultural or heritage destinations and the reasons why they are popular.

Research tip

Find out more about long-haul cultural holidays by looking through a long-haul tour operator's brochure or at some long-haul specialist websites, such as www.tropicalsky.co.uk

HOLIDAY TYPE

Each destination offers the customer a different type of holiday experience. Not all customers want the same experience from their holiday or enjoy doing the same types of activities. Due to the long flight time, many tourists may be looking for more than one type of travel experience within their long-haul holiday, and therefore they look for a destination that offers several different features. With this in mind, many long-haul destinations try to offer their customers a wide number of different activities and attractions. Long-haul holidays can be a range of durations. Apart from the short city break market, it is normal for a long-haul holiday

to be more than seven nights in duration. Some longer trips, which may include tours, cruises and stopovers, may be more than one or two months long, especially if the holiday involves a long flight.

Short break

The short break long-haul holiday market is increasing with a number of destinations becoming more accessible. These include purpose-built resorts like Dubai in the Middle East, countryside resorts like South Africa, and cities like New York. The flight time, time difference and easy accessibility to resort transportation may affect a tourist's decision to choose a destination for a short break. Short break resorts often appeal because of their facilities or due to a specific interest destination, and therefore they are booked by a range of different customers.

> **Think** Which other destinations are popular for short break long-haul holidays?

Multi-centre

Twin or multi-centres involve staying at more than one destination. Normally the destinations chosen are close to each other and transport between the two destinations is regular and easy to organise. Twin centres also offer a range of experiences in one holiday. Therefore, couples who like different types of holidays may choose a twin centre as a way of ensuring they are both happy with the destination choice.

A popular twin centre is a coach tour of China followed by a seven-night stay in Thailand. This combines a cultural tour with a beach resort. A multi-centre involves several different destinations, for example, Australia, New Zealand and Tasmania. These are generally longer holidays, often more than 14 nights, and may include a complicated itinerary that includes tours, cruises and a range of different accommodation types.

Multi-centre holidays offer tourists the opportunity to explore a region in depth, for example, a short stopover or city break in Bangkok, followed by a tour of Vietnam and transfer to a beach resort in Phuket could possibly be combined with a cruise or tour of China or Japan.

Stopover

Some cities like Bangkok are not large enough for a longer break, but can be built into an itinerary as a one or two-day stopover destination. These stopover destinations are often used to break a long journey. For example, Singapore is used to break the flight to New Zealand or Australia, and therefore helps tourists to avoid jet lag on arrival at the destination. Other stopover destinations have a specific visitor attraction that appeals to tourists, but they have few other tourist facilities and are therefore insufficient to appeal to a tourist for longer than a day or two.

Hotel-based/all-inclusive

There are a large number of purpose-built destinations in the Caribbean, Indian Ocean and the Far East. These are often all-inclusive and offer the tourist a wide range of facilities without leaving the resort. Some of these hotels have been developed into large resorts and have become attractions in their own right. A range of accommodation, for example, water bungalows, suites and luxury penthouses and views, attract customers who are looking for privacy. The convenience of having a range of tourist facilities in a safe environment appeals to some tourists. However, tourists who wish to experience local culture do not always enjoy an all-inclusive hotel-based holiday as there is no need to leave the hotel and opportunities to meet the local people are limited.

Special occasion

Many long-haul holidays are taken to celebrate special occasions, for example, honeymoons and wedding anniversaries. Many destinations also offer their customers the opportunity to get married while on holiday. Weddings organised by UK tour operators overseas are legal, and therefore

tour operators sell a range of wedding packages at different locations. These can vary from specialist packages, such as Elvis weddings in Las Vegas, to unique locations such as the Sydney Opera House or beach resorts in the Caribbean or Africa. A range of other special occasion holidays and events can also be booked, which could include blessings, special celebration meals for wedding anniversaries, birthdays or unique once-in-a-lifetime experiences like hot-air balloon flights or parachute jumps. Family and friends can also be invited to overseas events and group bookings, such as wedding parties, often attract a better price than individual trips.

Figure 8.2 A couple celebrate their wedding day on a Carribean beach

Activities

Some long-haul destinations offer a wide range of activities and sports that use the local resources. Some examples of these destinations include diving in the Seychelles, climbing and walking in Nepal, or adventure sports in New Zealand. These destinations become renowned for their sporting activities and attract tourists who are either interested in one specific activity or a range of different sports. Destinations offering walking, trekking or climbing can limit the types and number of tourists who visit in order to preserve their terrain and natural attractions. Facilities may be basic and may not appeal to all types of customers, especially those looking for luxury accommodation or extensive evening entertainment.

Visit friends and relatives (VFR)

A number of people book overseas holidays in order to visit friends and relatives. These may be people whose friends and family have moved overseas, or overseas residents who now live in the UK and wish to return home. Some charter flights can only accept bookings from UK passport holders, and therefore this limits the bookings that can be made on behalf of tourists who wish to visit friends and relatives overseas. These details need to be checked before booking.

Long-haul holidays that are based around visiting friends and relatives may be flight-only or a combination of flights, accommodation and free time. The choice of destination is often predetermined and the resort and destination facilities of secondary interest to the tourists. Accommodation may be chosen because of its location and closeness to the houses of friends and relatives.

Cruise/tour

One of the ways in which a tourist can visit several long-haul destinations at the same time is by taking a cruise. Long-haul cruises can be divided into two different types – general and specialist.

General cruises visit a range of different destinations and possibly different countries. Each cruise stops at a number of different ports and tourist attractions and offers a wide variety of onboard facilities and activities that appeal to different types of passengers.

Special interest or specialist cruises focus on a specific area of coastline or one country, and they offer passengers an in-depth experience of that area. These cruises are often accompanied by a guest lecturer who offers an insight into the region and points out areas of interest. Tours, ports and excursions are arranged to appeal to the passengers. These specialist cruises are often more expensive than general cruises, although some ports are visited by many different types of ships from small specialist cruises to large mass market ships.

Example

Princess Cruises (www.princesscruises.com) offers a wide range of specialist cruises as well more general cruises. One of the most popular of these is the 'Voyage of the Glaciers', which includes stops to see National Parks and famous glaciers.

In a similar way to cruises, long-haul coach tours also offer tourists the opportunity to gain detailed knowledge of one particular country or area. Like cruises, these may be special interest or general tours and offer an in-depth opportunity to visit that country. Normally these tours involve a range of different transportation methods, including coach, rail and internal flights, and many are accompanied by an English-speaking tour guide who often accompanies the customers from the UK. Different accommodation is used each night and most meals are included in the price of the tour.

Type of booking

The majority of long-haul travellers book their holidays through tour operators and travel agents, and they therefore travel on pre-arranged package holidays. These package holidays can be divided into mass market and tailor-made. Most tailor-made holidays are booked directly with the tour operator or by using a specialist independent travel agent. Mass market packages are often booked using high street travel agents, the Internet or directly with the tour operator using the telephone or the Internet.

A small number of tourists, gap year students and backpackers make independent travel arrangements or may only use a travel agent to book flights and their first night's accommodation. Due to government visa regulations, some long-haul destinations cannot be accessed by independent travellers. Tourists need to be advised of this in advance of their booking and the situation checked by their travel agent or reservation staff.

Research tip

Use the internet to find out about companies who offer backpackers and independent travellers assistance with planning their holiday.

Example

The Student Travel Association is a worldwide specialist service that offers a range of facilities for student travellers, including discounted flights and accommodation bookings. It can also help to plan trips, arranging travel visas and obtaining travel insurance.

VISITOR MOTIVATION

Reasons for going on a long-haul holiday can vary and the customer's choice of destination can depend on a number of different factors. These may include the tourist's age, budget and the number of people travelling together and their individual likes and dislikes.

Relaxation

One of the main reasons to travel overseas is relaxation and this type of holiday can be either leisure or activity-related as different people relax in different ways. Many destinations attract tourists because they are very different from the UK and offer a complete change and the chance for the tourists to escape their everyday life. The opportunity to experience luxury, good service and relax by the pool appeals to many tourists and some resorts build on this appeal factor by offering spa and beauty treatments.

Business

Sometimes a business trip is combined with a long-haul holiday or it may be the main reason for booking a flight. Often business travel and conference organisers at a long-haul destination will offer the opportunity to extend a business trip by a short holiday before or after the meeting, and family can fly out to join or accompany the person attending the meeting. The choice of destination and resort depends on the business meeting, event or conference and is often predetermined by the event organisers and not the business travellers. It is frequently the case that the people attending the conference or meeting are offered the chance to go on daily excursions to see the local area. This is encouraged by local tourist boards that may organise tailor-made excursions for the conference participants as it could encourage a return visit for a longer period of time.

Education/culture and history

Education and the opportunity to learn about different cultures and historical places often motivates educated people or those interested in culture to travel and visit different or unusual destinations. These are frequently people who enjoy having the opportunity to meet local people and see the local way of life, and who enjoy learning about the history and culture of the destination. Famous events in history, which have made the destination significant, may encourage tourists to visit them. Examples of this are Dallas, which receives many tourists who are fascinated by the death of J.F. Kennedy, and Vietnam, which attracts tourists who are interested in the Vietnam War.

Media influence

Resorts and destinations that have been featured in the media, either in newspapers or books, attract tourists who have read about the destination. In addition, movies and television programmes filmed in certain locations also attract tourists who want to see the original film locations or country. Many people who have seen spectacular scenery or a tourist attraction in a film or television programme are encouraged to visit. Some people may want to take photos of iconic locations like Born Free or re-enact scenes from films or television programmes. An example of this is *The Lord of the Rings* films, which were followed by a specific film-related tourism campaign run by the New Zealand Tourism Board in order to capitalise on the publicity created by the film.

Figure 8.3 The spectacular scenery of New Zealand, setting for The Lord of the Rings trilogy

TRAVEL FACTORS

Travel to a long-haul destination is very different to travelling within the UK or the majority of places in Europe and a number of different factors need to be considered. These may affect destination choice and customer appeal as certain factors called barriers to travel may stop a tourist from visiting a particular destination.

Key words

Barriers to travel – political, social and economic factors which stop people travelling to a particular destination

---

Think Choose one popular long-haul destination and identify some of the barriers to travel.

Weather

Some long-haul destinations have extreme weather conditions and this information needs to be checked in advance of making a booking and appropriate destinations selected. The temperature and amount of sunshine at a destination are not always indicators of the exact situation and other factors like rainfall need to be considered.

Some long-haul destinations are seasonal with rainy seasons called monsoons. These destinations may be cheaper at this time of the year, but not all customers want to go on holiday when it is raining. At some times during the year, destinations in the Caribbean and some places in the USA are more likely to be affected by hurricanes and tornadoes, so this should be checked before recommending the destination to a customer. Humidity and extreme heat can also affect a customer's enjoyment of a holiday. Some destinations appeal to tourists specifically because of their extreme weather conditions, for example rainforests, the Arctic and Antarctic.

Time zones

The length of the flight means that tourists will experience a change in their time zone. For example, California is eight hours behind UK time.

The website www.timeanddate.com can be used to find out the local times of destinations around the world.

A time difference means that the tourist may suffer jet lag, tiredness, difficulty sleeping and have problems adjusting to the time difference on arrival at the resort.

Health and vaccinations

One of the other risks of a long-haul flight is the possibility of deep-vein thrombosis (DVT), which can cause blood clots to form in a passenger's legs. However, this is very rare and airlines always offer instructions to passengers on the best ways to avoid both jet lag and DVT, including foot exercises and drinking plenty of water.

Another health issue that should be considered are the vaccinations that are sometimes required in order to enter the country. Some vaccinations, such as yellow fever, are compulsory for some destinations like Namibia and will require a vaccination certificate. Other destinations make recommendations for precautions like Malaria tablets or the Typhoid vaccination. However, these are voluntary and are recommended as a sensible health precaution. Customers should check with their GP a number of months before their departure to ensure that they have the correct vaccinations and health advice. It is important for customers to contact their GP plenty of time before their departure date as some vaccinations must be administered over a period of time. Some developing countries will recommend that tourists bring their own medical supplies, such as needles and syringes. If this is a requirement, medical kits can be bought from local chemists and packed into the passenger's main luggage, and not in the hand luggage. Customers should also be made aware that AIDS and the HIV virus are common in many developing destinations. As a result, sensible precautions should be taken, which are similar to those in the UK.

Visa regulations

In addition to checking health advice, customers should also check the visa regulations for entry into a country. Some tour operators and travel agents will offer assistance to their customers for obtaining a visa, especially if an invitation letter is required. However, the ultimate responsibility for obtaining the correct visa lies with the customer and not the tour operator or travel agent. Independent tourists and tourists travelling with tour operators who do not offer assistance in obtaining a visa will need to check the current visa regulations themselves. The best place to check the current visa regulations is the local Embassy or Consulate.

Safety and security

Not all long-haul destinations are as politically stable as the UK and occasionally political unrest, terrorist attacks and military conflicts may break out. In this case, the Foreign and Commonwealth Office will amend their travel advice and will also provide British passport holders who are overseas with advice and assistance. Most tour operators will offer alternative destinations to their customers in the event of a destination becoming unsafe and the Foreign Office advising against travel.

Research tip

Information on the state of security, health warnings, general visa restrictions and country specific travel advice can be obtained from the Foreign and Commonwealth Office's website www.fco.gov.uk, which is updated regularly.

Example

Thailand is a popular tourist destination, but in 2007 the Foreign and Commonwealth Office advised against travelling to some parts of the country due to outbreaks of Bird Flu and the delicate political situation in certain southern provinces. Approximately 75,000 British travellers choose to travel to Thailand every year and the majority of these tourists encounter no problems whatsoever.

Social situation

In addition to the physical aspects of travelling to a long-haul destination, tourists should also be prepared to expect some social and cultural differences. Many, but not all, long-haul destinations are located in developing countries, which have a different standard of living to the UK. Customers may be surprised by the levels of poverty and amount of begging that they observe during travelling and steps should be taken by the tour operator or travel agent to prepare customers for this. This could include issuing travel advice or guide books about the country to tourists in advance of their visit or providing tourists with written or verbal codes of conduct, which advise the tourists on particular social and religious customs. These codes of conduct may offer ideas to customers on how to assist the local population without, for example, encouraging begging by giving children sweets, money or pens. They may put customers in contact with the local orphanage or aid shelter or offer to take donations on their behalf.

CUSTOMER TYPES

Although perceived as expensive holidays, a wide range of different people travel to long-haul destinations and each different customer type is looking for something different from their holiday.

For example, some families may choose to travel to an all-inclusive resort with a mass market tour operator. This ensures that the holiday is at a fixed price with no extra costs and that there is a range of different activities and facilities for the children. The flight time, medical facilities and types of destination may also affect their holiday choice.

Couples of all ages travel long-haul. However, their choice of destination and means of travel vary depending on their age, budget, motivation and travel experience. Some young couples may travel independently, either backpacking or staying in cheaper local facilities that allow them flexibility and the opportunity to meet the local community. Other couples travel with a mass market tour operator to a range of popular destinations. This offers them the security of an organised booking. Older couples who have more disposable income may choose a more specialist and exclusive tour operator or destination and may look for places that offer the opportunity to learn about a different culture and history or to see a popular attraction. Older couples are generally less likely to travel independently and they prefer the security of a pre-arranged package or tour.

Independent travellers on a gap year or tourists whose aim in travelling is to visit friends and relatives may only book a long-haul flight or a flight and accommodation-only package. Gap year tourists are often students or young adults who are attracted to a destination because of its reputation and popularity within the backpacker community. Information on backpacker destinations can be found on the website www.lonelyplanet.com, which is a website run by Lonely Planet guide books.

Long-haul business travel may be to a conference or exhibition, for a business meeting or special event. Some colleges, schools and universities take their students on long-haul holidays and the rise of award schemes like the Duke of Edinburgh, fundraising hikes and expeditions have led to an increase in the number of younger travellers visiting long-haul destinations.

There has recently been a rise in the number of tourists going overseas for medical treatment. They find that operations with long waiting lists or expensive operations, which are not available through the UK health service, are quicker and cheaper overseas. Therefore, they make private arrangements with hospitals and clinics around their world. Some clinics and hospitals will also make travel arrangements for their customers. Popular medical treatments overseas include transplants and cosmetic surgery.

Research tip

Use the internet to examine the range of different tours/activities which are offered by charitable and expedition organisers.

EVIDENCE ACTIVITY

P1 – P2 – M1 – D1

1. Select four popular locations for each of the destination types below. Locate each destination or resort on a blank world map.

   - city destination

   - coastal or seaside destination

   - purpose-built destination

   - natural destination

   - historical or cultural destination. (P1)

2 Now choose one example for each destination type and describe the type of holiday that each destination offers to customers. Consider the different factors that influence a customer's choice. (P2)

3 Using the five different destinations or resorts chosen for Question 2, identify the different customers who might book holidays to these resorts. Describe each different customer's motivation in detail and the various travel factors that may have influenced their reasons for choosing this type of destination. (M1)

4 For each destination, you need to explore the reasons why the destination may or may not have been selected by specific customer types.

   a. Assess their success in attracting tourists.

   b. Identify the barriers to travel that stop customers visiting.

   c. Make specific recommendations on how these destinations could increase their appeal to different tourists and remove the barriers to travel that you have identified. (D1)

8.3 *Features of long-haul destinations that appeal to different customer types*

A range of different factors influence where the customer chooses to go on holiday. These can include the ease of getting to the destination, the accommodation and attractions at the destination and the local culture and way of life. Combined together, these factors are called destination appeal.

Key words

Destination appeal – factors that make a destination or resort attractive to customers

---

As long-haul holidays are often more expensive than holidays in Europe, the choice of destination and resort is very important. A destination that does not meet the customer's expectations leads to a disappointed tourist and may also lead to a complaint. Therefore, it is important to match the customer's expectations with a suitable resort and consider all of the customer's requirements when discussing their holiday.

ACCESSIBILITY

Some long-haul destinations are difficult to get to and involve a long journey with stopovers or a number of different means of transport. Although complicated journeys may appeal to more adventurous tourists, this may stop other people from booking.

Most long-haul journeys begin with a flight, which is often the most expensive part of the holiday.

Long-haul flights are mainly with scheduled airlines, such as British Airways, Emirates or Cathay Pacific, but some larger resorts like the Maldives, Goa and Cuba can also be reached by direct charter airlines like Monarch. Customers occasionally choose to travel by private jet.

Research tip

Use different airlines' websites to research the different stopover destinations/routes which can be used to reach Sydney, Auckland and Buenos Aires.

Services on a long-haul scheduled flight depend on which class the customer chooses to travel in. First class is only occasionally booked as it is the most expensive and very luxurious with larger seats, better food and excellent customer service. It is more common for tourists to choose to upgrade to business class on a long-haul journey as there is more leg room and a wider range of facilities for the tourist to enjoy. Overall, it is considered to be a more comfortable method of travel. First class and business class travel offer the additional benefit of access to private business or first class lounges, which include food, drinks, IT facilities and a range of magazines and newspapers that can be enjoyed while waiting for a flight. The standard way to travel, which is included in the tour

Figure 8.4 Scheduled airlines such as Emirates offer long-haul flights

operator's brochure price, is in economy where the seats are smaller and there is less leg room.

Scheduled flights run to a strict timetable and must take into account the time difference in the country where they are flying to. For this reason, journeys may begin early in the morning or late in the evening. Some tourists have a long journey to the airport and overnight accommodation must be booked in an airport hotel before an early morning departure. Alternatively, connections from regional airports may be required, for example, flights from Aberdeen to Heathrow before a flight to Montreal.

Charter airlines mainly offer only economy or standard travel. However, some do have a small number of premium seats, which offer more facilities to the traveller. The emphasis is on price and therefore the seats are closer together with less leg room than economy on a scheduled flight. Although often described as direct flights, some of these flights, such as the ones going east, stop for about an hour at an airport in the Middle East in order to re-fuel for the remainder of the journey. As charter airlines are owned and run by tour operators, only people who have booked a holiday with the tour operator can book tickets and the flight is included as part of their holiday.

Cruise ships around long-haul destinations such as the Caribbean also begin with a flight that is timed to correspond with the embarkation time for the ship. The cruise ship transport is seen as part of the holiday and the reason for booking. One of the few long-haul holidays that does not involve a flight would be a six-day cruise from the UK to New York, leaving from Southampton. This could be combined with a return cruise trip or a longer stay in New York, followed by a flight back to the UK.

DESTINATION FACILITIES

Destination facilities are the attractions and features that attract the tourist to visit that particular destination. Destination facilities include everything that a tourist can do within a resort, not just the visitor attractions, but also restaurants, shopping and accommodation, sport and leisure facilities.

Visitor attractions are divided into two types: Natural and man-made. Natural attractions occur in nature and examples include the Great Barrier Reef in Australia and the Grand Canyon in Arizona. Man-made or built attractions can vary from historic monuments like the Taj Mahal to theme and adventure parks like Disneyland in Florida. Man-made attractions also include museums and archaeological ruins, and may also include the local way of life and culture. Some man-made attractions such as theme parks appeal to a specific audience of families or younger people. Whereas, others have a wider appeal and are key visitor attractions that are visited by many different types of tourists as they are iconic like the White House in Washington DC. Natural attractions mainly attract people who are interested in wildlife and scenery. Many natural attractions are also used as the centre for activity and sporting activities. For example, the area around Mount Everest is used for walking, climbing and trekking and the calm waters of the Caribbean are suited to sailing.

One of the main features of many long-haul resorts is the climate, with destinations having guaranteed sunshine and hot weather for the majority of the year. This appeals to lots of people living in the UK, especially during the cold winter months. Not all long-haul destinations appeal to tourists for their hot weather and extremes of cold and snow. Winter sports destinations rely on cold weather for sporting activities. Other cold destinations attract tourists interested in watching related wildlife like polar bears or penguins or spectacular scenery like icebergs, which can only been seen in very cold destinations like the Arctic and Antarctic.

Example

Discover the World (www.dicover-the-world.co.uk) offers a range of holidays to places with extreme climates inluding specialist cruises using Icebreakers and touring holidays of Canada and Iceland.

The range of accommodation in long-haul resorts

Figure 8.5 A cruise ship in Antarctica

varies and many are purpose-built for a specific customer type. Some destinations will only try to attract rich five-star customers who are considered to be wealthy and more likely to spend money in the destination. For this reason, only five-star accommodation is available. Other resorts will offer a range of accommodation from cheaper hostels for backpackers and low budget tourists to more expensive all-inclusive hotels and luxury accommodation. Resorts that attract tourists for a specific activity like climbing or are visited due to an important tourist attraction may only offer a limited choice of accommodation and basic tourist facilities.

The range of in-resort amenities and activities will also attract tourists. This can include a wide selection of different bars, restaurants and nightlife, which offer customers a variety of food and drink at a range of different prices to appeal to all budgets. In some city destinations, shops are the main attractions to tourists, especially if the prices for goods are cheaper than the UK, like gold in Dubai or designer goods in Singapore. The exchange rate can influence tourist shopping behaviour as a good rate and good shops will have a direct impact on the number of people who visit and the amount of money they spend there. Tourists also like the opportunity to shop for local products and to barter with the locals for traditionally produced souvenirs and goods. Therefore, local shops and markets also appeal to tourists.

CULTURE

One of the most interesting experiences for many long-haul tourists is the opportunity to see a way of life and culture that is very different to their own. Tourists often book one-day excursions, which offer them the chance to visit the local communities and interact with the locals. For example, in Belize, tourists can book local excursions to the village of Dangriga-Hopkins where they can meet local villagers. These excursions may give them the opportunity to try on local dress for photographs, eat local food and to try the local drink. There may be the opportunity to visit cathedrals, mosques and synagogues, enabling them to learn more about the country's religion and way of life.

Evening entertainment, either in hotels or on evening excursions, can also offer the chance for tourists to listen to traditional music and watch traditional dances. These evening events are often accompanied by traditional food and drink, and are organised specifically for tourists with a view to providing an insight into the local culture and way of life. Some customers prefer not to book organised excursions or tours, and instead meet local people by walking around the city or destination. While it is safe to do so in the majority of long-haul destinations, tourists should however be made aware of any risks or security issues in advance of travelling.

Another way in which tourists can learn about the local culture is to watch local events or attend a traditional festival or annual event. These local events are not always advertised to tourists, although many, like the Rio De Janeiro Carnival in Brazil, are famous around the world and provide a specific reason to visit a destination at that time of the year. These events can range from the historical and traditional events, such as the Kumbh Mela Festival where pilgrims bath in the River Ganges, to more modern sports events, such as the Grand Prix circuit or world sporting events like the Olympic Games, which appeal to tourists with a specific interest in sports.

CUSTOMER TYPES

Some destinations and resorts attract a wide range of different customers. However, some aim to attract tourists from their target market and then adjust their accommodation, attractions and leisure facilities to reflect this; for example, Orlando in Florida targets families. Other destinations attract tourists for a specific reason. It may be that they have a world renowned spa, a historic monument, natural attraction or are famous for a particular event in history.

Destination features that appeal to families are children's clubs and a variety of activities including different sports for older children and relaxation for the parents. Sports instruction that is included in the price of a holiday is very popular as well as all-inclusive resorts where there are no hidden extras in the cost of the holiday. Other attractions that appeal to parents booking a holiday are swimming pools, beaches, a good range of visitor attractions and clean accommodation. Destinations that can be reached by direct flights are particularly popular and appeal to families due to the ease of travel. There are many long-haul resorts and tour operators that specifically offer resorts for families, such as Beaches and Club Med. Some families prefer activity or cultural holidays that also educate their children and some specialist tours, for example, safaris, have been created specifically for families with young and teenage children.

Couples sometimes prefer a children-free environment and hotels that guarantee this will appeal to them. Couples often book long-haul holidays as a celebration, for example, a wedding anniversary or honeymoon. For this reason, romantic locations like Bali and Fiji are popular. Other couples have specific interests such as sports, culture or an interest in history, and book their holiday around this. A wide range of long-haul holidays appeal to people with special interests, such as diving holidays, culture and historical holidays, or holidays that focus on wildlife or activities like trekking. These are aimed at couples without children or empty nesters.

Gap year travellers can either be travelling independently or as part of a semi-organised tour that includes some kind of voluntary work. Gap year travellers are often on a tight budget and they therefore stay in local accommodation and travel mainly using local transport. Some long-haul resorts like Australia have a thriving backpacker industry and many of the tourists are backpackers. Other resorts seek to minimise the number of backpackers who visit by limiting the number of cheap hotels and accommodation on offer. Gap year and backpacker tourists often choose their destinations by word-of-mouth from other backpackers or by the destination's reputation as a place that is good for backpackers. Therefore, the appeal of the destination is not always the destination, but the opportunity to meet and socialise with other backpackers and gap year students.

Business tourists are attracted to destinations that combine a number of attractions with good hotel and conference facilities including accommodation and conference rooms. Resorts wanting to attract business tourists should be easy to access from many different destinations with direct flights from major cities around the world. In addition, good communication links (Internet, telephone and fax) can also influence the choice of conference location.

CASE STUDY: THE MALDIVES

The Maldives are a group of islands in the Indian Ocean. Each island has its own purpose-built resort. A direct charter flight from the UK takes 11 hours. However, scheduled flights can also be booked and these can be combined with stopovers in Dubai and Sri Lanka. Individual customer requirements need to be considered in order to match each island to the customer and ensure customer satisfaction.

Customers are transferred to each purpose-built island on arrival at the airport. Transfers can either be by the local boats called Dhonis or by speedboats or sea planes. Transfers can be long and, on occasion, rough depending on the weather conditions. Although hot throughout the year, the Maldives do have a monsoon season and rainfall should therefore be checked before booking.

Each hotel, or purpose-built resort, offers the customer something different. Some are very luxurious and offer five-star facilities, while others offer the opportunity to get back to nature with cold sea-water showers and a 'no news, no shoes' feel.

Islands vary in size and in the facilities they offer. Some islands are so small that they take 10 minutes to walk around, while others are larger and can take over an hour. Some of the more basic islands have only one restaurant and bar for the customers to use and resorts that are far from the capital city may have limited menus, which rely on the locally caught fish and supplies arriving from the capital city on a weekly basis.

Accommodation ranges from suites and bungalows with views over the lagoons to water bungalows and private villas. A range of board types are available from bed and breakfast on the larger resorts where there is a choice of restaurants to all-inclusive or full-board on the islands that do not provide a large choice of food and drink outlets.

The main attraction is the opportunity to relax on the beach, although some resorts also provide spa and gym facilities. Some islands offer sporting activities, which include diving, snorkelling, windsurfing and jet-skiing. There are few opportunities for shopping. The chance to observe the local culture is restricted to organised excursions. There is little opportunity to meet local people away from the island hotels. Local evenings are normally organised by the resort owners and this includes the chance to watch the local dancing, Bodu Beru, and eat the local fish curry.

As relaxation is the main motivation for travel, the Maldives tend to attract couples and families with older children who may enjoy the sports on offer. The romantic appeal of a desert island attracts many special event holidays like honeymooners and wedding anniversaries and the Maldives can be combined with a Sri Lankan wedding or a tour of India.

While there is a long flight to consider, no visa is required for British passport holders and the recommended list of injections and health requirements is not lengthy. Although a dictatorship, The Maldives is considered to be a peaceful and safe holiday destination with little or no risk involved.

QUESTION

What types of customers do you think book holidays in the Maldives? Identify the barriers to travel that stop people from visiting the Maldives.

EVIDENCE ACTIVITY

P3 – M2 – D2

1. Choose one long-haul destination that is of particular interest to you. In order to keep this project manageable, specific cities, resorts or small countries would be best. For this destination, identify and describe the following:

- the destination's accessibility, including methods of transport, frequency of flights and example transport costs

- the destination's facilities, for example, the natural and built attractions, climate, different types of accommodation, food and drink outlets and the local sports and entertainment activities on offer

- the local culture, including any annual festivals and events, religion, customs and traditions, traditional music, dance, food and drink. (P3)

2. Now you must match the destination's key features and appeal that you have identified in Question 1 with the different customer types who visit the destination. Find some statistics about the different visitor types who visit the destination or who use the attractions and facilities in the destination. Try to identify the different reasons for their choice of destination. (M2)

3. You now know who the tourists are visit the destination. Now identify the tourists who do not visit the destination and make specific suggestions on how the destination can change and improve its facilities to attract different customer types. (D2)

8.4 *Be able to plan a long-haul tour*

Customers who book a long-haul tour will be booking an inclusive package in which flights, transportation, accommodation, visitor attractions and tour guides all have to be organised and booked in advance. Details of the tour are provided to the tourist in advance of the trip in the form of an itinerary, which includes their pre-arranged travel information. Each customer's itinerary is different and specific to them.

Tourists who are staying in one resort or hotel may also book day or evening excursions. However, this is not a tour and while itineraries containing flight and accommodation details are provided to these customers, they are less detailed than a full tour itinerary.

> ### Key words
> Itinerary – written details of the holiday booked

TRAVEL

When planning a long-haul holiday, one of the first factors to consider is how the tourist is going to get to the country. This involves researching the gateway airport and the connections either by transfer or public transport to the planned hotels. Local forms of transport should be researched and considered as some resorts may only be accessible by boat, sea plane, helicopter or taxi. Information about transfers must be advised to the customer in advance.

In complicated tours, customers may travel on both international and internal flights and may also travel by coach or rail. The journey times of each segment of the journey need to be considered and taken into account when planning the tour and details given to the customer. In addition, the transfer time between the different forms of transport, flight and journey times needs to be added and the customer needs to be given the correct arrival and departure times in local time. Time should be allowed for customers to make flight connections and overnight accommodation organised, where necessary.

If the customer has booked first or business class for their international flight, they may wish to upgrade for all parts of the holiday. This should be checked and booked in advance. It is possible that some internal flights will not offer customers the opportunity to upgrade and they must therefore travel in economy class.

If customers are booking car hire, then maps, distances and approximate journey times will need to be advised to the customer and the need for an international driving licence investigated.

Figure 8.6 Tourists consulting road map whilst abroad

ACCOMMODATION

Tour accommodation may vary and some destinations may not have a wide choice of accommodation available for tourists. Where possible, tourists should be given a selection of accommodation and the option of different board basis, for example, half-board, full-board or all-inclusive. In more developed long-haul destinations, for example, in Canada, America or Australia, customers are also able to choose self-catering accommodation, such as apartments or campsites like Kruger Park in South Africa.

Research tip

Discover more about the types of accommodation offered by Kruger Park in South Africa on their website www.krugerpark.org.

ATTRACTIONS

A long-haul tour may be special or of general interest, but normally a wide range of attractions are built into the itinerary.

The attractions are often the most important part of the tour and one of the main reasons for booking the tour. Therefore, enough time must be given for the tourists to see around each large and important attraction. Some smaller attractions may be used to break up a long coach journey, providing places to stop, possibly for lunch.

When considering the attractions that are included in an itinerary, a number of factors should be considered. One of the main factors to consider is the target market of the tour; for example, families may be more interested in theme parks than older couples. Another factor that is important is to have a range of different types of attractions, so that the tourists do not visit too many similar attractions on the same day. Other attractions like shops and markets offer the tourists the opportunity to meet local people and buy souvenirs. Any specific local festivals that take place while the tourists are visiting the destination should be advertised and offered to the tourist as a possible excursion.

VISITOR NEEDS

The visitor's specific requirements should be considered at all stages when planning a long-haul tour. Where possible, itineraries and travel arrangements should be tailor-made to each individual customer requirements. Tourists visit long-haul destinations for different reasons and the tour that they are offered should reflect this. The accommodation offered, the board basis and modes of transport, where possible, should be amended to reflect the tourist's motivation and budget.

Not all tourists are able to book a traditional two-week holiday and flexibility with regard to flights and transfers may need to be shown when making transport arrangements. For this reason, tours should try to offer a range of different accommodation types, flight times, gateway airports and joining points.

The option to upgrade both for accommodation (for example, to a suite, water bungalow or luxury tent) and flights should be offered to all tourists and additional excursions should also be considered and described to the customers in full.

Customers with specific travel needs, for example, disabled or elderly travellers may need additional assistance with regard to their travel arrangements. This could include porterage services for baggage, additional assistance at the airport or contacting visitor attractions or hotels in advance to check the access arrangements, availability of lifts or to book specific guides either in Braille or large print.

ITINERARY CONTENT

When booking a holiday, the terms and conditions of travel are made clear to customers and a certain amount of information is provided. Nearer to the time of departure, once all arrangements have been finalised, the tour operator will send an itinerary to the customers. This provides in-depth details about their booking and is often accompanied by visa and health information, although customers should not wait until this information arrives and should investigate these issues before the itinerary arrives by themselves.

EVIDENCE ACTIVITY

P4 – M3

1 Create a multi-centre tour for one of the customer types below. You will need to provide details similar to the itinerary shown including transportation, journey times, optional excursions and optional upgrades, details of accommodation and the attractions and events to be visited during the tour. Your tour should include flights to and from the UK and also a minimum of 4 different centres and last for 14 days.

You should keep a list of the different sources that you use when researching your tour to use as a bibliography. (P4)

- a group of students on a budget who want to travel around Australia, seeing the sights and meeting other young travellers

- an older couple who want to travel around South America, visiting several cultural and historical highlights

- a family with teenage children who want to travel and cruise on a relaxing holiday around the Caribbean

- a group of four friends who want to travel around the USA. They want to see as much as possible and are willing to drive while overseas

2 Once you have created your tour itinerary, justify why you have chosen this itinerary. Describe why you think this itinerary is appropriate for your customers. You might like to consider your choice of:

- flights and transportation methods

- accommodation and board basis

- attractions (M3)

Exotic
Tour Holidays

Passenger names: Mr C Jones
                    Mrs C Jones

.... Customers' full names as shown
                 on flight tickets

Taj Tour, Goa Extension plus additional night extension in Mumbai

Included in price:
- Air conditioned vehicles throughout
- All entrance fees to monuments and national parks
- Porterage on arrival and departure at each hotel and airport
- Escorted English-speaking guide whilst on tour and services of our local agents
and representatives during extension and city break

.... Items included in holiday
                 cost laid out for customers

Day 1 10th January 2008

Depart   London Heathrow (LHR) to Delhi
                  Virgin Atlantic flight number VS0330
                  Depart   : 21:00
                  Flight time: 8 hours, 15 minutes + 1 day
                  Upgraded to Business class travel

.... Flight details include flight
                 times, time difference,
                 journey time class of travel,
                 (Virgin Atlantic) and
                 flight number

Day 2
Estimated time of arrival Delhi (DEL): 10:45
Transfer to hotel by private car
Accommodation booked at: Taj Palace Hotel
                            1 night
                            Standard room
                            Bed and breakfast basis

.... Flight arrival details and
                 transfer arrangements

.... Accommodation details:
                 room type, number of
                 nights the accommodation
                 is booked for and meal
                 arrangements

Afternoon: meet tour guide and escorted tour of New Delhi
Evening: at leisure or optional evening excursion to Sound and Light show at the Red Fort.
Book and pay locally - approximate cost £10.00

Day 3
Morning: tour of Old Delhi
Depart after lunch for coach transfer to Agra. Approximate journey time 5 hours
Accommodation booked at: Oberoi Amarilas hotel
                            2 nights
                            Premiere room with balcony
                            Half board basis
Afternoon and evening: at leisure

.... Included and optional
                 excursions with
                 approximate prices and
                 method of booking

Day 4
Morning: early morning visit to Taj Mahal
Lunch in local restaurant near Taj Mahal
Afternoon: at leisure, chance to return to Taj Mahal or explore Agra

.... Major visitor attraction

Day 5
Morning: early departure by coach for Jaipur. Approximate journey time 6 hours
Afternoon: stop for included lunch and tour of the deserted Mughal city of Fatephur
Accommodation booked at: Oberoi Rajivilas
                            3 nights
                            Luxury tent
                            Bed and breakfast basis
Evening: at leisure

.... Lunch during journey
                 organised for customers
                 and costed into tour price.
                 Visitor attraction is en route

Range of different attractions. Optional excursions all clearly indicated in advance to customers

Free time for shopping at local bazaar. A common feature of many tours is a farewell dinner

Day 6
Morning: coach transfer and tour of Amber Fort
Included: Lunch at local restaurant
Afternoon: walking tour of city of Jaipur
Evening: optional evening dinner at local restaurant with traditional dancing and live music.
Book locally - approximate cost £12.00

Day 7
Morning and afternoon: day at leisure to explore Jaipur markets and bazaars
Evening: farewell group dinner at local restaurant

Following coach tour a beach resort extension has been added to the holiday

Day 8
Morning: departure by coach to Delhi. Approximate journey time 6 hours
Accommodation booked at: Taj Palace Hotel
                              1 night
                              Standard room
                              Bed and breakfast basis

Evening: at leisure

7 nights accommodation at beach resort on an all inclusive basis.
No excursions or tours included in this part of the tour, although these could be booked and paid for locally

Day 9
Morning: private transfer by coach to airport
Internal flight from Delhi to Goa   Air India flight AI235
                                           Estimated time of departure: 10:00
                                           Estimate time of arrival 13:00
Private transfer to Taj Exotica Hotel
Accommodation booked at: Taj Exotica Hotel
                              7 nights
                              Pool villa
                              All inclusive board basis

Additional extension to the city of Mumbai, which allows customers to visit another major city in India

Day 26
Morning: private transfer by coach to airport
Internal flight from Goa to Mumbai   Jet Air flight 9W474
                                            Estimated time of departure: 06:35
                                            Estimate time of arrival 11:55

Private transfer to Taj Mahal Palace and Tower
Accommodation booked at: Taj Mahal Palace and Tower
                              1 night
                              Standard room
                              Half board
Afternoon: escorted private tour of Mumbai
Evening: at leisure

Third different airline that the customers have travelled with – different airlines allow more flexibility to the tour but can increase the price

Day 27
Morning: at leisure
Private transfer to airport

Depart   Mumbai (BOM) to London Heathrow
                Virgin Atlantic flight number VS0350
                Depart: 14:55
                Flight time: 10 hours
                Upgraded to Business class travel
                Estimated time of arrival at London Heathrow (LHR): 19:25

Private escorted tour of city allows customers to fully experience the city in the short time available

Departure flight details

Edexcel
190 High Holborn
London WC1V 7BH

ISBN: 978-1-40586-807-5

Printed in the UK
Illustration by Oxford Designers & Illustrators Ltd
Indexed by Indexing Specialists (UK) Ltd

Acknowledgments
The Publisher is grateful to the following for their permission to reproduce copyright material:

ABTA; Alva.org.uk; BBC; EasyJet; EuroTunnel; Investors in People, for more information visit investsorinpeople.co.uk; Portland Holidays Direct; Ryan Air; Teignbridge District Council, for more information visit teignbridge.gov.uk; Hebridean Whale and Dolphin Trust; World Tourism Organization.

Blackwell Publishing for granting the inclusion of extracts from Richard Butler's Destination 'Product Life Cycle' in the Canadian Geographer Journal.

Crown copyright material is reproduced with the permission of the Controller of HMSO.

All visitbritain.com and tourismtrade.org.uk material courtesy of VisitBritain.

Every effort has been made to trace the copyright holders and we apologise in advance for any unintentional omissions. We would be pleased to insert the appropriate acknowledgement in any subsequent edition of this publication.
Picture Credits

The publisher would like to thank the following for their kind permission to reproduce their photographs:

Action Plus Sports Images: pg 137 (Mike Hewitt); Alamy Images: pg 12, pg 14 (Photick - Image and Click), pg 16(tr) (Julian Marshall), pg 28 (geophotos), pg 36 (John MacPherson), pg 45 (Anthony Kay), pg 50 (Peter Titmuss), pg 80 (Hideo Kurihara), pg 87 (Jack Sullivan), pg 91 (worldthroughthelens), pg 104 (Steven May), pg 109 (John Boud), pg 112 (Simon Vine), pg 132 (picturedimensions), pg 146 (Jon Arnold Images), pg 167 (Ace Stock Limited), pg 171 (Antony Nettle); Bahamas Tourist Office: pg 164; Britain on View: pg 68, pg 70 (Martin Brent); Corbis: pg 42, pg 44 (Mark Karrass), pg 65(l) (Aladdin Color), pg 75 (epa/Gary Penny), pg 128, pg 130, pg 145 (Eye Ubiquitous / Peter Seheult), pg 156, pg 158 (Bob Krist), pg 173 (George D. Lepp); DK Images: pg 19 (Rough Guides / Tim Draper), pg 30 (De Agostini Editore Picture Library), pg 71; Getty Images: pg 39 (Stringer), pg 56 (Christopher Lee), pg 177 (Ghislain & Marie David de Lossy); iStockphoto: pg 65 (r) (Bill Grove), pg 175 (Beate Weiner); Leeds Bradford International Airport: pg 18; PunchStock: pg 47 (Stockbyte), pg 55 (Brand X Pictures), pg 100, pg 102 (Thinkstock), pg 119, pg 149 (Blend Images); Reuters: pg 155 (Yiorgos Karahalis); Rex Features: pg 31, pg 58, pg 142.
Cover images: PunchStock: Digital Vision

All other images © Pearson Education

Picture Research by: Sarah Purtill

Every effort has been made to trace the copyright holders and we apologise in advance for any unintentional omissions. We would be pleased to insert the appropriate acknowledgement in any subsequent edition of this publication.